WOMEN, CELEBRITY, AND LITERARY CULTURE BETWEEN THE WARS

LITERARY MODERNISM SERIES
Thomas F. Staley, Editor

WOMEN, CELEBRITY, AND LITERARY CULTURE BETWEEN THE WARS

FAYE HAMMILL

University of Texas Press, Austin

Copyright © 2007 by the University of Texas Press
All rights reserved
Printed in the United States of America
First edition, 2007

Requests for permission to reproduce material from this work should
be sent to:
Permissions
University of Texas Press
P.O. Box 7819
Austin, TX 78713-7819
www.utexas.edu/utpress/about/bpermission.html

⊗ The paper used in this book meets the minimum requirements of
ANSI/NISO Z39.48-1992 (R1997) (Permanence of Paper).

Library of Congress Cataloging-in-Publication Data

Hammill, Faye.
    Women, celebrity, and literary culture between the wars / Faye
Hammill. — 1st ed.
        p.   cm. — (Literary modernism series)
    Includes bibliographical references and index.
    ISBN 978-0-292-72606-2
    1. American literature—Women authors—History and criticism.
2. English literature—Women authors—History and criticism.
3. Women and literature—History—20th century.   4. Women
authors, American--20th century—Biography.   5. Women authors,
English—20th century—Biography.   6. Fame—Economic aspect—
History—20th century.   7. Authorship—Economic aspects—
History—20th century.   8. Authors and readers—history—20th
century.   9. Popular culture—History—20th century.   I. Title.
    PS152.H36   2007
    820.9'928709042—dc22
                                                              2007009533

Contents

Acknowledgments

I am grateful in particular to Professor Phyllis Lassner for her detailed, encouraging, and immensely helpful comments on the draft of this book. I am also very grateful to several friends and colleagues: Rob Gossedge, Dr. Mary Grover, Dr. Louise Harrington, Dr. Anouk Lang, Professor Rick Rylance, and Dr. Keir Waddington, for reading draft chapters and offering many valuable suggestions. Especial thanks to my husband, Professor Jonathan Percy, not only for reading all the chapters, but also for his unfailing interest in my research and for love and support over the years in which I have worked on this project.

I appreciate the generosity of those who have kindly shared their research materials with me or sent me copies of texts: Dr. Cathy Clay, Ruth Collier, Mark Dusseault, Tauba Heilpern, Professor Avril Horner, and Dr. Daisy Neijmann. I thank especially Professor Lorraine York, for allowing me to read her work before publication, and Reggie Oliver, for corresponding with me about his aunt, Stella Gibbons, and for his encouragement and helpful information.

I have presented papers on the material included in this book at seminars at the Universities of Liverpool, Glamorgan, Hertfordshire, and Chichester, as well as at a meeting of the Modernist Studies Association. I have benefited greatly from these opportunities to discuss my ideas, and from the feedback offered by audiences.

I very much appreciate the encouragement and careful assistance of Jim Burr and Lynne Chapman of the University of Texas Press and Professor Tom Staley, director of the Harry Huntt Ransom Humanities Research Center and modernism series editor for UTP. I am also grateful to Paul Spragens for his meticulous copyediting.

Financial support for my research has been generously provided by the British Academy and the Cardiff University Young Researcher Travel Fund. Space and research support during my visit to the University of British Columbia were provided by the Centre for Research in Women's Studies and Gender Relations and also the International Canadian Studies Centre, and I am grateful to Professors Sneja Gunew, Richard Cavell, Laura Moss, and Laurie Ricou for welcoming and assisting me during my visit.

Material written by L. M. Montgomery is reproduced here with the authorization of the heirs of L. M. Montgomery. *L. M. Montgomery, Emily of New Moon, The Story Girl, The Blue Castle,* characters, names, and related indicia are trademarks of Heirs of L. M. Montgomery Inc. *Anne of Green Gables* and other indicia of "Anne" are trademarks and Canadian official marks of the Anne of Green Gables Licensing Authority Inc.

Quotations from letters written by Margaret Kennedy are included by kind permission of her daughter, Mrs. Julia Birley, and I am grateful for her supportive comments. I thank the Syndics of Cambridge University Library for permission to quote from the papers of the Femina Vie Heureuse Prize.

For access to, and assistance with, archival material, I am grateful to Mr. Godfrey Waller and Dr. Patrick Zutshi, of Cambridge University Library; Mr. Bernard Katz, formerly of the Archival and Special Collections, University of Guelph Library; Mr. George Brandak, Manuscripts Curator in Rare Books and Special Collections, University of British Columbia Library; and especially Miss Pauline Adams of Somerville College Library, Oxford.

Approximately four paragraphs from my chapter on Stella Gibbons formed part of an article I published in *Modern Fiction Studies* 47.4 (Fall 2001), entitled "*Cold Comfort Farm,* D. H. Lawrence and English Literary Culture between the Wars." A shorter version of my chapter on L. M. Montgomery was published in *Modern Language Review* 101 (2006) and is reprinted by permission. A shorter version of my chapter on Anita Loos appeared in *Critical Survey* 17.3 (2005) and is reprinted by permission.

WOMEN, CELEBRITY,
AND LITERARY CULTURE
BETWEEN THE WARS

INTRODUCTION

The Strand was seething with noise and confusion; then presently, to my bewilderment, I began to be aware that I, myself, was contributing to the hubbub. News vendors all along the way were barking out the headlines on the posters [. . .] and they carried my name in red and black lettering: "Anita Loos in London."

As I listened to those cockney voices, I was chilled by that new danger to my marriage. What if Mr. E were there to hear his [wife's] name being called out in the London street?

I sought refuge from that thought by going back to the hotel. By that time, the phones in both my rooms were ringing. While I answered one, my maid tried to cope with the other but, speaking only French, she added to the confusion. And from that time on, day and night, my phones never stopped ringing.

The British are prone to magnify writers. They pampered Noël Coward, Michael Arlen, Freddy Lonsdale, and Somerset Maugham as if they were matinee idols. And interest in me was heightened by the fact that I'd once lived in the magical world of D. W. Griffith, Douglas Fairbanks, Charlie Chaplin, and Mary Pickford.

ANITA LOOS, *KISS HOLLYWOOD GOODBYE* (73)

Literary celebrity, in this account, is part of the "hubbub" of everyday life, yet it also gives access to a "magical world." The celebrity author is magnified, elevated above ordinary mortals. At the same time, she is incorporated into the bewildering modern city, and cannot take refuge from the public, even in her bedroom. Simply by her known presence, she contributes to the chaos, but it is her name and not herself which circulates in the street. Shouted out and repeated, the name becomes part of the "noise and confusion"; its meaning and value are renegotiated as it is translated across languages, dialects, and cultures.

In the London of 1926, the arrival of Anita Loos was a newsworthy event, not only because her book *Gentlemen Prefer Blondes* had made such a sensation the previous year, but also because she was a conduit to the stars of Hollywood, who fascinated the British public. As her comparison with matinee idols suggests, the high-profile authors of the twenties and thirties were constructed in relation to new models of fame emerging from Hollywood. Literary celebrity was increasingly predicated on forms of public performance, and in her autobiographical text Loos deliberately enacts her own celebrity by exaggerating her impact: her name is being barked out "all along the way," and the phones "never stopped ringing." These excessive gestures coexist with an anxiety about her own status which is directly related to gender, and her attempted retreat from the exposure of the street to the private space of the hotel room evokes the ideology of separate spheres. Indeed, Loos's various autobiographical writings betray acute fear that her rise to fame has compromised her femininity and ruined the life of her less successful, envious husband.

This extract from *Kiss Hollywood Goodbye* (1974) touches on many of the aspects of literary culture and celebrity which will be explored in this study. The book concentrates on seven high-profile women whose books caused a sensation in the early twentieth century: Dorothy Parker, Anita Loos, Mae West, L. M. Montgomery, Margaret Kennedy, Stella Gibbons, and E. M. Delafield. This is a deliberately varied selection, and these authors are not usually compared in any detail by critics; each tends to be treated as an isolated literary or star phenomenon. Yet they can be connected in many ways, and such connections illuminate the complex transatlantic cultural interchange of the 1920s and 1930s. There are many affinities among these writers, in terms of their careers as well as the thematic and formal aspects of their writing, and they also influenced one another's work. The same cultural discourses surrounding sophistication, urbanity, and the economics of female survival in a man's world informed the work of all these women; and the same literary networks and systems of celebrity, centering on particular magazines, publishing houses, literary prizes, theaters, hotels, and Hollywood studios, structured their public images and professional lives.

Witty and highly individual novels such as Loos's *Gentlemen Prefer Blondes,* Gibbons's *Cold Comfort Farm,* or Kennedy's *The Constant Nymph* were literary events, surprise best sellers which provoked debate precisely because they could not be understood in relation to contemporary literary categories and hierarchies. On first publication, they were received as significant contributions to high culture; later their high sales led to their reclassification as commercial fiction. The same is true of Montgomery's *Anne of Green Gables* (one of the most widely read books of all time), and this novel, like Delafield's *The Diary of a Provincial Lady,* became a best seller on the strength of a very original central character, attractive enough to generate numerous sequels and achieve a remarkable longevity. The fame achieved by Montgomery and Delafield was contingent on the much greater renown of their heroines. West also invented several memorable characters, the best known being Diamond Lil, protagonist of a play, film, and novel. Yet she used her writing primarily to create and sustain her own celebrity image, and the "Mae West character" eventually eclipsed all her fictional heroines. Her three novels have been largely ignored, yet they were very significant to West's creation of herself as a celebrity. Similarly, Dorothy Parker is primarily remembered for her public personality, evolved through her journalism and disseminated via the sophisticated magazines of New York. The Parker persona—with its distinctive combination of sentiment and cynicism—is also recognizable in the speaking voice of her lyric poems and some of her stories; its allure was such that she achieved the remarkable feat of having a poetry collection in the best seller lists.

The most straightforward purposes of the present study are to reinscribe these fascinating writers into literary history, to probe their relationships with one another and with the canonized authors of their era, and to engage in detail with their writing, particularly those texts which reflect on cultural hierarchy, celebrity, publicity, and performance. Beyond these, the book will address a number of central questions, all with specific reference to the early decades of the twentieth century. First, what was the relationship between celebrity culture and literary culture, and how was this relationship inflected by gender? Second, how did the fame and commercial success of women writers in this period impact on their cultural authority and on the reception of their work? Third, what kind of agency did women writers have in the determination of their own celebrity images, and how far were they appropriated by the media into particular cultural discourses? The project is also concerned with developing more sophisticated critical approaches to middlebrow writing and with evolving a nuanced understanding of the middlebrow in relation to modernism and popular culture.

LITERARY CULTURE, STYLE, AND THE MIDDLEBROW

The personal style of these women, and their varying degrees of embodied visibility in early-twentieth-century culture, are among my concerns here. Most of them were frequently photographed, usually for publicity purposes; some also became the subjects of cartoons, while publicly exhibited paintings and sculptures provided more solid testimonies to the fame of Parker, West, and Kennedy. The marketing of authors through images was a fast-developing commercial strategy in this period, and it related in significant ways to the highly visual culture of Hollywood, which circulated pictures of stars through fan magazines, advertisements, and consumer products. But the personal style of this generation of female authors is, I would suggest, often a function of their literary style. The way in which these women presented themselves, and were presented by publishers and journalists, often relates to the style projected through the language of their texts and through their fictional characters.[1]

For Margaret Kennedy, Stella Gibbons, and E. M. Delafield, a conventionally elegant style of dress was part of their assertion of a civilized, commonsensical, broadly middlebrow identity, in contrast to the eccentric and unkempt bohemian characters depicted in their novels. Equally, a restrained, realist prose style is constructed as a norm in their texts, in contradistinction to overcolored or radically experimental modes of writing and conversation, which they render parodically. At the same time, they raise questions about these oppositions between civilized and bohemian, realist and experimental, and more broadly about the politics of literary style, and such questioning is very significant to my discussion. L. M. Montgomery collaborated with her publishers' efforts to market her, through photos and media texts, as a genteel lady writer, a suitable mentor for the adolescent girls who formed the principal audience for her wholesome, stylistically accessible stories. Her own rather Romantic aesthetic is tempered by her gentle mockery of Anne's overblown romanticism, flowery phrasing, and desire for frilly dresses with puffed sleeves, all of which are incongruous in prosaic Avonlea, where she lives. But in the early film versions of *Anne of Green Gables,* Anne's idyllic dreams become the primary reality, with Hollywood starlets embodying her fantasized, glamorous version of herself.

Anita Loos's success, like Montgomery's, was inspired by the image of a child. The diary of her most famous character, Lorelei Lee, is written in an infantile style; indeed, Lorelei's idiosyncratic, inaccurate, and yet oddly charming prose is the outstanding achievement of Loos's career. Lorelei deliberately plays on her youthful, blonde appearance, with its connotation of innocence. Yet, while she satirizes her heroine, Loos actually projected herself in similar ways, using Lorelei's style in her personal writing and endorsing cartoons which represented her as childlike and frivolous. She insisted on her identity as a "girl" even when she was well into middle age—her first volume of autobiography, published in 1966, is titled with one of Lorelei's phrases, *A Girl Like I.*

Dorothy Parker, like Loos, used her petite, pretty, feminine appearance to disarm, and to lend additional impact to her satire. Parker was adept at exploiting the incongruity between her vicious wit and her unexpectedly ladylike, demure appearance. Her literary style was so distinctive that even her anonymous fashion captions for *Vogue* are immediately recognizable. Mae West also based her appeal on wit, but in her case, this was combined with the more blatant attractions of a famously curvaceous figure, exaggerated by corsets and extremely high heels, and set off by a dazzling array of jewelry. Her literary style was similarly excessive, often to the point of self-mockery. Both the innuendo of her phrasing and her suggestive modes of dress and performance were honed in response to the interwar climate of censorship. Pungent dialogue is also crucial to West's novels, and she experimented with the representation of different dialects; like Parker and Loos, she was among the pioneers of colloquial, urban language in American fiction. Each of the seven authors chosen for this study, while not embracing a radical modernist aesthetic, is stylistically innovative; and style, in a broad sense, is thematized throughout their work.

The preoccupation with style, taste, imitation, and social performance which characterizes the work of all these authors can be tentatively identified with a middlebrow perspective. The middlebrow has been much abused. In her essay "Middlebrow," Virginia Woolf defines it as "this mixture of geniality and sentiment stuck together with a sticky slime of calves-foot jelly" (*Death,* 118), while Q. D. Leavis describes "the staple reading of the middlebrow" with distaste as a set of "respected middling novelists of blameless intentions and indubitable skills" who leave their readers "with the agreeable sensation of having improved themselves without incurring fatigue" (36, 37). More recently, Pierre Bourdieu has written dismissively that "middle-brow art [. . .] is characterized by tried and proven techniques and an oscillation between plagiarism and parody most often linked with either indifference or conservatism" (*Field*, 128). The term "middlebrow," in order to be an effective critical category for the consideration of interwar literature, needs to be detached from such limiting definitions as these and reconstituted as a productive, affirmative standpoint for writers who were not wholly aligned with either high modernism or popular culture. It is important to recognize the forms of stylistic experimentation which middlebrow writers engaged in, and which are often overlooked because they do not correspond to the experimental strategies of high modernism. In sum, a new critical approach to such material is needed.

Much middlebrow writing has been ignored by the academy because of a misperception that it is so straightforward as to require no analysis, while in fact, its witty, polished surfaces frequently conceal unexpected depths and subtleties. Alison Light says of interwar middlebrow culture that its "apparent artlessness and insistence on its own ordinariness has made it peculiarly resistant to analysis" (11). Further, middlebrow books, especially those which achieve a wide readership, are often denigrated as commercial products, with the highly questionable implication that only experimental art, addressed to a select audience, can escape the contamination of the marketplace. A final problem is that, while the middlebrow has always encompassed both male and female writers and readers, it has, along with popular culture, been persistently gendered feminine, with a belittling and exclusionary intention.[2] Nicola Humble, in her book *The Feminine Middlebrow Novel, 1920s to 1950s*, argues that one important reason for the "critical neglect of the major part of fiction published in Britain in these years is that it was largely written and consumed by women" (2). Her study encompasses some male authors, such as E. F. Benson, Evelyn Waugh, and Angus Wilson, who shared the concerns of their female contemporaries. Similarly, Light notes that the "cultural squint" produced by the literary establishment's "obsession with [. . .] elites" devalues interwar authors such as Noël Coward or P. G. Wodehouse, as well as many women writers. Nevertheless, both Light and Humble concentrate primarily on women writers, and their books demonstrate that the reinscription of the middlebrow into literary history is in part a feminist undertaking, since it involves attention to an undervalued literature which was, indeed, mainly produced by and for women. Humble also argues: "If this is a feminine literature, it is also very much the literature of the middle classes, paying a meticulous attention to their shifting desires and self-images" (3). This is indisputable, and yet many middlebrow texts also often subvert values which are taken to be constitutive of interwar middle-class ideology. The novels analyzed in the present study challenge and reassess the ideals of marriage, home, and family, and complicate class categories and lines of social discrimination. Of particular relevance to my project is the fact that writers who are preoccupied with celebrity often reassess the dynamic between private and public, and so represent a challenge to accepted notions of the inward turning of women's writing in this period.[3]

The increasing number of critics working on the nonmodernist literature of the early twentieth century are hampered by the lack of appropriate terminology to describe their specialism. The period is referred to by literary critics as the "modernist," while cultural critics concentrate on material such as music hall, Hollywood film, and mass-market magazines and novels. What, then, becomes of writing which cannot be easily accommodated to the paradigms of either high modernism or popular culture? This book is a study of that intermediate field of literary production from which some of the most fascinating and enduring texts of the period emerged. The recuperation of the middlebrow, and the development of more flexible and sophisticated approaches, have recently been initiated by critics,[4] and the present study seeks to advance this important project.

The middlebrow has been delineated, by more hostile critics, in terms of pretension and upward mobility—an aspirational form of imitation, an attempt to appropriate forms of culture which are not fully understood. Bourdieu describes this process:

> Pretension, the recognition of distinction that is affirmed in the effort to possess it, albeit in the illusory form of bluff or imitation, inspires the acquisition, in itself vulgarizing, of the previously most distinctive properties; it thus helps to maintain a constant tension in the symbolic goods market, forcing the possessors of distinctive properties threatened with popularization to engage in an endless pursuit of new properties through which to assert their rarity. (*Distinction*, 251–252)

Yet the primary satiric target of many of the broadly middlebrow texts considered in this study is precisely this: pretension, in all its forms.

Gibbons, Parker, Kennedy, and Delafield mock those who seek distinction through deliberate eccentricity, intellectual posturing, bogus bohemianism, and social climbing. In their writing for magazines, they trade in the delineation of social "types," which was a staple of periodicals such as *Vanity Fair, The New Yorker, Time and Tide,* and *Punch.* To conform to one of these types is to fail in the struggle for distinction. Loos's Lorelei Lee is also satirized for her inept imitations of authorship, virtue, refinement, and even blondeness; yet the text invites stronger contempt for those who are taken in by her act. All the authors chosen for this book flatter their readers by constructing them as culturally literate and sophisticated, not to be taken in by highbrow pretension or by lowbrow aspiration. Yet this construction of a position of superiority for implied author and implied reader is itself a bid for distinction and depends on the logic of sophistication. As Jessica Burstein notes: "Like the dynamic of fashion, sophistication works by relentlessly defining itself against its immediate past, or immediate context" (234). The ability to discriminate must be restricted to initiates; in claiming this ability for herself and her readers, an author seeks to distinguish herself from the unsophisticated mass.

More specifically, the early-twentieth-century discourse of sophistication depends on a privileging of urban over rural and metropolitan over provincial. Parker and Loos, prime exponents of New York style, continually identify their texts in this way. Suburban bores are caricatured (though sometimes with a touch of pathos) in Parker's stories for *The New Yorker,* a magazine which declared it was "not edited for the old lady in Dubuque" but for "persons who have a metropolitan interest."[5] Loos chose Little Rock, Arkansas, as the home of her blonde adventurer because her beloved H. L. Mencken described it as "the Sahara of the Bozart."[6] Lorelei disguises her unpromising origins in her campaign to conquer New York high society, though she occasionally plays on her identity as a "little girl from Little Rock" (*Blondes,* 92) to generate sympathy.

The privileging of the metropolitan exists, however, in tension with the contemporary urge toward the simple life, and the pastoral fantasies which resulted. All the authors discussed here engage with these oppositions. *Cold Comfort Farm, The Constant Nymph,* and *The Diary of a Provincial Lady* are all structured by an exaggerated opposition between London and a rural setting (respectively, Sussex, the Austrian Alps, and Devon), while the island idyll of Montgomery's novels is threatened by the dangerous allure of urban opportunities and visitors from the city. This preoccupation with the city is just one of the many ways in which the authors analyzed in this book engage with the concerns of modernity. Another significant element of their rhetorical modernness is a willingness to address previously taboo subjects, including contraception and teenage sexuality, and even—in the cases of Parker and West—to invest their own celebrity images with a transgressive sexuality.

MODERNISM AND THE MIDDLEBROW

Engagement with the modern, for some of the seven writers, is formal as well as thematic. It is true that, on the whole, they tended to regard experimental and avant-garde art with a certain bewilderment, amusement, or even hostility, yet Montgomery was the only one to be wholly intolerant of it. Several of the others responded to modernist innovation in serious ways, and some of their texts have affinities with experimental narrative projects: West's impressionistic evocations of New York, for example, or Loos's emphasis on the materiality of language. A parodic approach is more characteristic of these authors, however: parody of stream of consciousness and free verse occurs in Gibbons, Loos, Delafield, and Parker. Drawing on the more expansive definitions of modernism and modernity which are being developed in recent theory and criticism,[7] it is possible to read them as participants, however tentatively, in modernist experiment. They also interacted textually with canonical modernist authors. Loos's writing, for example, has interesting resonances with the work of both T. S. Eliot and Gertrude Stein, while Delafield implicitly responds to Virginia Woolf's work in her own texts, with a mixture of admiration and opposition. Gibbons's books have many affinities with those of Evelyn Waugh (who is ambiguously located in relation to modernism), and she also establishes complex intertextual connections with D. H. Lawrence.

A theoretical framework for studying the interaction between modernism and the middlebrow has not yet been fully established; such a framework needs to take account of, whilst also challenging, existing theories of modernism's relationship to mass culture. One of the classic accounts is Andreas Huyssen's 1986 book *After the Great Divide*. Huyssen summarizes his influential theory with the statement that "modernism constituted itself through a conscious strategy of exclusion, an anxiety of contamination by its other: an increasingly consuming and engulfing mass culture" (vii).[8] A later book, focused on English literature, is John Carey's *The Intellectuals and the Masses* (1992), which argues that "modernist literature and art can be seen as a hostile reaction to the unprecedentedly large reading public created by late nineteenth-century educational reforms" (i) and that "the pressure of mass culture [drove] intellectuals to invent new proof of their distinction in a world which increasingly found them redundant" (72). These oppositional models of elite and popular have, however, been questioned or modified by other critics. Some demonstrate that many modernist writers were intensely preoccupied with the marketplace,[9] while others point to the interdependence and mutual borrowings between avant-garde and popular forms in the period.[10] Michael North includes in his 1999 book *Reading 1922* a chapter entitled "Across the Great Divide." It opens with an account of Gilbert Seldes's simultaneous involvement, in 1922, in two projects: the publication of *The Waste Land* in *The Dial* (of which Seldes was then managing editor) and the planning of a new book, *The Seven Lively Arts,* which established American popular culture as a legitimate object of critical enquiry. North argues that Seldes's career demonstrates "the larger social and cultural connections between popular culture and literary modernism," revealing both as "part of a larger cultural change in which public life and private came to be dominated by representations, by images" (141).

While North persuasively counters Huyssen's construction of modernism as antipathetic to popular entertainment, he does not move beyond Huyssen's conception of early-twentieth-century cultural production as entirely composed of modernist art and popular entertainment.[11] Huyssen defines the popular culture of the period as "serialized feuilleton novels, popular and family magazines, the stuff of lending libraries, fictional bestsellers and the like" (49), and high culture in terms of modernist writing, making no mention of the vast area of literary production which falls into neither category. North, although demonstrating the connections between the two supposed opposites, maintains the dualistic understanding of early-twentieth-century culture, not acknowledging the presence of a middle ground. Yet the rise of middlebrow culture in this period performed the very task of destabilizing the categories of high and low which North himself seeks to achieve. Nicola Humble argues: "Middlebrow fiction laid claim to the highbrow by assuming an easy familiarity with its key texts and attitudes, while simultaneously caricaturing intellectuals as self-indulgent and naïve" (29). This is an important point, yet middlebrow fiction did not always simply "lay claim" to the highbrow, it frequently expanded and challenged earlier definitions of art and intellectual work. In borrowing from both modernist and mass cultural forms, it diminished the apparent distance between them. Instead of simply responding to high culture, the middlebrow, I would argue, changed the ways in which high culture was understood. The large audience which many middlebrow authors reached gives some indication of the likely impact of such reformulations of cultural hierarchy.

Drawing on the work of Jeffrey Weiss, Michael North also argues that "music hall [. . .] provides a formal model for the avant-garde, a model of ironic juxtaposition in which quick transitions between the high and the low, the comic and the bathetic, the artistic and the commercial deflate pretensions and level out specious distinctions" (152). This deflation and leveling, I would argue, are also accomplished by some middlebrow texts. Indeed, North's description applies perfectly to *Cold Comfort Farm*, with its sudden switches between an Austenian style and the purple prose of the popular rural novel; or to Dorothy Parker's poetry, which combines the disciplined formal purity of Horace and Catullus with the idioms of New York cocktail parties. Texts such as *The Constant Nymph* or *The Diary of a Provincial Lady*, which are obsessively preoccupied with fine distinctions between cultural levels and between different conceptions of taste, art, and culture, ultimately render those distinctions suspect. And the ambiguous cultural status of these texts, with their peculiar and unstable cross-class appeal, itself works to disrupt boundaries between high and low, commercial and artistic. These books critique the commodification of art, yet as highly profitable commodities they become part of the cultural battle which is dramatized in their pages.

The journals in which the work of my chosen authors was published and reviewed also had complex attitudes toward modernism. *Vanity Fair*, the New York magazine where Dorothy Parker was a staff writer and Anita Loos also published, devoted a significant amount of space to experimental artists and writers, even as it satirized their excesses and those of their imitators. Its attitude is epitomized in the anonymous paragraph of introduction prefixed to Stein's "Have They Attacked Mary. He Giggled," published in its pages in 1917:

> Somehow, it seems as if the surest test for the detection of a modern philistine is the poetic work of Gertrude Stein. The reader who takes a delirious joy in the poem which we publish here, who constantly stops

his reading to say "Isn't it great—" "Isn't it wonderful?," etc., is not a philistine. On the contrary, the individual, male or female, who begins foaming at the mouth at Miss Stein's second "page," who shrieks "This is insanity" at the third or fourth, and ends by writing a letter of protest to the Editor of *Vanity Fair*, IS one. Decidedly this second individual is one. Is one decidedly. (Amory and Bradlee, 20–21)

The reference to letters of protest is not an idle one—*Vanity Fair* in fact drew criticism from some of its advertisers for reproducing paintings by Van Gogh, Matisse, and Picasso which were thought to be "decadent and distorted" (Bradlee, 11), and the editor, Frank Crowninshield, had to negotiate between aesthetic principles and commercial considerations. *Vanity Fair*'s choice to print this poem invites serious attention to "difficult" writers such as Stein, while its parody of her encourages a healthy detachment. Gently ridiculing both the champions and the detractors of modernism, the magazine implicitly advocates a balanced approach and seeks to attract both enthusiastic and skeptical readers of modernist writing.

In Britain, the literary weekly *Time and Tide,* where E. M. Delafield was a regular contributor and Stella Gibbons an occasional one, published essays and stories by Bloomsbury Group authors and reviewed their novels favorably, but also featured comic cartoons representing them and printed correspondence from readers who found their work unreadable. In the balance they struck between mockery of highbrow pretension and serious attention to avant-garde writing and art, periodicals such as *Time and Tide* or *Vanity Fair* can be identified with the middlebrow, as I have defined it. The middlebrow provided a vantage point from which high culture, popular culture, and middlebrow culture itself could be critically observed, and permitted the magazines to publish a range of material to appeal across a fairly broad audience, without risking identification as a mass market product. *Vanity Fair* and its sister publication *Vogue* (which had American and European editions) were also important vehicles of the expanding culture of celebrity, featuring many portraits of successful artists and entertainers, as well as nominations for the hall of fame. This was easily reconciled with the sophisticated ethos of the editors; in effect, they encouraged readers to distinguish themselves as culturally literate and socially aware by dropping the right names, and such strategies constituted a resistance to the forms of celebrity available through mass popularity, as opposed to serious artistic or public achievement.

The middlebrow is fundamentally connected with the history of literary celebrity. Most recent studies of celebrity authors, however, make only passing reference to middlebrow culture. The exception is a book by Joe Moran, who points out in *Star Authors* that literary celebrity is "the product of a historically close relationship between certain kinds of authors and a 'middlebrow' print culture, which was ultimately answerable to the marketplace but which also aimed to make literature accessible to the broader populace" (33–34). Moran explains further: "Since they tend to straddle the divide between the restricted and extended subfields of cultural production, celebrity authors are ambiguous figures. As cultural signifiers they often contain elements of the idea of the charismatic, uniquely inspired creative artist associated with the autonomization of the cultural field, but they also gain legitimacy from the notion of celebrity as supported by broad popularity and success in the marketplace" (7). Questions of "brows" and cultural hierarchy are, indeed, intimately linked to literary celebrity, and their relationship is complicated by issues of gender. I understand the term "literary culture" to include all these subjects, and in this study, I analyze gender and celebrity as dimensions of authorship and as aspects of Anglo-American literary culture in the early twentieth century.

CELEBRITY AUTHORS

The history of literary celebrity has been rendered in strikingly male terms. Leo Braudy, in *The Frenzy of Renown: Fame and Its History* (1986, revised 1997), discusses famous writers, politicians, and public figures from Alexander the Great to the present. Of the thirty-eight individuals mentioned in the list of chapter and section headings, only one (Emily Dickinson) is female. Even very recent—and extremely valuable—studies pay only limited attention to famous women. Aaron Jaffe's *Modernism and the Culture of Celebrity* (2005) concentrates on T. S. Eliot, James Joyce, Ezra Pound, and Wyndham Lewis, though it does include illuminating discussion of women modernists, arguing that they were ill-served by modernist modes of self-fashioning and publicity. Loren Daniel Glass's *Authors Inc.: Literary Celebrity in the Modern United States* (2004) is centrally concerned with gender, but argues that literary celebrity is intimately connected with masculinity, since masculine posturing allows celebrity authors to protect themselves from the supposedly feminized mass audiences who in fact ensure their success. His chapters are on Mark Twain, Jack London, Gertrude Stein, Ernest Hemingway, and Norman Mailer. Joe Moran's *Star Authors: Literary Celebrity in America* (2000) likewise includes chapters on four male authors and one female (Twain, Mailer, John Updike, Philip Roth, and Kathy Lette). Both Glass and Moran concentrate on America, and only Jaffe adopts a transatlantic approach. Whilst these books, then, will certainly inform the critical framework of this study, they do not touch on the specific field of literary production which it concentrates on. Limits of geography, period, genre, or gender have excluded the material and the writers I am working with from these, and all other, existing books on celebrity.[12] In general terms, these seven writers have received very limited critical attention, and more specifically, the effect of their fame and commercial success on the reception of their writing has rarely been considered, even though their careers can be seen to represent new paradigms for female literary success.

In recent years, a series of books and articles have immensely improved our understanding of the processes by which celebrity images are constituted and circulated, and the meanings which are invested in them. But in this burgeoning field of celebrity studies, literary celebrity is still only a small subsection, developing rather belatedly.[13] Most specialists in celebrity work in the fields of media studies and sociology, rather than literature, and concentrate on film and the media, or music and sport stardom.[14] Some of this work offers very useful methods, theories, and precedents for the analysis of celebrity authors. But as with the books on literary celebrity, most of these studies concentrate exclusively on America, and there is also a distinct emphasis on the contemporary. Only a few critics have adopted a systematically historical perspective on fame, though several influential theorists (notably Boorstin, Cawelti, Lasch, and Schickel) have looked backwards only to trace a narrative of decline. According to these models, which show the influence of Adorno, the advent of mass media transformed "genuine" artistic fame based on achievement into a culture of high-profile yet disposable celebrities, whose renown is founded more on their personality than their work. More recently, other critics have challenged this line of thinking on the basis that it is too uniformly hostile to popular culture, and that it dismisses the actual achievements of authors, artists, and actors by exaggerating the role of marketing and packaging in producing their fame (see Gamson; Marshall; Moran).

The nature of celebrity is a current obsession in the media as well as the academy, with the result, as Moran writes, that celebrity has become "an unstable, multifaceted phenomenon—the product of a complex negotiation between cultural producers and audiences, the purveyor of both dominant and resistant cultural meanings, and a pivotal point of contention in debates about the relationship between cultural authority and exchange value in capitalist societies" (3). In the specific context of the early twentieth century, celebrity became entangled in the complex relationship between modernism and mass culture, since, as Jaffe argues, these "two systems of cultural production long alleged to be at odds" actually overlap "where the elite promotion of authorial originality meets with the mass phenomenon of celebrity" (88). He explains further:

> The same way modernists and modernism's literary economists fetishize authorship, celebrities and their publicists fetishize the production of self. The rhetoric of both insists on alleged indifference to consumption, studied insensitivity to existing tastes of consumers, readers, audiences, and publics. Yet, both presume a notion of production that cannot be confined to a single productive source but that instead measures production in terms of both the circulation and the relative valuation of its commodities. (90–91)

These tensions can also be discerned in the self-fashioning texts (including autobiography, interviews, letters, and also self-reflexive fiction) published by the authors considered in this book. Partaking of and yet mocking the modernist fetishization of authorship which Jaffe identifies, they also frequently value their own work in terms of its circulation and the profit it generates.

On the whole, though, the authors considered in this study endorse and aspire to a traditional concept of fame as a reward for genuine achievement, as opposed to a more cynical, modern idea of the celebrity as simply "well-known for his well-knownness," as Daniel Boorstin put it (97). Such celebrities were epitomized, during the interwar era, in royalty, or women notorious for their sexual liaisons, such as Peaches Browning in the twenties or Mrs. Simpson in the thirties.[15] There are, though, significant differences in the extent to which the authors studied in the book actually sought fame: West and Montgomery, at one end of the scale, were confessedly determined to become famous, while for Gibbons, at the other, fame was as unexpected as it was undesired. All seven, however, became involved in an active relationship with their own fame. Lorraine York notes that Montgomery "developed a strategic and remarkably intelligent negotiation with the celebrity processes that surrounded her and in part tried to define her" (99). This comment could also be applied to the other authors, and York's approach is a useful corrective to theories which deny any agency to celebrities themselves. Certainly, these writers all capitalized on their fame to at least some extent, and they attempted to exercise a degree of control over their own celebrity images, as well as exploring celebrity culture in their writing.

Literary celebrity, as Moran points out, "is different in significant ways from the celebrity produced by commercial mass media," because the "encroachment of market values on to literary production [. . .] forms part of a complicated process in which various legitimating bodies compete for cultural authority and/or commercial success, and regulate the formation of a literary star system and the shifting hierarchy of stars" (3–4). Therefore, the best-selling and fashionable authors of the interwar years often became the focus of debates about literary value and cultural hierarchy. The terms of this debate are, though, intimately connected with the rise of cinema, and this is one reason why literary celebrity, in spite of its distinctiveness, should not be treated in isolation from other kinds of fame. In the early twentieth century, Hollywood had an immense impact on the operations of literary celebrity. First, and most straightforwardly, films made from novels raised the profile of their authors, even though the studios gave little credit to the original books. Gibbons, Kennedy, Montgomery, West, and Loos all had films made from their work, and these impacted significantly on the status of their texts and the later critical response to them. The film version of *Gentlemen Prefer Blondes,* for example, a sumptuous fifties musical starring Marilyn Monroe and Jane Russell, functioned to detach Loos's novel from its period, obscure its gender politics, and associate it permanently with the sphere of popular entertainment.

Second, hundreds of writers went to Hollywood after the introduction of sound, to work on dialogue.[16] Most of these were men, with a few exceptions such as Dorothy Parker, Lillian Hellman, and Rachel Crothers. (Anita Loos was virtually the only author to begin in Hollywood and then move to a New York–based literary career.)[17] Many of the authors who went to Hollywood prospered financially, but, as Richard Fine argues, almost every one was "disquieted or unnerved by the experience" (13), because "the profession of authorship as he had known it" was under attack there (14). Writers were not much respected in Hollywood; they had no creative control over the films they worked on, and their scripts were often completely rewritten by others. Producers often paid only for the cachet of a well-known author's name, rather than for his or her actual input to the film. This debased authors' achievements by measuring their worth in terms of renown rather than quality.

Third, the star system of Hollywood affected the systems of literary celebrity. To keep labor costs under control, early silent films avoided crediting or publicizing actors or creative personnel. But as demand for new films increased, along with public interest in screen actors, stars began to be named and rapidly became the most powerful figures in the industry. Their rising salaries helped inflate the pay of other workers, including writers, and win them credits and acknowledgment. More importantly, it was Hollywood which made the twenties "a period of unprecedented public fascination with celebrity culture in America" (Helal, 78), a fascination nourished through the media and advertising. This prompted a growth of interest in celebrities outside the film industry, including authors. Richard Schickel describes Scott Fitzgerald as "a pioneering paradigm, the beginnings of a model that now holds controlling sway over the way we apprehend cultural work, which is primarily through cults of personality, through authorial image, and not, primarily, through the work itself" (212). This analysis is unduly bleak and clearly derives from a view of late-twentieth-century culture as degenerate. Nevertheless, I would agree with Schickel's dating of a paradigm shift in literary celebrity to the 1920s; developments in that era certainly do inform current constructions of celebrity authorship.

TRANSATLANTIC EXCHANGE

The influence of Hollywood rapidly became international, inducing the expansion of celebrity culture in countries such as Britain and Canada. Admittedly, in interwar Canada, the cult of personality did not take hold to quite the same extent as it did in the States: owing to Canada's vastness and sparse population, it did not have the large-scale media, entertainment, and distribution infrastructures which in the United States allowed images of celebrities to be circulated through mass-market magazines and films shown in every town. Nevertheless, the growing interest in celebrities in Canada was fed by Hollywood, and the near-saturation of Canadian markets with American cultural products meant that many of the authors and actors most widely recognized in Canada were in fact from the States. (L. M. Montgomery, Mary Pickford, and Norma Shearer were exceptions, and their international success led, ironically, to the frequent misidentification of all three as American.)

In Britain, Hollywood film was highly significant. While the early development of the moving image was led by British and European innovators, by 1920, 80 percent of films shown in British cinemas were American. During the interwar years Hollywood had, of course, many advantages over European film industries, most notably the West Coast sunshine and space, as well as levels of capital unavailable in damaged postwar European economies. The lack of British film stars was another important reason why the industry became somewhat moribund in the UK. British entertainment celebrities, in fact, were often created through the cheaper medium of radio. Whereas radio broadcasting in North America was highly fragmented and localized, Britain established a national corporation, the BBC, in 1922. The network's national coverage and immense popularity made it a highly effective conduit for celebrity culture, and it launched music hall singers and comedians such as Gracie Fields, Elsie and Doris Waters, and Beatrice Lillie into stardom. Lillie was actually from Canada, but because the entertainment industry (and hence the celebrity system) were so undeveloped there, she moved to London and later to New York.

The systems of literary celebrity were on a larger scale in America than elsewhere. While the interwar years might be seen as the great age of American literary celebrity, when writers such as Stein, Fitzgerald, and Hemingway became major stars, it is difficult to identify British equivalents (unless T. S. Eliot is counted as British). It can be argued, though, that some of the best-known names in British literature were famous for reasons connected with scandal, with personality and style, or with marketing. Lawrence, Joyce, and Radclyffe Hall, for example, were celebrated primarily because their books had been banned or put on trial for obscenity. Writers associated with Bloomsbury and bohemia, including Woolf, Vita Sackville-West, and the Sitwells, were also fairly visible, but this was partly because of their unconventional lifestyles and because their modes of dress and décor became fashionable in certain circles. They were not, however, publicized anything like as widely as their American contemporaries. The faces of Hemingway and T. S. Eliot appeared on the cover of mass-circulation magazines *Time* and *Life,* while Stein's name was illuminated in Times Square, but the Sitwells and the Bloomsbury Group were deliberately marketed to an elite audience only.[18] Glass comments that in early-twentieth-century Europe,

> the split between the avant-garde and bourgeois was concretely un-
> dergirded by well-established cultural hierarchies and institution-
> ally separated markets for art and literature. In the modern United
> States—with a much-less-established tradition of high culture and a
> far-more-developed mass cultural public sphere—many authors [. . .]
> found themselves having to adapt to the marketing strategies and au-
> dience sensibilities of large-scale production. (6)

In Canada, high culture was largely imported from Britain, France, and the States, and mass culture almost entirely from America. Publishing and literary culture were not well established at this period, which meant that most Canadian authors—including Montgomery—launched their careers with American periodicals and publishing houses, and many moved to America or Europe.[19]

While all the authors included in this study published best-selling, celebrated books, the Americans achieved a far greater degree of personal fame than the British women. Anita Loos found the British "prone to magnify writers," but as she herself notes, those who were associated with Hollywood, or at least with the theater (she mentions Maugham, Coward, and Lonsdale), attracted by far the most attention. But in America, the institutions by which celebrity was generated—magazines, publishers, film studios—operated on a different scale. Richard Fine writes that in the Twenties, authors who traveled to New York from provincial America or from abroad "discovered a world where [. . .] a writer was a person of consequence" and would receive "prestige, respect, and celebrity" (41). He analyzes the "remarkable richness and vitality of New York's literary life" during the 1920s, "a time of unparalleled prosperity in the literary marketplace" (23–24), when on average 225 new Broadway productions opened each season, and 18 new publishing houses were established in ten years, with the number of new titles doubling between 1920 and 1925. This was partly due to the self-confidence of postwar America and the voracious new appetite for American (rather than European) writers. In Britain, literary culture was not quite so well financed. Many new periodicals sprang up only to collapse after a short period, and journals tended to pay contributors badly. Most British publishers remained very conservative, with their lists largely composed of reprint titles from the Victorian era (see Feather; McDonald). While the Depression severely damaged many British writers' careers, American writers flocked to Hollywood during this period to ensure their incomes. Broadly speaking, during this period, literature became more rapidly and extensively commodified in the States than in Britain or Canada, although as was so often the case, both countries were soon following America's lead.

North American and British middlebrow culture shared many features, but also differed in significant ways. In terms of cultural and book history, the term "middlebrow" generally refers to a set of institutions and initiatives, including book clubs, extension courses, circulating libraries, lists of "great books," radio book programs, and "outline" books (or accessible introductions to subjects such as philosophy or history), which aimed to make high culture available to a broad public.[20] All of these were present in both Britain and North America, although there were differences in their relative importance and the rate at which they developed. The circulating library originated in Britain, and library networks—both free and commercial—were very well established in the UK during the early twentieth century. Boot's Book Lending Service, for example, was established from 1898 onwards in hundreds of local shops, and exchanged over 25 million volumes by 1925 and 35 million by 1938. Library provision, especially in rural areas, was more comprehensive in Britain than in America, due of course to the relative size of the two countries.

Although library usage was very significant to the development of American middlebrow culture, there was perhaps a greater emphasis on book ownership in the States than in the UK, particularly in the earlier decades of the century. In 1923, President Calvin Coolidge exhorted the American population to improve their minds, become more successful in their work, and develop spiritually. To achieve these things, he advised, "you must read books. And you must do more than read them. You must own them, make them part of you. And you must choose the *right* books" (Coolidge). As Megan Benton comments: "Ownership of books, which had traditionally bestowed a certain elite cultural credential, meant less and less per se as unprecedented numbers of Americans began to buy books for a host of reasons, including explicitly for their iconographic powers" (270). The equivalent book-buying boom in Britain did not occur until the 1930s, stimulated in particular by Penguin's introduction of the sixpenny book in 1935. The introduction of book clubs did much to stimulate sales in both countries. While Britain had the Times Book Club as early as 1904, this was not really a book club in the modern sense, as it began as a lending library and only sold retired library titles rather than new books.[21] It was the Book-of-the-Month Club, established in America in 1926, which was the progenitor of the series of successful and profitable book clubs and societies set up on both sides of the Atlantic. Members benefited from reduced prices and advice on choosing what to read, while publishers gained publicity from the discussion generated by the clubs. Book clubs brought significant popularity to many women authors, and novels by most of the writers considered in this study were book club choices during the twenties and thirties.

WOMEN WRITERS

Although the interwar years were marked by various forms of hostility toward women's writing in all three countries, this was also a time when new generations of female authors gained an increasing share of the Anglo-American literary market, and they left a rich legacy of work in all genres. A summary of the vast and diverse literary production of women during the early twentieth century cannot, of course, be attempted, but the outlines may be traced. The best-remembered interwar Canadian women writers, aside from Montgomery, are the poet Dorothy Livesay and the novelists Mazo de la Roche, Nellie McClung, Martha Ostenso, Laura Goodman Salverson, and Lily Adams Beck. With the exception of Livesay, these are all authors of series of high-selling books. Indeed, Anglo-Canadian women's writing of the period might be broadly characterized in terms of popular or middlebrow fiction, rather than landmark texts belonging to "high culture" or the avant-garde. A clear tendency toward regional writing, romantic tropes, and stylistic conservatism is also visible.

The literary production of American and British women during the early twentieth century was more diverse. In the United States, regional authors such as Willa Cather, Edna Ferber, or Zona Gale and realists like Edith Wharton flourished alongside stylish urban writers like Loos, West, and Parker, as well as the Harlem Renaissance authors (among them Nella Larsen and Zora Neale Hurston), and also a highly experimental group including Anaïs Nin, Gertrude Stein, Amy Lowell, Mina Loy, Djuna Barnes, and H. D. Progressive modern writers such as Susan Glaspell and Ellen Glasgow were also successful, and among the best-known poets of the era were Elinor Wylie and

Edna St. Vincent Millay. Popular and children's novelists included Jessie Fauset, Fannie Hurst, Margaret Mitchell, and Laura Ingalls Wilder. The work of British women during this period is also wonderfully exciting and various. Among the best-remembered are the Bloomsbury writers and the modernists (Virginia Woolf, Vita Sackville-West, Sylvia Townsend Warner, Nancy Cunard, Dorothy Richardson, Bryher), the romantic and detective novelists (Daphne du Maurier, Ethel M. Dell, Barbara Cartland, Agatha Christie, Dorothy L. Sayers), the children's authors (Enid Blyton, Richmal Crompton, Beatrix Potter), the political writers of the thirties (Winifred Holtby, Vera Brittain, Naomi Mitchison, Rebecca West), the writers of empire (Rumer Godden, Jean Rhys), and a group including Rosamond Lehmann, May Sinclair, Elizabeth Bowen, and Rose Macaulay, who are now beginning to be reread as participants in the modernist project.[22]

This fascinating and until recently underanalyzed body of writing is now attracting increasing attention from critics. A whole range of books and articles on the Anglo-American women's writing of the wartime and interwar years has appeared over the past twenty years, and many others consider both women and men authors of the period. It is impossible to list them all here, but a sample of the most recent may be mentioned. In the short period since the turn of the century, important monographs by Phyllis Lassner, Jane Garrity, Deborah Parsons, Nicola Humble, Kristin Bluemel, Jane Dowson, and Diana Wallace have been published, as well as edited collections by Lisa Botshon and Meredith Goldsmith, Stella Deen, and Ann Ardis and Leslie W. Lewis. Most books on interwar literature concentrate on either American or—more frequently—British literature; a few recent books take a comparative approach (Ardis and Lewis, Deen, Parsons); none includes Canada in its frame of reference. The transatlantic comparison, and the inclusion of Canada, allow for a much more nuanced understanding of the role of celebrity in Anglo-American literary culture, especially because the celebrity images of the authors were invested with different meanings in the three countries. Canada is currently a very significant site of celebrity authorship (Margaret Atwood and Michael Ondaatje, for example, are major international stars), but the history of literary celebrity in Canada is not simply a late-twentieth-century phenomenon, since L. M. Montgomery is one of the most high-profile and widely read female authors of all time.

Despite the recent flowering of scholarship on interwar writing, most of the authors chosen for this study have been the subject of very little criticism. Yet their names are among the most widely recognized among women authors of their era, and in some senses, they are still celebrities now. Books such as *Cold Comfort Farm* or *The Diary of a Provincial Lady* continue to be highly popular, while Anne of Green Gables retains her iconic value and the Prince Edward Island tourist industry inspired by Montgomery is burgeoning. Owing to their involvement with the high life of New York and Hollywood, the three American authors are identified with popular cultural visions of the interwar decades, and the received idea of the twenties and thirties conjures the kind of glamor which they embody. Indeed, nostalgia for the 1920s and 1930s is currently at a new height—witness the proliferation of books, Web sites, and college courses about the Jazz Age or the Thirties; the republication of interwar lifestyle and etiquette manuals;[23] the revivals of twenties and thirties fashions; the increasing interest in early cinema and silent film; the numerous new productions and films of musicals such as *Chicago, Cabaret, The Boyfriend, Bugsy Malone, On Your Toes, No, No, Nanette!,* and *Guys and Dolls;* and the recent films set in the twenties and thirties, such as *Gosford Park* (2001), *O Brother, Where Art Thou?* (2000), *The Newton Boys* (1998), *Sky Captain and the World of Tomorrow* (2004), and *The Aviator* (2004). This book, then, takes account of the growth in both academic and popular interest in the early decades of the twentieth century, and contributes to the cultural and literary history of the period through attention to authors whose work is intriguing, popular, and yet insufficiently understood or analyzed.

METHODS AND STRUCTURE

My critical framework positions Parker, Loos, West, Montgomery, Kennedy, Gibbons, and Delafield in relation to intersections among gender, authorship, celebrity, and cultural value, issues which are of immense and growing importance in modern literary studies. I analyze the rhetorical strategies these authors adopt to project their celebrity personae, both in their writing and in interviews or public appearances. Through extended close readings, I also trace the tensions relating to gender and celebrity, and to publicity, performance, and cultural hierarchies, which inform their fiction, journalism, and autobiography. The impact of fame and high sales on the authors' cultural capital is explored through attention to the reception of their most celebrated texts and their self-positioning in relation to high and popular culture.

Although the topics and concerns I have outlined above run throughout the book, the emphasis is deliberately different in each chapter. This is partly because of the varied nature of the authors' careers and literary production, and the differing kinds of published and archival material available in relation to each writer. More importantly, the careers of these particular authors were selected as case studies because each illuminates a different aspect of the ways celebrities were constituted in interwar literary culture. Magazines and newspapers, theater and cinema, prizes and censorship all come into focus in specific chapters. I read the work of the seven writers alongside a variety of other texts, including memoirs, book and film reviews, obituaries, cinema publicity material, newspaper profiles, personal letters and diaries, literary and glamor magazines, and the minutes of a prize committee. In these ways, the project expands beyond the seven chosen authors to engage with the broader cultural and literary discourses of the period.

The book is arranged by country, with American writers considered in the first three chapters and British writers in the last three. The chapter on L. M. Montgomery, placed centrally, situates Canada in relation to American and British literary culture and draws together many of the book's key concerns. Born rather earlier than the other authors, Montgomery achieved success before the First World War. My discussion in this chapter therefore extends back to the 1910s, but is primarily concerned with Montgomery's celebrity in the postwar period, when her books began to be filmed. Through close readings of newspaper profiles and book and film reviews, the chapter considers the values invested in Montgomery's celebrity image and in the images of the Hollywood actresses playing Anne, especially Mary Miles Minter, who starred in the first film in 1919.

Four of the chapters offer case studies of particular books, considering the relationship between the fame of a novel or its heroine and the fame of the author. *The Constant Nymph, Cold Comfort Farm, The Diary of a Provincial Lady,* and *Gentlemen Prefer Blondes* have all become isolated by literary history, which has difficulty explaining and incorporating them into its structures. An analysis of the conditions of production and reception of these books provides many insights into the literary culture of the interwar years, while accounts of the changing status of the novels and their authors in later years can illuminate shifting critical priorities. Close reading of these novels reveals the extent of their preoccupation with celebrity itself, with performance and publicity, with questions of taste and cultural value, and with the gendered aspects of authorship. Material from several significant archives, which have not been consulted by previous critics, informs these chapters. Of particular importance are: first, Kennedy's letters to a close friend, detailing her responses to the success of her work and to her sudden fame, and second, the minutes and correspondence of the Femina Vie Heureuse prize committee. Kennedy was a member of the committee, and one of its annual prizes was awarded to Gibbons; the papers illuminate the processes by which books are consecrated through literary prizes.

Two chapters are devoted to authors whose invention of themselves as public figures takes precedence over the significance of any of their individual books: Mae West and Dorothy Parker. Parker refused to collaborate fully with the commercial agendas of the magazines she published in; instead of promoting the products they endorsed (whether haute couture or Broadway shows), she instead promoted herself through her fashion captions and theater reviews. Interacting with her own celebrity image in complex ways, she became a mistress of self-satire, yet even this became a way of consolidating her trademark persona. West, like Parker, is remembered principally for her personality and her memorable quips; and in their self-construction as public figures, verbal wit and sexual innuendo were crucial. What is there to choose between West's "A hard man is good to find" and Parker's excuse for uncompleted reviews, "too fucking busy and vice versa"?[24] West's career offers insight into the relationships between literary celebrity and cinematic and theatrical celebrity. Her extension of cultures of performance into the realm of fiction is an unusual trajectory, and her three novels reinforce her celebrity image, as well as reflecting on the ways in which it was circulated.

Many of the women authors who were popular, admired, and influential in the interwar years have subsequently been neglected in favor of their more avant-garde contemporaries. The highly important contribution of such writers to the shaping of interwar literature and culture urgently requires reassessment. While the discussion centers on particular books and authors, the conclusions are intended to apply more broadly, and to advance understanding of the cultural history of the early twentieth century, and particularly of the meanings of celebrity authorship in that period. Finally, while the close readings are designed to draw out the intellectual significance of the texts discussed, the quotations should also give an idea of the enjoyment which the books afford. These texts are not only highly significant elements of interwar culture; they also continue to appeal widely to modern readers. This project was inspired by my own pleasure in the witty, original, and versatile writing produced by these women, and I hope to communicate this pleasure in what follows.

1 | "HOW TO TELL THE DIFFERENCE BETWEEN A MATISSE PAINTING AND A SPANISH OMELETTE"

Dorothy Parker, Vogue, and Vanity Fair

The Dorothy Parker persona has come down to us not only through her own writing but via biography, scholarship, film, memoir, and popular nostalgia for the 1920s. The creation of Dorothy Parker as celebrity was begun through her own cultivation of an identifiable style, by means of her journalism and her social image, especially her highly publicized association with the Algonquin Round Table. But her writing soon became subordinated to the mythologized image of the viciously witty "Mrs. Parker," and eventually the Parker legend exceeded her control and eclipsed her actual literary achievements.

Parker's work has been further marginalized by her own anxious relationship to the literary. Many of her poems and stories are ambivalent and self-conscious about literary value. While she needed to sell her work in order to survive, she nevertheless refused to conform to literary fashions and popular audience requirements, and satirized popular novels, critics, fictional heroines, and profits.[1] Like some of the other authors discussed in this study, Parker tended to underrate her own work. Yet her career was highly successful: she published in the most prestigious American magazines, and her theater and book columns were popular and influential. Her first poetry collection, *Enough Rope* (1926), made the best seller lists, an almost unprecedented achievement for a book of verse, and her next volume, *Sunset Gun* (1928), followed suit. Her story "Big Blonde" won the coveted O. Henry Award for 1929, and she also worked on the scripts for several films which became classics, including *A Star Is Born* (1937), *Nothing Sacred* (1937), and *Saboteur* (1942).

In selecting from her magazine publications to compile volumes, Parker consolidated her celebrity persona; as Stuart Silverstein says of *Enough Rope:* "she deliberately chose to include those verses whose substance and style reflected what she hoped to project as her own, that is, the scarred and astringent modern woman [. . .] experienced in sex but cynical of love" (32). Silverstein, editor of *The Uncollected Dorothy Parker,* himself contributes to the mythologizing of Parker by collecting her witticisms and attempting to define her legend. Other recent revisions of the Parker myth have similar emphases: Arthur F. Kinney refers to "the recognizable Dorothy Parker persona, that of the woman who is both exploited and thick-skinned, who is put upon but can equally well put down others" (91), while Nina Miller notes that "By the time of her first best-selling collection in 1926, she had made a national career for herself as the most luckless and sardonic woman lover on literary record" (763).

These recent characterizations of "Dorothy Parker" are evidently based on the speaker of her lyric poems. Parker's contemporaries wrote much less about her rhetorical and literal role as lover and emphasized instead her manners, brain, and dangerousness. Anita Loos remembered: "we never became friends. I was overawed by her brilliant mind and had no desire to be a target for her irony" (*Girl,* 149). Somerset Maugham recalled his first meeting with her, "demure in black silk, but with a demureness fraught with peril to the unwary" (599). Lillian Hellman refers to Parker's "behind-the-back denunciations of almost comic violence" of most of those she met (*Unfinished Woman,* 172), but also recalls: "Her view of people was original and sharp, her elaborate, overdelicate manners made her a pleasure to live with, she liked books and was generous about writers, and the wit, of course, was so wonderful that neither age nor illness ever dried up the spring" (173). The best-known description of Parker is by Alexander Woollcott, one of her Round Table companions. In August 1933, Woollcott published a profile of her in *Cosmopolitan* titled "Our Mrs. Parker,"[2] which was reprinted the following year in his best-selling essay collection *While Rome Burns.* It was at this point that Parker herself (as opposed to her work) became a "marketable commodity of distinct proportions" (Silverstein, 12). Woollcott labeled his profile a "Portrait of a poet attempted by one who, abashed by the difficulties of the undertaking, breaks down and weakly resorts to a hundred familiar quotations" (142), demonstrating that Parker's witty sayings were already the stuff of legend in the early Thirties. The profile itself contributed substantially to the myth of "Mrs. Parker," and Woollcott's memorable description of her as "so odd a blend of Little Nell and Lady Macbeth" (149) has been much quoted.

Parker has received much attention from memoirists, biographers, filmmakers, collectors of quotations, and even compilers of dictionaries (as she was the first to make use of certain new colloquial phrases in print).[3] But since her writing has been sidelined by her celebrity image and her widely quoted epigrams, literary critics have—until very recently—given her little acknowledgment. In an article on Parker and Mina Loy, Jessica Burstein suggests: "Perhaps Parker has been overlooked in scholarly circles not only because she is understood as neither hard nor grim, but because she is already familiar. That familiarity is reflected in the probability of our having access to some shard of Parkeriana" (233). Indeed, many people can quote the brief poem "Men seldom make passes / At girls who wear glasses" ("News Item") or Parker's response when challenged to construct a sentence containing the word "horticulture": "You can lead a horticulture, but you can't make her think."[4] Regina Barreca, in her introduction to a 1995 edition of Parker's stories, argues that "Parker has been slammed for at least thirty years," accused of being a commercial writer and of confining herself to narrow topics. Barreca counters: "Parker's work is anything—anything—but slight, concerning as it does life, death, marriage, divorce, love, loss, dogs, and whisky" (x). The work of Burstein and Barreca is part of a recent, if still limited, growth of critical interest in Parker,[5] which has taken place in the context of increasing attention to the women's writing of the modernist period and of expansive redefinitions of the categories "modern" and "modernist." Two further articles, by Nina Miller and Kathleen Helal, have offered important new insights into Parker's rhetorical relationship with her audience.

These essays concentrate primarily on Parker's poetry and, to a lesser extent, her short fiction. The valuable analyses they offer can be significantly extended and developed through consideration of Parker's uncollected journalism, especially her contributions to *Vanity Fair* and also her early work at American *Vogue.* Like her verse and fiction, her journalism mediates the discourses of sophistication, sentiment, and Modern Love,[6] and also relates in complex ways to Parker's public persona. Her magazine writing deserves examination for the insights it offers into the construction of Parker's celebrity image. More broadly, this material throws light on the ways in which New York magazines participated in celebrity culture and literary culture in the early twentieth century.

"Some Brief Statements Regarding Lingerie"

Parker's talent was first recognized by the influential Frank Crown-inshield (also Anita Loos's mentor). In 1915, Crowninshield got Parker her first literary job with *Vogue* and two years later took her on as a staff writer for *Vanity Fair*, which he edited. Most critics and biographers pass rapidly over her period at *Vogue*, since it was not until she moved to *Vanity Fair* that she became a star. But it was at *Vogue*, I would argue, that Parker first began to develop her distinctive literary persona, even though she rarely contributed signed pieces [7] and was largely employed in composing captions for fashion drawings.

Picture captions printed in American *Vogue* during the 1910s are never attributed, and only this famous one is known to be Parker's: "From these foundations of the autumn wardrobe, one may learn that brevity is the soul of lingerie, as the Petticoat said to the Chemise." [8] Nevertheless, it is relatively easy to guess which are hers. The standard idiom of the *Vogue* fashion caption of this era is exemplified in the following, chosen at random:

> Summer isn't really summer unless one has a silk frock. This one is of white tub silk cross-barred with any of various colors and combined with white Georgette crêpe with charming results. [9]

> Excellence of material and making mark this slip-on blouse of flesh or white batiste trimmed only with ruffles of itself. [10]

Interspersed with such bland endorsements can be found some rather different captions. On 1 June 1916, a page was devoted to dresses by "Jenny," one of which is labeled:

> A rose organdy frock fully believes in meeting every extremity with a frill of black Chantilly; in fact, a good part of its skirt is given over to black Chantilly, through which one sees, as through a glass, darkly. Whenever she could think of nothing else to do to the frock, Jenny embroidered strange designs on it in black. [11]

This is surely Parker. Who else would incorporate a biblical quotation into a description of a summer dress? The skeptical tone refuses the usual function of such write-ups, which is to collaborate with fashion houses (which also make up a large proportion of *Vogue*'s advertisers) in selling their wares. The majority of *Vogue*'s fashion stories, then as now, are commercials thinly disguised as news, but Parker turned hers into an eccentric literary genre.

The rest of the fashion captions during the magazine's early years are anonymous in all senses; they draw attention to the picture rather than to themselves. But those which I attribute to Parker take a far more personal tone, suggesting individual authorship through a distinctive combination of allusion, punning wit, and double entendre. One feature in 1916 is headed: "Premet Makes Some Brief Statements Regarding Lingerie, Fully Covering the Subject with Two Tea-Gowns," and one of the sketches is labeled:

> "Other times, other knickers," remarked Premet, and behold the result. They are of taffeta changing from yellow to rose, and their width is due to pockets, for even harmless necessary knickers are knee-deep in pockets these days. At the knees, tasseled rose and yellow cords draw their own conclusions. As for the bodice above—well, there it is, "sans peur et sans support."[12]

Parker is said to have written several captions *Vogue* would not print, but its editors did permit many which are definitely risqué. In one issue, she evidently captioned the regular feature on clothes for adolescents:

> There is only one thing as thrilling as one's first love affair; that is one's first corset. They both give the same feeling of delightful importance. This one is planned to give something approaching a waistline to the straight sturdiness of the twelve-year-old. It is of cotton tricot, boned a bit in back, and those shoulder-straps are more than mere mementos of the corset waist our infancy knew—the whole affair hangs on them.
>
> This tricot corset may be had in white or flesh color, and there are two elastic bands at the top so that one may bend when and where and as far and as often as one pleases.
>
> A corset of flesh colored tricot, slightly boned, is particularly suitable for the extremely young person who is also the ardently athletic

person; and it is equally to be desired should one be less young but just as athletic. It starts off with a narrow band of thread lace at the height of its career, but all the rest of the way is plain sailing.[13]

Parker is here developing the combination of innuendo with a superficial feminine demureness which would later characterize both her social image and her poetic persona, giving rise to Woollcott's remark about Little Nell and Lady Macbeth. While Mae West gave apparently innocent lines a sexual charge through the way she delivered them, Dorothy Parker reversed this strategy, and is remembered for cultivating a quiet, ladylike appearance, which gave added piquancy to her suggestive and bitchy remarks. According to Woollcott: "She has the gentlest, most disarming demeanor of anyone I know. [. . .] But Mrs. Parker carries—as everyone is uneasily aware—a dirk which knows no brother and mighty few sisters" (149).

In May 1916, *Vogue* featured a page of photos of actresses currently starring on the New York stage, and their captions are strongly suggestive of Parker:

> Lola Fisher is not always being photographed with an uncomfortable cat. In between times, she can be found making a success of herself as Nan in "Rio Grande," Augustus Thomas's new play.

> Anne Murdock, that young person of whom dramatic critics are never able to write without using the words "Billie Burke," appears in the title rôle of "Suki," Winchell Smith's latest comedy.

> Like truth, intelligence crushed to earth will rise again—even the intelligence of the theatre-going public. Proof: Galsworthy's "Justice," in which Cathleen Nesbitt plays the only feminine role.

> Phyllis Neilson-Terry played Lady Harding in "The Great Pursuit," in which there were so many stars that the footlights were practically superfluous.[14]

Just as *Vogue*'s fashion captions promoted the wares and services of particular dress designers, shops, and interior decorators, so its photograph captions were usually wholly admiring, "puffing" show business celebrities and reinforcing the preeminence of high society women. They thus take on a function akin to advertising. Once again, Parker refuses to cooperate with this agenda, and instead works to hone her personal style. Her labels for the pictures of actresses function as mini-reviews, even entering into dialogue with other reviewers; and they foreshadow the epigrammatic, polished, yet frequently contemptuous tone which she adopted when she actually became a theater critic. Although not attributed, the *Vogue* theater and fashion captions are recognizable as Parker's precisely because they represent the first stage in the consolidation of her style, and thus, in the invention of her legend.

"WE NOMINATE FOR THE HALL OF FAME"

Parker's mocking tone offended *Vogue*'s conservative, supremely ladylike editor, Edna Woolman Chase. As Parker's biographer Marion Meade points out, what she was actually doing during this period was "training herself to write in the Frank Crowninshield genre" (43), and certainly, her work was much more appropriate for *Vanity Fair* than for *Vogue*. Although the two magazines, both owned by Condé Nast, shared preoccupations with fashion and the famous, they differed significantly in emphasis and attitude. American *Vogue*, established in 1892, concentrated on women's clothes and dressmaking, supplementing this with features on interiors, gardens, etiquette, and entertaining. It published no fiction and little poetry, and its coverage of the arts was limited to columns in the back pages entitled "Seen on the Stage" and "What They Read." These headings suggest a conception of plays and books as mere accoutrements of fashionable society. Indeed, the columns' implicit purpose is to advise readers as to which plays to be seen at, and which books to be seen reading, while art exhibitions are treated primarily as events in the fashionable calendar. *Vanity Fair,* which appeared from 1914 until 1936,[15] offered far more extensive coverage of the arts. There were reviews, photographs, serious discussions, and comic pieces, encompassing both experimental and traditional art forms, and all addressed to culturally literate readers.

Both magazines were preoccupied with social image, but in different styles. The ideal *Vogue* reader would project her image through clothes, accessories, quiet good taste, and correct behavior, and the *Vanity Fair* reader through sophistication, wit, provocative opinions, and a wide cultural knowledge. While *Vogue* was a women's magazine, *Vanity Fair* included regular features on cars, men's clothing, and masculine accessories, had many male contributors, and addressed its advertisements to readers of both genders: "if, despite your youth, you are becoming an old fogey, or an old maid, or an old bachelor, or an old bore; if your *joie de vivre* is dying at the roots—then you must read *Vanity Fair* and presto! you will be nimble-witted and agile-minded again."[16] *Vanity Fair* also published witty cartoons, satires, and parodies, often mocking particular social and artistic "types," together with light essays and varied features. The magazine was initially modeled on British papers like *The Sketch* and *The Tatler*,[17] and in its early years, it nostalgically idealized Englishness, running features on English country houses, English humorists, and so forth. But *Vanity Fair* rapidly became identified specifically with New York. As Miller notes: "the development of a distinctively urbane New York sensibility arose with a more general commodification of style in the consumerist 1910s and 1920s" (764), and *Vanity Fair* was a pioneer in this field. *Vogue,* on the other hand, associated itself with European style; it was a showcase for French haute couture, and in one 1916 issue, the contents page proclaimed: "IT comes from Paris."[18]

When *Dress and Vanity Fair* (as it was initially called) was launched, a series of adverts for it appeared in *Vogue.* The established status of the earlier magazine was invoked to guarantee the quality of the new one, but *Dress and Vanity Fair* was identified as having a "broader field" than *Vogue,* and was marketed in terms of exclusivity and sophistication:

> Our ambition is not towards a popular magazine with a big subscription list. We don't expect everybody to be interested in "Dress and Vanity Fair," and, frankly, we shall not try to interest everybody. On the other hand, there are, we believe, a great number of people, who will thoroughly enjoy the cleverness, the variety, the dash and appreciate the fastidiousness and luxuriousness that shall in time make "Dress and Vanity Fair" the most distinctive among all American magazines.[19]

Each monthly issue began with a one-page text without a byline, ostensibly an editorial, but actually a promotional exercise. Witty and light-hearted, these pieces took various dramatic and fictional forms, and "negotiated a terrain defined by sophistication and gender relations, with the strong implication that the two were inexorably intertwined" (Miller, 765). This, of course, was precisely the terrain which Dorothy Parker made her own, and she began to do so when working at *Vanity Fair*. Indeed, she wrote some of these pseudo-editorials herself, claiming authorship by signing them D. P., instead of leaving them anonymous, as was usual.

In May 1919, her text "The Story of a Warrior's Return" recounts the arrival in New York of a soldier who, owing to his long absence, can no longer find his way about and does not recognize the current celebrities: "He realized that he could not distinguish a musical comedy star from a débutante, could not tell a mannequin from a social light. He [. . .] could not tell which were imagist poets, and which moving picture heroes; he did not know the steel magnates from the golf professionals" (D. P., "So This Is"). Parker's implication is that scales of cultural value (from imagism to Hollywood cinema) are in fact defined by discriminations of style and fashion, rather than by inherent "quality." Cultural hierarchies, she suggests provocatively, are constructed in a similar way to scales of social value (from débutante to mannequin); both are known through their celebrity representatives, and all that is required to understand them is current knowledge and urbanity. In the story, the soldier, whose prewar savoir faire is now worthless, suddenly feels provincial: "It seems as if wisps of hay were sticking out of my hair." He exclaims: "If only I could just get a good working knowledge of the places to go and the people who go there!" Naturally, his problem is instantly solved by a newsstand girl, who hands him a copy of *Vanity Fair,* explaining: "Here's a whole course of study in the art of being a New Yorker. It's a Who's Who in New York" (D. P., "So This Is").[20]

Both the Condé Nast magazines were important conduits of the expanding culture of celebrity in the early twentieth century (though *Vanity Fair* was distinctive in that it also reflected critically on celebrity culture, as Parker's soldier story demonstrates). Each magazine featured numerous full-page portraits in every issue, together with several galleries of smaller photographs. In *Vogue,* the pictures were mainly of society women: there were many posed portraits of brides or of mothers with small children, captioned with details of genealogy and connections. Groups of pictures documented horse-race meetings, social events of the New York Season, the clientele of summer resorts or luxury hotels, and the interiors of great houses. American *Vogue* also included one or two pictures of actresses or female dancers in each issue and occasionally ran photo features on creative artists. In *Vanity Fair,* by contrast, almost all the large portraits were of performers: stage and screen actors, singers, and dancers, both male and female. The photo features were as likely to focus on sets of successful novelists, playwrights, artists, or composers as on film stars. The contrast is much less marked, however, if *Vanity Fair* is compared to British *Vogue*. As Jane Garrity points out, the British edition showcased the Bloomsbury Group as "celebrity tastemakers," printing portraits of them and their houses ("Selling," 40), while many modernist writers and artists "willingly participated in the selling of high culture to *Vogue*'s elite female audience" (32). The readers of British *Vogue* were elite in class rather than intellectual terms, but as Garrity demonstrates, the magazine encouraged them to seek distinction in all aspects of their lives.

The achievement of some form of distinction is the criterion for inclusion in *Vanity Fair*'s regular feature "We Nominate for the Hall of Fame," but it purveyed a strikingly broad concept of fame. In March 1919, for example, the four nominees were Edward F. Albee, owner of the Keith vaudeville circuit; Lady Patricia Ramsay, daughter of the Duke of Connaught; Dr. Simon Flexner, director of the Rockefeller Institute; and David H. Greer, Bishop of New York. The photograph captions offer a diverse range of reasons for the nominations, from financial power and justice toward employees (Albee) through birth, beauty, and charm (Lady Patricia) to "energy, inspiration" and advocacy "of the destruction of false conventionalism" (Greer). But while this suggests a fairly traditional idea of fame as something which must be earned by unusual ability, virtue, and effort, the magazine also participates in the search for novelty and gossip typical of more lowbrow publications. The four figures chosen for March 1919 were currently "in the news": Lady Patricia had just got married, Simon Flexner had just been awarded the Legion of Honor, and so forth.[21]

Even as it pandered to public interest in the famous, *Vanity Fair* maintained a certain skepticism toward the celebrity system. The "Hall of Fame" feature was occasionally replaced by a "Hall of Oblivion," nominating people who should be quickly forgotten, and satire of celebrity behavior was a staple of the magazine. The witty cartoons by "Fish" (Anne Harriet Fish, later Sefton) were particularly effective in this respect. Her themed sets of illustrations were always captioned, at first anonymously but increasingly (from 1920 onwards) by a named author, often by Dorothy Parker. (This suggests that magazines were beginning to recognize captions themselves as a creative form—maybe because writers like Parker had turned them into one.) The cartoon features reduced the stars of the social and artistic worlds to a series of "types," denying them the distinction and individuality which is the supposed hallmark of fame. For example, in December 1920 a set of sketches illustrated various difficult celebrity marriages. Among the characters are "two great opera-stars," who cannot agree which of them should sing first, leading to "harmony distinctly à la Stravinsky"; a "feature-film star of the first magnitude" who marries into the aristocracy; a "famous man-modiste" in a relationship with his mannequin; and a "leading lady who insists on hitching her wagon to a male star" ("Mysterious Marriages," 66, 67). These illustrations and their captions interpret fame in terms of social visibility or notoriety, and—like Parker's story about the soldier—they discriminate between sculptors and oil millionaires or between actresses and débutantes purely on the basis of personal style. The subtitle of the piece, "A Scientific Search into Certain Matings and Mis-matings," indicates the contemporary rhetorical appeal to science. The piece attempts a "taxonomy" of social types, while the exaggerated gestures of the cartoon figures turn all the social roles into predictable displays. There is a continuity between these cartoon features and Dorothy Parker's fiction and poetry, with their preoccupation with social performance and celebrity behavior.[22]

"FREE SPEECH, AND FREE VERSE, AND FREE LOVE, AND FREE EVERYTHING"

In 1920, a selection of Fish's illustrated features was published in book form, with the title *High Society: The Drawings by Fish. The Prose Precepts by Dorothy Parker, George S. Chappell, and Frank Crowninshield.* The title page describes the book as offering "Advice as to Social Campaigning, and Hints on the Management of Dowagers, Dinners, Debutantes, Dances, and the Thousand and One Diversions of Persons of Quality." This title, suggesting a parodic version of an etiquette manual,[23] is a little misleading, since the book contains as many pictures of sculptors, poets, and bohemians as of aristocrats and socialites, and one of its primary satiric targets is artistic pretension. On the pages entitled "Advice to the Lovelorn: What Every Girl Should Know Before Choosing a Husband," the pictures include a young man declaiming dramatically to a bored-looking girl, captioned as follows:

> Beware the modernist poet. There is a time in every girl's life—usually around Spring—when she falls in love with the Professional Poet. He wears his hair in the manner made popular by Irene Castle, and he believes in free speech, and free verse, and free love, and free

everything. His favorite game is reading from his own works—such selections as his "Lines to an Un-moral Tulip." (Fish, 40)

The girl is equally bored by "The Futurist—with a Past," whose caption runs:

> Then there is the Futurist Artist. He is really a great factor in a girl's education; he can show her how, at a glance, to tell the difference between a Matisse painting and a Spanish omelette, and he knows just what the vorticists are trying to prove. He dresses like the property artist in musical comedies and he is simply ripping at designing costumes—he tells you how Lucile is battling to engage him, if he would only descend to commercialism. Avoid them, girls, avoid them! They always have a past! (Fish, 41) [24]

The fraudulence of these two figures consists not only in their unjustified claims to specialized knowledge and talent, but also in their pretended denunciation of the commercial (in reality, they want to be given "free everything"). Their recognizability as "types" destroys their claim to distinction.

As well as publishing Fish's visual mockery of celebrities, *Vanity Fair* also included prose features and stories lampooning would-be stars or analyzing cultures of publicity. In 1927, Walter Lippmann's essay "Blazing Publicity" refers repeatedly to the "machinery" of publicity, pointing to mechanical reproduction as a precondition for the new celebrity culture, and suggesting that it detaches publicity from any kind of moral function. The machine, he argues, cannot be made "to regulate itself in a civilized fashion" (121) since it is "guided by newspaper men. They are the watchers who scan the horizon constantly looking for the event which may become the next nine days' wonder" (121). By publishing this piece, *Vanity Fair* might be seen to be implicitly comparing itself (favorably) to the newspaper men; proposing that, in honoring only those who have achieved something significant in fields such as art, sport, or public affairs, and not writing about scandals, murders, and the like, the magazine is in fact regulating the publicity machine in a civilized fashion.

Another article, "Putting Over a Prima Donna," which appeared in *Vanity Fair* in 1919, argues that a prima donna does not achieve the pinnacle of fame by "soaring up, up, above the common crowd" but by being "properly merchandised" by her manager and press agent

(Ross, 100). In the same year, Dorothy Parker herself, under the pseudonym Helen Wells,[25] wrote a spoof entitled "The Autobiography of Any Movie Actress, Set Down in the Regulation Manner," featuring a relentlessly self-promotional starlet. Obeying the modern logic of celebrity, the supposed actress exaggerates the extent of her own publicity in order to generate more: "you know the rest, [. . .] all you who flock to see every 'film' that I appear in, who eagerly read every line about me that is printed in the papers, and who besiege me with requests for my photograph, signature, and 'cast-off' clothing" (Wells, 33). These, and numerous similar articles, demonstrate *Vanity Fair*'s determination to reflect on celebrity culture, as well as participating in it, and this doubtless informed Parker's own critical analyses of the star system, as well as her acute awareness of how she, as the celebrated "Mrs. Parker," was expected to behave.

"MY INTENSE SUFFERING DURING THE PERFORMANCE"

For the magazines of postwar New York, Dorothy Parker's name had an increasing value. Back at *Vogue,* her name had been worth little, not only because she was then at the start of her career, but also because of the magazine's approach to authorship. In its early decades, *Vogue*—in its American and European editions—showcased photographers (such as Edward Steichen, Cecil Beaton, and George Hoyningen-Huene) rather than authors. Staff writers were referred to as "editors" (that is, contributors to editorial content), and a fairly uniform writing style was required from them. According to Diane Vreeland, the staff of American *Vogue* were expected to conform to the extent of personally embodying its style: "all editors wore hats in the office [. . .] Editors were encouraged to lead the life and appear as images represented in the magazine" (n.p.). The contents page of each issue simply lists features by title, under the headings "Costume," "Society," "Arts and Decoration," and so forth, without giving the authors' names.

By contrast, the contents pages in newer publications such as *Vanity Fair* or *The New Yorker* prominently identified the author of each piece, and articles were often illustrated with a photograph of the writer. Such magazines promoted themselves on the basis of the individuality of their contributors. *The Smart Set,* for example, then edited by W. H. Wright, advertised itself in 1913 as maintaining "the highest standard of literary excellence" and addressing "readers who [. . .] are capable of appreciating genuineness and virility in modern letters."[26] Wright introduced, among others, D. H. Lawrence, James Joyce, and Frank Wedekind to the American public. Subsequently, under the editorship of H. L. Mencken and George Jean Nathan, *The Smart Set* published the early work of writers including Scott Fitzgerald, Eugene O'Neill, Sinclair Lewis, and Dashiell Hammett.[27] At *Vanity Fair,* while the Frank Crowninshield genre had identifiable parameters, variation and individuality were nevertheless crucial to the magazine's appeal. Crowninshield's ventures into experimental work led him to publish Jean Cocteau, Djuna Barnes, Gertrude Stein, Amy Lowell, and e. e. cummings, but the magazine's staple fare was provided by regular contributors such as Parker, P. G. Wodehouse, Robert Benchley, and Edmund Wilson, supplemented by work from Loos, Edna St. Vincent Millay, Aldous Huxley, and many others.

Parker rapidly became one of the best-known names in *Vanity Fair* and went on to publish in numerous other prestigious magazines, including *Life, The New Yorker, The Smart Set, New York World,* and *Esquire.* Parker and many of her contemporaries became celebrities partly through the dissemination of their work and their names through these periodicals; in turn, their growing fame sold copies of the magazines. Posts such as theater critic or book reviewer for these magazines were sought-after and high-profile. *Vanity Fair* placed review essays prominently, giving more emphasis to the name of the reviewer than that of the author or playwright under review. Parker was honored when, in April 1918, Crowninshield chose her to replace Wodehouse as theater columnist for *Vanity Fair.* As New York's only woman drama critic, she brought an instant distinctiveness to the magazine, whose staff had been announced by Crowninshield in his first editorial in 1914 as "determined and bigoted feminists" (Crowninshield). Parker quickly began to evolve a highly individual style of theater criticism, characterized by a witty, informal, but rather cynical tone, varied by occasional bursts of enthusiasm and exaggeration. Making no pretense at objective judgment, she emphasized her personal response to the plays and placed the figure of the critic centrally.

In a 1919 column, for example, Parker wonders why attending the theater has become so much less enjoyable in recent years:

> Is it that the dizzy whirl of modern life has made us cold and blasé? Or is it, perhaps, that the plays themselves are just naturally poisonous?

Personally, I am a trifle inclined towards the latter theory—and the new plays are certainly backing me up in my opinion. There is *Tiger! Tiger!*, Edward Knoblock's drama at the Belasco, for instance. Somehow, I cannot feel that the dizzy whirl of modern life had anything to do with my intense suffering during the performance—I hold the play itself directly responsible. The plot concerns the affair of a Member of Parliament with a cook,—an affair which goes on for nearly three years. When, at the end of that time she decides to leave him, he makes a frightful scene [. . .] It seemed most unreasonable of him to behave that way; how could he expect a cook to stay in the same situation for more than three years? [. . .]

The MP finally goes to war—where he should have gone early in the play—and gets himself killed. As far as I was concerned, he was unlamented. [. . .] Goodness knows that I appreciate thoughtfulness and attention, in a man; but when a large, strong, able-bodied Britisher won't go to war because a perfectly self-supporting woman says that she would miss him if he went—well, it seems to me to be a trifle over-obliging of him. ("Plays of War," 33)

Although this article is illustrated by a picture of the actress Jane Cowl and mentions a series of other performers, it is not they who are constituted as celebrities through the review. It is Dorothy Parker herself; her public personality saturates the piece. The plays simply become illustrations of Parker's personal theories, and it is her experience of watching them, rather than the nature of the performances, which forms the focus. In her next column, she even imaginatively intervenes in the show: "Fay Bainter is so persistently kittenish in the leading role that it was all I could do to keep from rising in my place and appealing to her personally,—'Please, Miss Bainter, won't you stop being cute for just two minutes? You don't know how I should appreciate it'" ("The Midwinter Plays," 39, 74).

This particular piece opens with a long paragraph on the life of a critic, once again placing the reviewer, rather than the actors, center stage: "There are long, quiet stretches when he hasn't a thing to do with his evenings, and then there are sudden outbursts of such violent activity that he nearly succumbs to apoplexy" (39). Parker also develops a strategy of personal address to the reader: "I don't know whether you feel that way about it, but I think [*Dear Brutus*] is a far better play than *A Kiss for Cinderella* was. I will admit that I got a bit sunk in the whimsicalities of *A Kiss for Cinderella*, but *Dear Brutus* never cloys for a moment" (39). Rhetorically, this reinforces *Vanity Fair*'s claim to know exactly who its readers are and to be address-ing only a particular, precisely defined kind of audience. In terms of Parker's own persona, the piece exemplifies what Helal refers to as Parker's "complex renunciation and recuperation of femininity" (79). Whilst exploiting the supposedly feminine privilege of the personal, intimate tone, she also rejects several other qualities traditionally as-sociated with the feminine (cuteness, kittenishness, whimsy, cloying sentimentality), and finally, she emphasizes her own distinctiveness as a woman drama critic through the disjunction between the masculine pronoun ("he hasn't a thing to do") and her evidently female persona.

Parker's theater columns constituted, as Meade points out, a "re-jection of the prevailing standards for female writing and thinking" (45), and her outspokenness and sarcasm contributed to her popular-ity by lending her an attractive modernness. Indeed, it was not through the "unfeminine" aspects of her behavior that she came to grief; it was through the threat she posed to the economic basis of *Vanity Fair*. In December 1919, she savaged three high-profile plays, and ended with a paragraph of uncanny prescience: "Sometimes, while pondering over the earnings of Dr. Frank Crane or musing on the royalties accumu-lated by Mrs. Eleanor H. Porter, one wonders whether this glad out-look is not the right ideal, after all. A backward glance through the pages of history reveals the fact that none of the World's Greatest Crabs ever amassed anything really noteworthy in the way of a bank account" ("The First Hundred," 35). This particular piece of crabbing cost Parker her job. In an interview in 1956, she recalled: "The plays closed and the producers, who were the big boys—Dillingham, Ziegfeld, and Belasco—didn't like it, you know. *Vanity Fair* was a magazine of no opinion, but I had opinions. So I was fired" (Capron, 4). Her reviews may not have been quite so influential as this implies, but the three producers—all advertisers in *Vanity Fair*—had indeed complained to Condé Nast. Parker could not, ultimately, be tolerated at either *Vogue* or *Vanity Fair*, since her contributions did not underwrite the prod-ucts of the advertisers, whether dresses or dramas.

But by the time of her departure from *Vanity Fair* she was suffi-ciently well known to trade on her name in the literary marketplace, and the publicity already generated through her association with the Algonquin Round Table worked in her favor. The *New York Times* im-mediately ran a news story by Woollcott announcing and lamenting the dismissal. Next, Robert Benchley and Robert Sherwood resigned from the magazine in sympathy, and Franklin P. Adams wrote in his *New York Herald Tribune* column "The Conning Tower": "R. Benchley tells me that he hath resigned his position with *Vanity Fair* because they hath discharged Dorothy Parker, which I am sorry for" (Adams, 241). The influence of "The Conning Tower" was such that writers could become well known through a single mention, and he gave special emphasis to the sayings and doings of the Algonquin Round Table, of which he was a member. "The Conning Tower," in fact, was a crucial factor in the consolidation of Parker's reputation as a wit, and although she repeatedly rejected this designation,[28] she nevertheless capitalized on it in her career.

Following the loss of her post, Parker rapidly began to pick up freelance work, including writing features for the *Ladies' Home Journal* and film subtitles. She was soon taken on as theater critic for *Ainslee's,* a good literary magazine but with a smaller, and more middle-class, readership than *Vanity Fair* had. Her unconventional writing, then, caused some damage to her career, since she had to move to a less prestigious magazine, but it also gave her a new sort of cachet and widened the circulation of her name and celebrity image. She became so important to *Ainslee's* that after she resigned in 1923, she was replaced, as Meade notes, "with a writer who aped her literary mannerisms" (108). Such imitations revealed the marketability of the Parker style, but no one managed to copy it very successfully, which confirmed her distinctiveness. Indeed, for most of the writers considered in this study, this paradox was crucial to their achievement of fame.

"YOU CAN PICK ME OUT OF ANY CROWD, THESE DAYS"

Some years later, in 1931, Parker substituted temporarily for Robert Benchley as drama critic for *The New Yorker*. Arthur Kinney considers that "Benchley was always more concise, [. . .] always less self-conscious" than Parker (155). But I would argue that she raised self-consciousness to an art form, and that it is crucial to the success of her journalism. The theater reviews she published in *The New Yorker* engage in dialogues, not only with the reader, but with other drama critics, with the correspondents of the magazine, and with Benchley himself. The first piece ends *"Personal: Robert Benchley, please come home. Nothing is forgiven"* ("Kindly Accept," 437). The joke is continued through the rest of the columns, with Parker dramatizing the supposed suffering which the necessity of attending and reviewing the plays has caused her. In reference to a character in an A. A. Milne play tapping out the message "I love you" in individual letters, she writes: "He tapped on through 'v,' and then did an 'e.' 'If he does "y,"' I thought, 'I'm through.' And he did. So I shot myself. It was, unhappily, a nothing—oh, a mere scratch—and I was able to sit up and watch that dream go on through all the expected stages" ("Just around Pooh Corner," 439). In explanation of why she has written at such length about the play, she states that it is from "bewilderment," since "On the morning after its unveiling, the critics of the daily papers went into a species of snake-dance over its magnificence" (440). She adds: "If *Give Me Yesterday* is a fine play, I am Richard Brinsley Sheridan. And there was yet another reason for my dwelling so much more than lingeringly upon the Milne work. Frankly—ah, let's not have any secrets, what do you say?—there wasn't anything else to write about" (440–441). The following week, she began with: "One more week's crabbing out of me, and I fear that you will take to throwing eggs. Yet I am forced again to tell a tale of woe, for I have no other. And I can't, you will admit, just stand up here in front of you and make faces, to earn my princely salary" ("No More Fun," 441). In her *New Yorker* reviews, then, Parker dramatizes herself—in the act of attending the theater and writing up her notices—to an even greater extent than she did in her *Vanity Fair* columns. In her final piece, she also asserts the superiority of her own judgments, writing that to "that mostly anonymous and largely feminine legion of Milne-lovers and Pollock-fanciers who took paper by the ream to inform me that they were every bit as good critics as I was [. . .] I can but toss what may sound like a kiss" ("Valedictory," 447–448). Unlike the Milne-lovers, she is not "anonymous," and her judgments are astute.

She further emphasized her own distinctiveness in another column: "If you want to, you can pick me out of any crowd, these days. I am the little one in the corner who did not think that *The Barretts of Wimpole Street* was a great play, nor even a good play. It is true that I paid it the tribute of tears, but that says nothing, for I am one who weeps at Victorian costumes" (Parker, "Kindly Accept," 434). Jessica Burstein, quoting this remark of Parker's, comments:

> Because sentimentalism is understood by misogynist and feminist critics alike as a common and commonizing tendency, [. . .] it is worth

noting how Parker distinguishes herself as *uncommon* by ironically parading her tendency to weep. This activity is distinctive precisely because of its context, the urbane and critical milieu of the Algonquin Round Table. Amid readers of *The New Yorker* and *Vanity Fair,* Parker plays the trump card of the sophisticate by at once naturalizing her actions and distinguishing herself from all the hicks who cling to a clinical intellectualism. (234)

Importantly, then, Parker can be at once sentimental and sophisticated; indeed, this rather unexpected combination became her trademark.

In asserting that she can be picked out of the crowd, Parker reaffirms her own celebrity status and recognizability. But her fame was rather localized; it was tied to the literary high society and urban chic of New York, as constructed and disseminated by sophisticated magazines. Outside this sphere, she was relatively unknown. The overlap between the spheres of movie celebrity and literary celebrity was very limited, and it was generally only the Hollywood star system which brought truly international fame. Meade notes that when Parker went to Hollywood in 1929 to bolster her finances by writing screen dialogue, "she glimpsed an MGM publicity release that referred to her as 'the internationally known author of *Too Much Rope,* the popular novel.' She was further dismayed to meet Irving Thalberg, production head of MGM, and realize that he had no idea who she was or why she had been hired" (197). Later in 1929, Parker visited London. Since she was not yet publicly associated with Hollywood, her fame did not precede her to any great extent, and she certainly did not receive the rapturous reception which Anita Loos experienced three years before. It was only on her return to New York in January 1930 that Parker was welcomed by a crowd of reporters.[29]

From 1927 to 1933, Parker wrote a weekly book review column for *The New Yorker,* signed "Constant Reader" (but generally known to be Parker's). Its fresh approach and personal tone won her a wide readership, and her literary criticism is of a high order—the judgments of "Constant Reader" have been largely endorsed by later generations. Parker achieved increased cultural authority through her book reviews, but she also used them to reinforce her trademark combination of sentiment and acerbity. In the piece in which she famously wrote: "The affair between Margot Asquith and Margot Asquith will live as one of the prettiest love stories in all literature," she also remarked of Asquith's *Lay Sermons:* "grudge it though I do, there is a disarming quality to it and to its author. (There I go, getting tender about things again; it's no wonder men forget me.)" (Constant Reader, 456, 457). Margot Asquith is displaced from the center of the piece, as Parker herself (or rather, her familiar persona) becomes—once again—the actual subject of her own writing. She constructs her femininity here in interesting ways: assigning herself several conventionally "feminine" qualities (bitchiness, softheartedness, and a preoccupation with men), but countering these with cynicism and self-mockery, and rejecting that crucial component of the supposedly typical woman, vanity.

Most of Parker's fiction, however, contrasts with her journalism in that her personality is erased from the text. As Brendan Gill comments in his introduction to the 1973 *Collected Dorothy Parker*: "Not the least hint of the Round Table is detectable in the stories [. . .] The author keeps her distance, and sometimes it is a distance great enough to remind one of Flaubert. She has written her tales with grave care and given them a surface as hard and smooth as stone, and there is no need for her to flutter about in the foreground and call attention to her cleverness" (xix). This is certainly true of a majority of her stories, yet in others, the Parker personality is emphatically present, and these stories are quite as successful as those described by Gill. In two of her monologues, she even inserts herself as a named character. In "The Garter" (1928), she imagines herself with a broken garter, forced to sit still holding up her stocking: "I certainly must be cutting a wide swath through this party. I'm making my personality felt. [. . .] Oh, have you met Dorothy Parker? What's she like? Oh, she's terrible. God, she's poisonous. Sits in a corner and sulks all evening" (101). She goes on to reference the less flattering rumors which were circulating about her at the time: "You know, they say she doesn't write a word of her stuff. They say she pays some poor little guy, that lives in some tenement on the lower East Side, ten dollars a week to write it and she just signs her name to it" (101). While the story's narrator is ostensibly mocking herself, as the victim of a peculiarly feminine embarrassment, the real targets of her satire are the readers of gossip columns, who would actually believe that a woman could not write the way Dorothy Parker does and that she must therefore be stealing a man's work. In the second monologue, "But the One on the Right" (1929), the narrator is placed next to a tedious man at a dinner party and imagines her hosts having said to one another: "we can stick him next to Mrs. Parker—she talks enough for two" (132). She is deliberately silent, refusing to behave as expected. The story points to various aspects of Dorothy Parker's public image, including her alcohol consumption ("I could do a little drinking, of course, all by myself. There's always that" [133]) and her suicidal tendencies ("All right, you baskets, I'll drink myself to death" [133]). Kathleen Helal comments on the narrator's "imprisonment in her own autobiographical text," adding: "Parker simultaneously dramatizes this identification problem and mocks the audience that would expect her to conform to that image. 'Mrs. Parker' remains inaccessible [. . .] because of the ubiquitous image that precedes her" (84).

"The Garter" and "But the One on the Right" are the only stories in which Parker explicitly names herself. Yet there are others in which she offers a similarly calculated performance of her own celebrity image, and it makes sense to compare such texts with her theater and book reviews, since she both projects and mocks the celebrated persona through all these forms of writing. The entertaining, acerbic voice in "The Little Hours" (1933), for example, has clear affinities with our received image of "Dorothy Parker." The speaker is awake at 4:30 in the morning, and having inadvertently remembered a couple of the sayings of La Rochefoucauld ("if nobody had ever learned to read, very few people would be in love" and "there is always something a little pleasing to us in the misfortunes of even our dearest friends"), she is unable to get him out of her head. At one point, she mentally addresses him:

> Ah, come on, son—how about your going your way and letting me go mine. I've got my work cut out for me right here; I've got all this sleeping to do. Think how I am going to look by daylight if this keeps up. I'll be a seamy sight for all those rested, clear-eyed, fresh-faced dearest friends of mine—the rats! My *dear,* whatever have you been doing [. . .] Oh, I was helling around with La Rochefoucauld till all hours; we couldn't stop laughing at your misfortunes. [. . .] If I can only sleep now. If I can tear my mind away from a certain French cynic, *circa* 1650, and slip into lovely oblivion. 1650. I bet I look as if I'd been awake since then. (207)

The speaker, highly literate and articulate, blames her wakefulness on too much reading. Yet she tries to put herself to sleep by repeating "slowly and soothingly, a list of quotations beautiful from minds profound" (207). Although she does not include any Dorothy Parker epigrams, the quotations do circle around Parker's favorite literary subjects, especially that of death ("But none, I think, do there embrace,"

"I think I will not hang myself today," and so forth), which brings the persona of the story closer to the authorial persona.

Parker's fictional monologues tend to be considered as a group by critics, but they can in fact be divided into two distinct kinds. In texts such as "The Little Hours" and "The Waltz," although the speaker is not named as "Mrs. Parker," nevertheless the voice unmistakably evokes the Dorothy Parker persona, and while the narrator mocks herself, she also elicits sympathy. These contrast markedly with monologues given in the voices of quite different characters, such as "A Telephone Call" (1928) or "Lady with a Lamp" (1932), in which the narrator is satirized. The opening lines of "Lady with a Lamp" exemplify Parker's technique of creating intensely annoying fictional narrators: "Well, Mona! Well, you poor sick thing, you! Ah, you look so little and white and *little,* you do, lying there in that great big bed. That's what you do—go and look so childlike and pitiful nobody'd have the heart to scold you. And I ought to scold you, Mona. Oh, yes, I should so, too" (144). There is a clear distinction: the "Dorothy Parker" narrators are witty and self-deprecating; the wholly fictional ones are neither. It is important to recognize this, since Parker's investment of her own celebrated personality in certain of her stories, poems, and articles has unfortunately led some critics to interpret all her work as autobiographical. Meade, in her otherwise excellent biography of Parker, insists: "In her verse as in her fiction, she always wrote about herself, or else drew portraits of people she knew. [. . .] She was almost incapable of doing purely imagined characters or situations" (99). There is much reason to dispute this; indeed, I would argue that one of her great strengths, in both fiction and poetry, is the dramatic monologue, in which she imagines herself into the minds of a range of quite different characters.

"THEY ARE DANCING IN THE STREETS, MRS. PARKER"

Parker, I have argued, sometimes uses her stories in the same way as her critical pieces, to reaffirm herself as a recognizable and famous "character," whilst also reflecting critically on her celebrity image and on the culture which circulates it. This is primarily true of the stories written in the first person, which perform the same work as her first-person lyric poems in delineating the trademark persona. I have concerned myself in this chapter with her prose writing, which has received rather less attention than her poetry, but it is also important to note the role of Parker's verse in her public self-construction. While it is difficult to summarize the nature of her poetry succinctly, it can safely be stated that the vast majority of the poems are in the first person and (in contrast to the short stories) give the impression of being spoken by a fairly unified voice corresponding to our notion of the Dorothy Parker persona. However, as Kinney notes, "by puns, clichés and unhappy word choices, her poems invite us to reflect on the sharp difference between poet and persona" (114), and the speakers of the poems are often "self-condemning," clearly revealing their own "hollowness" (115). This does not, though, alter the fact that the recognizability of Parker's poetic persona informed her public image as a celebrity.

The persona's most notable traits are a skepticism about love (resulting from a tendency to fall in love frequently, with disastrous results), a flippant defiance of accepted standards of behavior, and a world-weary resignation. The poetic voice mockingly takes on a variety of tones, briefly imitating more conventional love poetry, but usually adds a witty and unexpected punch line which inverts the sentiments expressed earlier in the poem. The relationship between speaker and listener is always important. Nina Miller writes: "Foregrounding the listening audience which lyric poetry conventionally suppresses, she transforms the solitary musings of a speaker addressing only herself or the figure of her lover into essentially public space and speech" (772). This is an illuminating comment, but Miller also argues that "For Parker as a writerly persona, [. . .] love itself proves to be her only means of entry into public speech" (780). To some extent, this is a reasonable assertion in relation to the poetry: much of it is indeed about love, although there is an almost equally significant focus on death, together with numerous reflections on writing, reputation, ambition, and independence, and even poems on Queen Victoria, Harriet Beecher Stowe, Guinevere, and the Virgin Mary. Miller's claim does not, though, hold true for Parker's stories and journalism, in which she ranged into quite different territory, even as she consolidated the "writerly persona" of the poems.

In terms of form, Parker's poems (with the exception of her parodies of free verse, which she omitted from her published collections[30]) are rhymed and in regular meter. These accessible forms, together with the novelty and wit of her poetry, led to high sales, as well as acclaim from respected critics writing in serious magazines such as *The Nation* and *The New York Herald Tribune*. Parker's best-selling volume

Enough Rope was—like *Gentlemen Prefer Blondes*—brought out by the respected publisher of modernism, Horace Liveright. Harriet Monroe's important periodical *Poetry: A Magazine of Verse,* which published many of the authors who eventually formed the canon of literary modernism, printed a review of *Enough Rope* by Marie Luhrs, who had won *Poetry*'s annual prize for verse the previous year. She wrote: "Mrs. Parker has her own particular field of frank American humor. She is slangy, vulgar, candid, and withal subtle, delicate and sparkling. The soul of wit distinguishes most of her pieces" (53). This account exemplifies the tone of critical response to the book. The categorization of Parker as a humorist places her firmly in a minor genre, but the very fact that *Poetry* reviewed the book increased Parker's cultural capital.

Edmund Wilson, reviewing *Enough Rope* in *The New Republic,* commented that Parker's work "has its roots in contemporary reality, and that is what I am pleading for in poetry." But at the same time, he suggested that her focus on the contemporary was limiting: "Her wit is the wit of her particular time and place, but it is often as cleanly economic at the same time that it is flatly brutal as the wit of the age of Pope; and, within its small scope, it is a criticism of life" (256). Wilson was an astute and admiring critic of Parker's work, but his reference to her small scope betrays that he considered her a minor poet, and it may also be a gendered judgment, since women writers were often criticized for confining themselves to the domestic and personal. Wilson's review certainly influenced later critics. Brendan Gill, for example, wrote in 1973: "Readers coming to Mrs. Parker for the first time may find it [. . .] hard to understand the high place she held in the literary world of forty or fifty years ago" (xv), and although he defends her adroitly, he claims we should admire her because she could "ably sum up her time and place" (xix), an argument often used to retrieve an author considered minor, on the basis of historical interest. Arthur Kinney, by contrast, inscribes Parker into a much broader poetic tradition, identifying her influences as Catullus, Martial, and Horace, as well as A. E. Housman and Edna St. Vincent Millay.[31] As Kinney writes of Catullus and Parker, "Confessional yet highly disciplined, conversational yet poetically rendered, the work of both poets displays a controlled imagination" (104). He adds that while she learned much of her technique from the Catullan tradition (which included poets such as Housman), "it was the Horation tradition that taught her the inevitability of man's failings and that led to her rueful and cocky tones" (106–107).

By 1928, Parker was being described by John Farrar, in *The Bookman,* as "a giantess of American letters, secure at the top of her beanstalk" (quoted in Meade, 178). In the same year, Neysa McMein painted a portrait of Parker, and in 1932, Edward Steichen photographed her full-length; both pictures were printed in *Vanity Fair.* Instead of writing about top celebrities for the magazine, Parker had now joined their ranks and become an object of scrutiny herself. The playwright S. J. Perelman wrote: "Dorothy Parker was already a legend when I first met her in 1932" (171). Yet there was a definite chasm between the public's estimation of Dorothy Parker and her own. Her book of short fiction *Laments for the Living* (1930) went through four editions in the first month, but although most reviews were good, some criticized the stories as slight. Her response was to cable her publisher, George Oppenheimer, that the reviews seemed "beyond words awful" and that she was "pretty discouraged about ever writing again." Oppenheimer's reply subtly chides her for being melodramatic: "They are dancing in the streets, Mrs. Parker, and drinking magnums of champagne in your honor, and yet you sit there and say you will never write another book for shame" (quoted in Meade, 212).

During the 1930s and 1940s, as Meade notes, both her reputation and her work suffered from her involvement with left-wing politics (302). She was blacklisted in Hollywood, questioned by the FBI about whether she had joined the Communist Party, and eventually called before a New York state joint legislative committee. This aspect of her life has also become part of her legend, although it is often only her brave criticism of the House Un-American Activities Committee (HUAC) which is remembered, and not her Stalinist sympathies. The suspicion of her association with the CP may have been one reason why it was not until the late 1950s that Parker "finally began to reap long overdue professional rewards from the literary establishment" (Meade, 362). These included an election in 1959 to the American Academy of Arts and Letters, and also the receipt of their newly established lifetime achievement award. But such honors arose from the respect of an older generation. Younger readers, including the students she taught in 1963 and 1964, during a period as a visiting professor at the California State College, Los Angeles, had not heard of her. Parker became increasingly self-critical as her style became less fashionable. She said in a 1956 interview: "My verses are no damn good. Let's face it, honey, my verse is terribly dated—as anything once fashionable is dreadful now." She added that "precision" is "all I realize I've ever had in prose writing" (Capron, 8).

She was, unfortunately, taken at her word by some critics in the middle and later twentieth century, and her abilities and achievements have, on the whole, been underestimated. Even critics who have worked extensively on editions of Parker's work still appear somewhat embarrassed by their own pleasure in it. Gill writes that she came much less near to greatness than Edna St. Vincent Millay, because she "worked less hard" and "flinched from thorough self-examination: the depths were there, and she would glance into them from time to time, but she was not prepared to descend into them" (xviii). This rather critically regressive tendency to pronounce confidently on Parker's character in an attempt to explain the supposed failures of her work is also evident in Silverstein's 1996 introduction to *The Uncollected Dorothy Parker.* He refers to Hollywood producers' mistaken assumption that Parker was an "artist," adding: "Dorothy, who never possessed that extraordinary creative spark, was only a diligent craftsman" (37). He even asserts that "imagination [. . .] was a quality she lacked" (37). These defensive gestures apparently represent a continuing anxiety about contamination by the middlebrow. The vocabulary of "craft" rather than art, the patronizing use of Parker's first name, the insistence on confining her relevance to her own age, the criticism of her lack of commitment, and the suggestion that only a lowbrow such as a Hollywood producer would consider her an artist, all work to diminish Parker's own cultural capital and protect that of the male editor, who arrogates to himself the authority to decide on "greatness." It is not to these critics that we should turn for a just assessment of Parker's merits, but to the feminist critics and theorists of modernism cited in this chapter, to those of her contemporaries who understood the achievement of her style, and also to the readers whose unabated demand for Parker's work has kept it continuously in print for eighty years.

Vanity Fair and *Vogue,* in their quest for distinction, were antagonistic toward universal appeal and mass fashions (whether in painting, literature, or clothing). At the same time, *Vanity Fair*'s balancing between serious attention to experimental writing and art and mockery of it is actually characteristic of the middlebrow. Crowninshield and his staff would doubtless have rejected any association with the middlebrow, as the term was understood at the time. Yet if it is defined in the way I suggested in my introduction, as a productive place from which to reflect on the commerce between high and popular culture, a place of intellectual curiosity and cultural aspiration combined with a healthy skepticism about pretension, then *Vanity Fair* fits perfectly into this category. So, indeed, does Dorothy Parker's own writing, although this designation does not close down readings of her in relation to literary modernism. This is because middlebrow writing itself engages with, and sometimes partakes of, modernist experiment; and Parker's journalism, fiction, and poetry are all, to varying extents, formally innovative.

Self-consciousness is a central component of the middlebrow as I have defined it. This self-consciousness often includes the text's awareness of its own cultural status, together with the author's awareness of her celebrity image. Parker repeatedly referenced her own public image. Much of her writing works to reinforce and develop her increasingly well-known and marketable persona, that distinctive combination of tenderheartedness and acidity. Some have identified her self-consciousness as a flaw,[32] but for me, it is a highly effective element of her literary aesthetic.

From an early stage, Parker's work exhibits a tendency to self-mockery, as well as an awareness of the way she herself has been commodified through the widespread quotation of her witty lines and the public circulation of her celebrity image. In her 1919 poem "Our Office: A Hate Song," purporting to give "An Intimate Glimpse of *Vanity Fair*—En Famille," as the subtitle announced, Parker refers back to (and misquotes) her own celebrated picture caption written a few years earlier for *Vogue*:

> Then there is the Editorial Department;
> The Literary Lights.
> They are just a little holier than other people
> Because they can write classics about
> " 'Brevity is the soul of lingerie,' said this little chemise to itself."

Parker very rarely quoted her own lines, and she only did so—as in this instance—with parodic intent. (By contrast, Mae West—as I will discuss in Chapter 3—continually recycled her own lines, thus contributing to the commodification of her personality much more blatantly than Parker ever did.) Parker's friend Lillian Hellman commented: "She never in her life repeated her own witticisms, perhaps sure that other people would do it for her" (Introduction, xxiv). They did, of course; even at the height of her career, Parker was primarily famous for her much-quoted epigrams, and the same is true today.

Parker's sophisticated aesthetic was nourished by, and contributed to, *Vanity Fair*'s New York urban chic. Partly through the self-consciousness of her own writing, and partly through the publicity which surrounded her and her associates at the Algonquin Round Table, Parker herself effectively became a fictional character. The speaking voice in her poems, some of her stories, and her journalism was clearly the "Mrs. Parker" persona, so recognizable that from 1925 onwards, creative writers were basing characters on her. Six plays and a novel feature versions of her,[33] and the dark-haired, attractive, and dangerously witty Dorothy Shaw in Anita Loos's *Gentlemen Prefer Blondes* is also suggestive of Parker. In the late 1950s, Parker had refused Columbia's offer to make a film about her life (Meade, 360), but in 1994, this idea eventually came to fruition in the form of *Mrs. Parker and the Vicious Circle,* directed by Alan Rudolph.[34] Curiosity about 1920s New York, and about the Algonquin Circle, continues to grow, and "Mrs. Parker" is still being reinvented, not only by critics and biographers but also in popular forms: the latest show to feature Dorothy Parker as a character is the 2002 musical *Thoroughly Modern Millie.* Dorothy Parker manipulated and exploited her celebrity image during her career, though she had only limited control over the various versions and impersonations of her which circulated, and at times, the expectations they imposed became oppressive. Yet her legendary personality and her witty one-liners have ensured her continuing fame, and in the decades since her death, her literary afterlife has been vigorous.

2 | "BRAINS ARE REALLY EVERYTHING"
Anita Loos's Gentlemen Prefer Blondes

Anita Loos's writing, like Dorothy Parker's, was shaped by the discourses of sophistication and cosmopolitanism, which were mediated by magazines such as *Vanity Fair, The New Yorker, Harper's Bazar,*[1] and *The Smart Set.* Her best-selling novel *Gentlemen Prefer Blondes* (1925) was initially serialized in *Harper's Bazar;* when it appeared in volume form, its astonishing sales made Loos a millionaire and a celebrity. Also a successful and well-connected screenwriter, she had an intimate knowledge of Hollywood as well as the literary high society of New York. She was introduced to the Algonquin Round Table, and remarked in her autobiography: "I dismissed them as being without interest, except for Dorothy Parker and Herbert Bayard Swope. I thought the others very naïve indeed" (*Girl,* 147). Loos has affinities with Parker, both in terms of writing and personal style. Both were diminutive, dark-haired, elegantly dressed, witty, sophisticated, and very much identified with New York chic. More significantly, the verbal echoes and thematic parallels between the work of the two authors suggest a certain mutual influence.

Loos's heroine, Lorelei Lee, starts out as a film star before turning her performance skills to new ends in her quest for a rich husband. Lorelei bears a definite resemblance to an earlier fictional actress, the narrator of Dorothy Parker's spoof "The Autobiography of Any Movie Actress, Set Down in the Regulation Manner," published in *Vanity Fair* in 1919. Both characters are aspiring authors, yet entirely unqualified to write. Lorelei describes her error-strewn diary as "literary work" (*Blondes,* 123), and considers that to be a writer, "you do not have to learn or practise" (5). Parker's film star claims: "I have never had time to write, although it has always been my ambition. Ever since I can remember, I have felt that 'the pen is mightier than the saw'" (Wells, 33). Just as Lorelei describes herself as the "little girl from Little Rock" (*Blondes,* 92), so Parker's narrator writes: "at last, the little girl from Twin Falls was a 'star' of the 'silent drama'" (Wells, 33). The characters refer to their obscure birthplaces in order to elicit sympathy and emphasize their achievements in breaking into film and into the upper echelons of New York society; the authors, meanwhile, invoke metropolitan prejudices against provincial America. Loos, who certainly read *Vanity Fair,* may well have seen Parker's text, and both authors are parodying the emerging genre of the celebrity movie autobiography, represented, for example, by the silent star Pearl White's untrustworthy *Just Me* (1919).[2] Like Parker, Loos repeatedly mocks celebrity behavior, and her four novels include satires of cinema starlets, Follies girls, best-selling writers, and members of the Algonquin Round Table.

Further evidence for Parker's possible influence on Loos might be found in a 1918 piece in *Vanity Fair,* "Extracts from a Secretary's Diary," signed L. L. Jones but very probably by Parker.[3] It contains jokes and details which directly anticipate *Gentlemen Prefer Blondes.*[4] But while some of Parker's early work, especially her contributions to *Vanity Fair,* could have informed Loos's novel, the influence may have worked both ways. Rhonda Pettit suggests that Parker's famous short story "Big Blonde" (1929) is a "response" to *Gentlemen Prefer Blondes,* since its narrative of a kept woman's descent into alcoholism and depression could be read as a rejection of Loos's "false depiction of female success within a capitalist economy" ("Material Girls," 53).[5] Laurie J. C. Cella also compares these two texts, in relation to the main characters' performance of a "deliberately constructed blonde spectacle" (47). More straightforwardly, certain fictions by Parker which appeared after the publication of *Blondes* use exactly the same jokes as Loos does, and echo her satire of particular types, notably the American abroad. A character in her 1929 *New Yorker* story "The Cradle of Civilization," for example, when told that a friend lost 85,000 francs at a French casino, asks, "How much is that in money?" (130), just as Lorelei notes that she and Dorothy, shopping in Paris, "do not seem to be mathematical enough to tell how much francs is in money" (*Blondes,* 53). Lorelei likes London, because "you would really think it was New York because I always think that the most delightful thing about traveling is to always be running into Americans and to always feel at home" (33). The woman in "The Cradle of Civilization" appreciates France for similar reasons: "I'm crazy about the Splendid. It's just like the Desert Club, back in New York" (130).[6] The provincial ignorance of New Yorkers, as presented in these stories, contrasts markedly with the urbane, cosmopolitan style which the magazines of interwar New York sought to project. Loos and Parker contributed to the invention of this style, through their writing, their personal self-presentation, and their rejection of provincialism. At the same time, they both satirize the image-obsessed culture which was at once nourished and critiqued by the magazines they published in.

Gentlemen Prefer Blondes was admired by eminent writers and thinkers including James Joyce, Edith Wharton, Sherwood Anderson, William Empson, George Santayana, and Rose Macaulay. But their praise was balanced by some ambiguous or hostile responses, notably those of William Faulkner, H. L. Mencken, Q. D. Leavis, and Wyndham Lewis. Their rejection or undervaluing of *Blondes* can be explained in terms of contemporary attitudes to a range of interrelated issues, namely: comic writing, sexual morality and censorship, female authorship, mass culture, and the commercialization of literature. Intriguingly, all these subjects are actually thematized in Loos's writing. *Gentlemen Prefer Blondes* and its sequel, *But Gentlemen Marry Brunettes* (1928), are wide-ranging satires of interwar American culture, including among their targets consumerism and conspicuous consumption, psychoanalysis, Hollywood, New York high society, flapper culture, the discourses of self-improvement and positive thinking, Prohibition, and censorship. The novels are narrated by the blonde Lorelei Lee, but much of the satire is conveyed through the cynical discourse of her brunette friend Dorothy Shaw, which is faithfully recorded (often with prudish disapproval) in Lorelei's diary, in her own unforgettable idiom. As Barbara Everett argues, the "peculiar force and flavour" of *Gentlemen Prefer Blondes* "comes from the brilliant invention of its personal style" (255).

Loos works the border between high and popular culture, never fully identifying herself with either. Her books are apparently aimed at a fairly educated audience, since their primary satiric target is a semiliterate, philistine lowbrow, but they also satirize the pretensions of highbrow culture in its various forms. Loos's engagement with the interwar debate about "brows" emerges in her ironic commentaries on the pretensions of the male literary elite, the seductiveness of popular entertainments, and the "puritanism" of American culture, a term which in the Twenties, as Malcolm Bradbury notes, "becomes the great abuse-word to assault the total lack of interest in, the total lack of effective environment for, the creative arts" (13). These are major themes of *Gentlemen Prefer Blondes* and its sequel, and similar preoccupations are evident in her two other novels, *No Mother to Guide Her* (1930, revised 1960) and *A Mouse Is Born* (1951), as well as in her volumes of unreliable but revealing autobiography and memoir. She uses both her fictional and autobiographical texts to negotiate her relationship to the literary establishment and the popular culture of her period.

"FUN IS FUN BUT NO GIRL WANTS TO LAUGH ALL OF THE TIME"

For many years, Loos was one of the best-known women in America, but today, while everyone recognizes the title *Gentlemen Prefer Blondes,* very few people can give the name of the author. This testifies to the extent to which the 1953 musical film version has eclipsed the novel, detaching it both from its author and from its period. The director, Howard Hawks (in collaboration with Loos herself, as scriptwriter), abandoned the historical location of the original text and transformed its girlish flapper heroines into what Susan Hegeman describes as "the larger-than-life feminine ideal of the postwar period: big, buxom, glittery" (547). Hegeman notes that while the film "has been an important site for feminist scholarship," Loos's original book has not: "critics who have addressed its popularity have done so with barely disguised embarrassment" (525).[7] Film and popular culture are now, of course, legitimate objects of academic study; yet in the field of literary studies, the commercial success of a book still tends to preclude it from serious critical consideration, even in the case of so sophisticated a text as *Gentlemen Prefer Blondes.* In recent decades, feminist scholarship has reinstated the American authors who were eliminated from the canon under the influence of the post–World War I hostility to women's writing,[8] among them: Willa Cather, Edith Wharton, Nella Larsen, Zora Neale Hurston, H. D., Amy Lowell, and Edna St. Vincent Millay. The rehabilitation of Anita Loos has been slow in comparison, and *Gentlemen Prefer Blondes* continues to occupy a marginal position in the canon.[9]

The literary status of Loos's novel has, in fact, been ambiguous from the moment of its publication; during the late 1920s and the 1930s, *Gentlemen Prefer Blondes* elicited a surprising range of both admiring and censorious comments from writers and critics. Loos was particularly pleased by a 1926 fan letter from Aldous Huxley: "I was enraptured by the book [and] have just hugely enjoyed the play" (quoted in Loos, "Memoir of Aldous Huxley," 89). James Joyce wrote to Harriet Shaw Weaver in the same year that he had been "reclining on a sofa and reading *Gentlemen Prefer Blondes* for three whole days" (Joyce, 246), while Edith Wharton praised the book extravagantly in several letters. She demonstrates a surprisingly broad concept of great literature, noting that during an Aegean cruise, she and her friends read aloud to one another in the evening from "*The Odyssey* or *Blondes.*"[10] Wharton also described the book as a masterpiece in two unpublished letters,[11] and she remarked to Frank Crowninshield: "I am just reading the Great American Novel *(at last!) Gentlemen Prefer Blondes,* and I want to know if there are—or will be—others, and if you know the funny woman, who must be a genius."[12] Her expectation of "others" presciently anticipates the replication of *Blondes* in various forms (sequel, musical and film adaptations, spin-off products).

George Santayana named *Blondes* the best philosophical work by an American (R. W. B. Lewis, 468), and a similar half-amused, half-serious response is discernible in William Empson's 1937 poem, "Reflection from Anita Loos." He explains in a characteristically gnomic footnote that he was inspired by "the fine character of Dorothy" (362), and his poem represents men as constantly motivated by ambition and women as limited by their prescribed social roles: "Gentlemen prefer bound feet and the wasp waist" (85). He glosses this theme in his note: "The way earlier societies seem obviously absurd and cruel gives a kind of horror at the forces that must be at work in our own" (362). The layers of irony in Empson's notes caution the reader against unduly literal interpretations of his poems; nevertheless his comparison of the various methods of remaking the female body as male fantasy (foot-binding, tight-lacing, and—by implication—hair dyeing) suggests that he has perceived a darker underside to Loos's novel. This presumably consists in its analysis of the relationships among economics, sexuality, and female freedom. The darkness of the poem itself is, however, relieved by its singsong rhythm and humorous refrain: "A girl can't go on laughing all the time," taken from Loos's line "Fun is fun but no girl wants to laugh all of the time" (*Blondes,* 63). This is rather typical of Empson: a number of his poems about tragedy and disaster have a disconcerting element of comedy in their manner. In this case, his deliberate mismatching of form and content may replicate his perception of the generic instability of *Blondes* itself. Susan Hegeman suggests that Empson considered Loos's novel as "a tragedy problematically dressed up as satire," and she also notes that the comic/satiric mode of the book adversely affected its literary status. Comparing it to *The Great Gatsby* (1925), she comments that while both books are entirely of their time and "address similar preoccupations with changes in the social conditions of '20s America," critics in later decades judged *The Great Gatsby* "to have transcended its moment [. . .] redeemed by the cultural authority of tragedy" (532), while *Blondes* was dismissed as a period piece.

In fact, while Rose Macaulay's description of *Gentlemen Prefer Blondes* as "probably the funniest book that has appeared in England or America" was used by the publishers to promote early editions,[13] the devaluing of the novel on the grounds of its comic genre began as soon as it was published. The influential critic and editor H. L. Mencken, Loos's close friend and the man whose admiration for a series of vacuous blonde women inspired the story, commented in his unsigned review in *The American Mercury:* "This gay book has filled me with uproarious and salubrious mirth. It is farce—but farce full of shrewd observation and devastating irony" (127). His statement evinces sincere admiration, but the terms "gay," "uproarious," and "farce" consign the novel firmly to the nonserious, popular realm of literature.[14] In a 1965 interview, Loos recalled that Mencken declined to publish *Blondes* in *The American Mercury* for fear he would "besmirch" it, and suggested she send it to a women's magazine instead (Kobal, 90). She also reports that Mencken described the probable audience for *Gentlemen Prefer Blondes* as "a frivolous public" (*Girl,* 267), a clearly gendered phrase. Such judgments are informed by the age-old hierarchy of tragedy over comedy, which persistently manifests itself in an association of tragedy with the masculine and comedy with both the feminine and the childlike.

The language of Loos's reviewers and male friends frequently reduced her to the status of a girl or a child. Although Loos mocks Lorelei's calculatedly childlike behavior (epitomized in her addressing her gentleman friends as "Daddy"), she is at times complicit with the view of herself as a child, and also with the more general infantilization of women prevalent in her culture. She includes in the picture insert in *A Girl Like I* a cartoon drawing of herself by Ralph Barton, which represents her as a diminutive figure sitting at a typewriter, her feet dangling in midair, with an enormous bow on the back of her dress and a vacant expression. The illustration originally appeared in a series of advertisements in *Harper's Bazar* promoting the forthcoming sequel to *Blondes,* and, as Sarah Churchwell points out, these adverts "promoted and simultaneously disavowed her resemblance to her characters" (154). Loos seems happy to endorse this image of herself, merely adding the caption: "The only thing wrong with this picture is that an authoress like I never learned to type," deliberately distancing herself from mechanized methods of cultural production (the typewriter) and from association with low-grade forms of female work (the secretary) whilst retaining the image of herself as childlike. In her 1963 introduction to *Gentlemen Prefer Blondes,* "The Biography of a Book," she recalls: "I began to write down my thoughts; not bitterly, as I might have done had I been a real novelist, but with an amusement which was, on the whole, rather childish. I have always considered grown-ups to be figures of fun, as children generally do, and have never been deceived by their hypocrisies" (xxxviii). She lists as "real novelists" Anderson, Dreiser, Faulkner, Fitzgerald, and Hemingway, making no mention of her female contemporaries. Despite her tongue-in-cheek tone, it is difficult not to suspect that she has internalized a conception of literature and high art as a male preserve. That this assumption was fundamental to the ideology of her period has been persuasively argued by recent theorists of modernism. Andreas Huyssen, for example, comments: "It is indeed striking to observe how the political, psychological, and aesthetic discourse around the turn of the century consistently and obsessively genders mass culture and the masses as feminine, while high culture, whether traditional or modern, clearly remains the privileged realm of male activities" (47).[15] Loos's perception of the male novelists of her generation as "real" writers and herself simply as a producer of popular culture (film scenarios, magazine fiction, and best-selling novels) certainly reaffirms this gendered hierarchy of cultural forms.

In the area of fiction, the association of the popular and the feminine had some statistical basis. In the 1920s, the best seller was indeed largely the preserve of women readers and writers, and this was also the period in which specialized genres of fiction and specialized magazines, all designed to appeal to women, began to proliferate (Melman, 45; Clive Bloom, 9). Of the ten best sellers of 1925 in America, eight were by women, though these eight covered a diverse range from Edna Ferber to Edith Wharton (Rosen, 82). However, Loos's attitude goes far beyond a simple acknowledgment of women's taste for, and success in, popular forms. Its most extreme expression comes in *A Girl Like I:* "I had no pride in authorship because I never thought that anything produced by females was, or even should be, important. It is horrible to think what sort of monster Shakespeare might have been as a woman. [. . .] The only authoresses I ever respected were women first of all [. . .] That they happened to take up writing was beside the point" (181). This emphatic reinscription of high culture as male conflicts, however, with her account of herself in the same text as a "cérébrale" (61) who is the intellectual peer of her male contemporaries and shares their knowledge of serious literature and their contempt for American mass culture:

> To me book learning didn't mean a thing unless it became an ingrained part of life. The majority of Americans don't realize what they're reading (unless it happens to be cheap pornography), hearing (except for rock and roll music), looking at (with the exception of television), or even tasting (unless it be hot dogs powerfully accentuated by mustard). [. . .] At any rate, a girl like I who never got past high school can take modest pride in making out quite well with the highbrows. I was once asked to preside over a symposium at the Faculty Club of Harvard University, where the professors asked such impertinent questions as: "Where did you get the sex experiences that are indicated by your writing?" [. . .] I told them, "From Baruch Spinoza, Immanuel Kant, and George Santayana." (*Girl*, 62–63)

She apparently believed that a woman could be an entirely adequate audience for high cultural forms, but not a producer of them, since her destiny as a woman was incompatible with a serious literary career. This view is informed both by her personal circumstances and by the ideological climate of America between the wars. Regina Barreca connects these two factors: "Told by her husband and illustrator [Ralph Barton]—and in myriad ways by the culture at large—that women could not write and still be truly feminine, that women's writing was therefore by definition unnatural, even aberrant, Loos [. . .] considered herself monstrous" (Introduction to *Blondes*, xxiii–xxiv). Loos's respect for her husband lessened dramatically when she saw he felt threatened by her ability to write material which she herself considered as relatively valueless. Yet she also experienced severe guilt because she felt her success had ruined his life.

Loos's experience is in some respects typical. Elaine Showalter writes that for American women in the 1920s and 1930s, "Encountering the real tensions between their writing and their personal lives led to disillusionment," and that "hostility towards female authorship and feminine values in academia and the literary establishment further stigmatized women's writing" (824). Although many of the admirers and readers of *Gentlemen Prefer Blondes* were men,[16] a hostility toward women's writing is evident in the comments on the novel made by certain male intellectuals. William Faulkner wrote to Loos in 1925:

> Please accept my envious congratulations on Dorothy—the way you did her through the intelligence of that elegant moron of a corn-flower. Only you have played a rotten trick on your admiring public. How many of them, do you think, will ever know that Dorothy really has something [. . .] My God, it's charming [. . .] most of them will be completely unmoved—even your rather clumsy gags won't get them—and the others will only find it slight and humorous. The Andersons [Sherwood and Elizabeth] even mentioned Ring Lardner in talking to me about it. But perhaps that was what you were after, and you have builded better than you knew: I am still rather Victorian in my prejudices regarding the intelligence of women, despite Elinor Wylie and Willa Cather and all the balance of them. But I wish I had thought of Dorothy first.[17]

At first unwilling to reduce Loos to the level of her mass readership, Faulkner creates a complicity between her as a witty, intellectual writer and himself as a perceptive, discerning reader, understanding the humor which the generality of the "public" will miss. But this is immediately modified, as he begins to suggest that the author herself may not have recognized the subtlety he sees in the text ("you have builded better than you knew"). Initially, Faulkner rightly associates Loos with the witty Dorothy, but subsequently he seems to consider her as another Lorelei—clumsy in her jokes and usually funny by accident rather than design.[18]

"Unvirtuous and Mercenary Intentions"

Evidently, by Faulkner's own admission, a sexist outlook is one reason for his unwillingness to credit Loos's achievement fully. John T. Matthews mentions another factor: "Faulkner's deprecation of Loos and her novel in the very letter meant to flatter them substantiates the serious modernist's contempt for popularity with the masses" (214).

The simple fact of Loos's immense popular success probably did count against her in the eyes of highbrows, but it should be remembered that a number of books by serious, "literary" writers had themselves recently become best sellers, among them E. M. Forster's *A Passage to India* (1924); Edith Wharton's *The House of Mirth* (1905), *The Age of Innocence* (1920), and *A Mother's Recompense* (1925); Sinclair Lewis's *Main Street* (1920), *Babbitt* (1922), and *Arrowsmith* (1925); and Willa Cather's *The Professor's House* (1925).[19] Besides these, several other American literary novels had achieved both high sales and critical acclaim, notably John Dos Passos's *Three Soldiers* (1921) and *Manhattan Transfer* (1925); Theodore Dreiser's *An American Tragedy* (1925); and Scott Fitzgerald's *This Side of Paradise* (1920). Presumably, therefore, commercial success alone would not necessarily preclude an author from being taken seriously. In Loos's case, high sales did have a damaging impact on her literary status, and I would suggest that this was partly due to the perception of her as mercenary. Writers with an established reputation for serious literature, such as Forster or Wharton, were unlikely to be suspected of purposely attempting to write a best seller, whereas Loos's thirteen years' experience as a Hollywood screenwriter and film producer inevitably associated her with a materialistic, commodity-based culture. Early reviewers of the novel associated it with cinema; the reviewer for *Vogue*, while admiring the book, noted that it would "probably find its way into the 'movies'" ("What They Read," 152).

Although the nineteenth-century ideal of the author as anonymous gentleman or lady amateur was an anachronism by 1925, "the spectre of the hack," as Clive Bloom puts it (12), still haunted serious writers. Popular fiction was already perceived as the expression of mass consumer and industrial society and was therefore condemned by authors who wished to dissociate themselves from the world of commerce. The judgment of Loos as commercial hack underlies Q. D. Leavis's remark, in *Fiction and the Reading Public* (1932), that *Gentlemen Prefer Blondes* is a book "whose slick technique is the product of centuries of journalistic experience and whose effect depends entirely on the existence of a set of stock responses provided by newspaper and film" (218). Loos recalls that H. L. Mencken said her story should be published in a glossy magazine, "in among the ads" (Kobal, 89). This deliberate association of her fiction with the commercial is intriguing because, as Churchwell argues, the text itself is "pervaded by contemporary anxieties about cultural capital, advertisement, imitation, and the middlebrow" (135). Such anxieties evidently inform the hostile or ambiguous responses of

Mencken, Leavis, and, most strikingly, Wyndham Lewis in his chapter on Loos and Gertrude Stein in *Time and Western Man* (1927). Lewis points to the "identical" tone and verbal tricks adopted by the two writers and describes them as "fundamentally alike" (56), yet distinguishes between them as follows: "Miss Stein [. . .] is a ponderous romantic of the Conrad type; whereas Miss Loos is a lightly ballasted best-seller only, working on the same lines. In perspective the latter will appear as a small mercenary practitioner of the school of Stein" (57). Lewis adds: "Miss Stein has certainly never had any unvirtuous and mercenary intentions of the kind besetting Miss Loos; she has never needed to be a best-seller" (59). The early publication history of *Blondes* does not, however, suggest a designedly commercial venture. It was, according to all available sources, written as a short story to amuse H. L. Mencken, and extended and published in installments at his instigation. A small edition in book form, of 1,200 copies, then appeared, but not with one of the middlebrow or popular fiction houses, rather with the prestigious Boni and Liveright, an important publisher of modernism, which had the work of Hemingway, Dreiser, Pound, and Eliot on its lists.

Certainly Loos took full advantage of the opportunities for profit and publicity provided by the unexpected success of her story,[20] but so did Gertrude Stein when her *Autobiography of Alice B. Toklas* became a best seller six years later (although Lewis could not have predicted this). Stein embraced the supposedly "unvirtuous" world of Hollywood celebrities to which Anita Loos belonged, noting in *Everybody's Autobiography* (1937):

> We were to go to dinner at Beverly Hills which is the same as Hollywood this I have said we were to meet Dashiell Hammett and Charlie Chaplin and Anita Loos and her husband and Mamoulian who was directing everything and we did. Of course I liked Charlie Chaplin [. . .] we both liked talking but each one had to stop and be polite and let the other one say something. (282–283)

In becoming a celebrity, Stein, as Loren Glass notes, "entered into an already-established authorial star system. [. . .] Authorial celebrities from Jack London and Edith Wharton to F. Scott Fitzgerald and Anita Loos had become loosely integrated into the larger market in 'personalities.'" He adds: "Although many high modernist authors dismissed the American culture of celebrity, Stein's fame confirmed that the modernist 'genius' could easily become a star" (2).

Stein also immersed herself in consumer culture: "in six weeks I wrote *The Autobiography of Alice B. Toklas* and it was published and it became a best seller and [. . .] I bought myself a new eight cylinder Ford car and the most expensive coat made to order by Hermes [. . .] I had never made any money before in my life and I was most excited" (*Everybody's Autobiography,* 40).[21] She here explicitly characterizes her work as a rapid production, in the same way that Loos describes herself as having dashed off her fictions and scenarios. This doubled gesture evinces both a disarming modesty about the value of their work and a concealed pride in their ability to judge public taste and satisfy it with so little effort.

At the time when Wyndham Lewis wrote his piece, however, Loos had already achieved commercial success while Stein was still appreciated only by the avant-garde, and on the basis of this distinction between the two authors, Lewis makes assumptions about their respective levels of "virtue" and extends this into a judgment of their literary value. Lewis's strategy for privileging modernist experimental writing over other forms is a classic example of one of the processes of consecration described by Bourdieu:

> The value of works of art in general—the basis of the value of each particular work—and the belief which underlies it, are generated in the incessant, innumerable struggles to establish the value of this or that particular work [. . .] these struggles [. . .] almost always involve recognition of the ultimate values of "disinterestedness" through the denunciation of the mercenary compromises or calculating manoeuvres of the adversary, so that disavowal of the "economy" is placed at the very heart of the field, as the principle governing its functioning and transformation. (*Field,* 79)

Lewis ignores the fact that *Blondes* includes sustained critiques of anti-intellectualism, censorship, consumerism, and the commodification of art. These critiques focus primarily on Lorelei. In her autobiography, Loos describes her heroine as "a symbol of our nation's lowest possible mentality" (*Girl,* 266), and she continually mocks Lorelei's philistinism and her attempts to disguise it:

> Well today Mr. Spoffard is going to take me all around to all of the museums in Munchen, which are full of kunst that I really ought to look at, but Dorothy [. . . is going] to the Half Brow house which is

the world's largest size of a Beer Hall. So Dorothy said I could be a high brow and get full of kunst, but she is satisfide to be a Half Brow and get full of beer. But Dorothy will never really be full of anything else but unrefinement. (*Blondes,* 86)[22]

Predictably, Lorelei can't take much "kunst" and soon deflects Mr. Spoffard into other ways of spending his time. She has no stamina for serious literature either: when one of her admirers presents her with a set of Conrad's novels, she has to get her maid to read them and tell her what they are about. Refinement, for Lorelei, is a euphemism for strategic concealment or discretion; she combines lowbrow taste with a pretense at culture, and through her Loos satirizes the emergence of middlebrow taste, which was represented by its detractors as a bourgeois attempt to hijack and commercialize elite culture.

"I WAS NOT ALWAYS SO REFORMED AS I AM NOW"

Lorelei's diary records her supposed longing for intellectual improvement, and claims to believe that "brains are really everything" (99), but in fact, her repeatedly expressed wish to improve her mind is simply a strategy to impress rich men and thus a function of her desire for economic gain. The novel can be read, as T. E. Blom argues, as "a classic send-up of the American myth in which a nobody from nowhere defeats the old European values of class and education, and wins all that is thought worth winning—money and fame" (40). Her definition of what is "educational" is the reverse of anyone else's—when visiting Paris, she writes:

> in only a few blocks we read all the famous historical names, like Coty and Cartier and I knew we were seeing something educational at last and our whole trip was not a failure [. . .] So when we stood at the corner of a place called the Place Vandome, if you turn your back on a monument they have in the middle and look up, you can see none other than Coty's sign. (*Blondes,* 52)

Lorelei quite literally turns her back on the solid "monuments" of history, literature, and culture in order to admire the depthless icons of consumerism and luxury. Her only use for cultural products is as a means to enhance her social status. For instance, in *But Gentlemen Marry Brunettes* she decides to help her husband, Henry Spoffard, improve his standing among New York intellectuals: "I gave Henry a supscription to the Book of the Month Club that tells you the book you have to read every month to make your individuality stand out. And it really is remarkable because it makes over 50,000 people read the same book every month" (135). In this brief intervention in the complex debate about the emergence of middlebrow culture in the interwar years, Loos depicts the Book-of-the-Month Club (which was founded in 1926) as an agent of the leveling-down and commodification of culture, since it ensures the commercial success of certain books and standardizes the reading choices of mass audiences.[23]

By marrying Mr. Spoffard, Lorelei achieves wealth and social respectability, but can continue to participate in the popular culture industry. She works as both a film actress and a fiction-writer, using her husband's money to finance her projects. Mr. Spoffard's respectability is, however, as much a sham as Lorelei's. "He always gets his picture in all of the newspapers because he is always senshuring all of the plays that are not good for peoples morals" (76), and he "cut[s] out all of the pieces out of all of the photoplays that show things that are riskay. So then they put all the riskay pieces together and they run them over and over again" (102). Mr. Spoffard has turned his appetite for the culture of distraction to his advantage—policing it becomes his métier and his route to fame. In the climate of censorship developing during the interwar years in response to the film industry, many films which are now considered classics were severely cut or had new endings appended, particularly if they depicted transgressive women who did not pay for their sins. This replacement of aesthetic values with rather regressive moral considerations is one of Loos's primary satiric targets.

Like the cartoon strips and West End plays decimated by Mr. Spoffard, Lorelei's autobiographical text is a popular cultural product which has to be made respectable. Lorelei is not only the creative impulse behind the story she narrates, she is also its censor: "I told [Gerry] things that I would not even put in my diary" (11). The unwritten narrative is at times intriguing: "And then we all got together [. . .] and the gentlemen brought their own liquor. So of course the place was a wreck this morning and Lulu and I worked like proverbial dogs to get it cleaned up, but Heaven knows how long it will take to get the chandelier fixed" (7). It is not explained how the chandelier was broken.

She revises the narrative of her own past until it almost fits the pattern of a Puritan spiritual autobiography:

> So I found out that Miss Chapman had been talking against me quite a lot. So it seems that she has been making inquiries about me, and I was really surprised to hear all of the things that Miss Chapman seemed to find out about me [. . .] So then I had to tell Mr. Spoffard that I was not always so reformed as I am now [. . .] So I really cried quite a lot. [. . .] So I told Mr. Spoffard that when I left Little Rock I thought that all of the gentlemen did not want to do anything but protect we girls and by the time I found out that they did not want to protect us so much, it was to late. [. . .] So then I told him how I finaly got reformed by reading all about him in the newspapers. (*Blondes,* 92–93)

Lorelei also frequently attempts to censure Dorothy's unruly speech: "I overheard her say to Major Falcon that she liked to become intoxicated once in a 'dirty' while. Only she did not say intoxicated, but she really said a slang word that means intoxicated and I am always having to tell her that [. . .] she really should not say 'dirty'" (22). But Lorelei's efforts to suppress Dorothy are disingenuous, since she records all her friend's rebellious pronouncements, thereby preserving the subversive elements of her story under a veneer of respectability.

Ironically, Loos's male friends tried to censor *Gentlemen Prefer Blondes* itself. She cites Mencken's opinion that the story would "shock" some readers, reporting that he said: "do you realize that you have committed the great sin of making fun of sex in America? I don't think anybody would publish it" (Kobal, 89). In the first volume of her autobiography, Loos relates that "Lorelei [. . .] was considered by my mentor, Crownie, as such hot stuff that she would smirch my reputation," adding that Crowninshield told Loos's husband John Emerson: "I wish little Anita had never written that story" (*Girl,* 270). These are further indications of the 1920s tendency to associate feminine virtue with privacy and modesty and to distrust women who entered the public sphere through writing. Even several decades later, in the early 1950s, Loos was still drawing attention to the taboo on women writing about sex. Effie Huntriss, heroine of Loos's novel *A Mouse Is Born*, requests some examples of books by "other Authoresses who were born Sexy" to help her write her memoir of her screen career, and is told by the bookseller that he has innumerable books about "how men feel in the presents of Sex Appeal" but that "the opasite point of view, telling how girls who have got it, feel the presents of men's reactions, has not been very adequintly covered" (82).

"THEY ALSO HAVE A MORE UNEXCLUSIVE DINING ROOM FOR THE BENEFIT OF THE MASSES"

Both *A Mouse Is Born* and Loos's other little-known novel, *No Mother to Guide Her,* are set in Hollywood. These texts expose the mercenary foundations of movie culture and the ignorance and lack of taste of those who work within it, but also point to the hypocrisy of writers who attempt to profit from Hollywood whilst preserving an attitude of educated disdain. Loos's satire encompasses both the hypocrisy of the high-minded but avaricious intelligentsia slumming in Hollywood in bad faith *and* the reverse: the tabloid fantasy of soulful and intellectual starlets. A similar multiplication of satiric targets occurs in *But Gentlemen Marry Brunettes,* in which Loos develops her strategy of simultaneously satirizing highbrow and popular culture. In this novel, Lorelei tells Dorothy's life story, and at one point gives an account of Dorothy's reception at the house of Mrs. Breene, mother of a rich young man who wishes to marry Dorothy. Lorelei emphasizes throughout the generosity of Mrs. Breene's conduct, not recognizing its patronizing and cruel intentions:

> Mrs. Breene [. . .] made conversation just as if Dorothy were an equal. And first she asked Dorothy her opinion of quite a few rare old first editions of anteek classic books they had in their libery. [. . .] Well, after Mrs. Breene saw that Dorothy had become as uncomfitable as she could be in a libery, she invited her into the Art gallery, to show her a new picture [. . .] And Mrs. Breene told Dorothy to look it over carefully, and then tell her what she thought of its "chiarusquero." Mrs. Breene was so sweet to Dorothy that she picked out the most titled aristocrats to introduce her to, even if Dorothy did not know what to call them. But instead of taking the opertunity of making friends, Dorothy only let everybody see her misery. (199, 202)

Dorothy is not, however, the only person at the party who is uncomfortable with highbrow taste: Mrs. Breene's other guests, supposedly "music lovers," talk loudly over a string quartet, and only the butler actually enjoys the music. The guests are far more appreciative of Dorothy's impromptu performance of a comic song and a dance routine she learned at the Ziegfeld Follies. Mrs. Breene, anxious to distance herself from popular culture, considers the Follies as "about the same as red ants" (202), an attitude reflecting the interwar association of uniform, coordinated dance troupes with mechanization and mass consumption. But her high-society guests let her down: they are more susceptible to the seductions of lowbrow entertainment than are their servants. The passage is not a rejection of high art in favor of the culture of distraction, but rather a critique of the hypocrisy of upwardly mobile people with pretensions to culture and a tendency to use that culture to subdue their social inferiors. The episode also demolishes the myth that taste and appreciation of art are confined to the wealthier classes.

In another episode of *But Gentlemen Marry Brunettes,* Dorothy and Lorelei attend "a literary party" in Jersey, whose guests include "Mr. H. L. Mencken, Theadore Dreiser, Sherwood Anderson, Sinclare Lewis, Joseph Hergesheimer and Ernest Boyd" (138). Lorelei's ignorance of serious modern literature is demonstrated by her initial reluctance to attend this event, but she eventually decides to go "because some of them do write quite well-read novels" (138). Her preference for widely read rather than artistically superior authors is emphatically lowbrow. She is disappointed, however: the party does not match her idea of a "literary salon," since the guests "did not even *mention* their literary work" (138). In marked contrast with the modesty of the Jersey authors is the self-promotion of the Algonquin Round Table, the members of which Loos criticizes using the classic satiric method of having her naïve heroine admire them. The self-dramatizing elitism of the Round Table emerges clearly in Lorelei's account of the waiter "who holds a velvet rope across the doorway of a small exclusive dining room to keep people who do not apreciate genius from going where they do not belong. For they also have a more unexclusive dining room for the benefit of the masses" (139). Lorelei finds the conversation of the Algonquin set to be friendly and generous, but inadvertently reveals it to be pretentious and far more vacuous than Lorelei's own: "first one genius said to another, 'What was that screamingly funny remark you made last Tuesday?' So then *he* told it and they all laughed. And then it was *his* turn to ask, 'And what was that terribly clever thing *you* said on Friday?' So then the other genius got *his* chance" (142). The ignorance and parochialism of the Algonquin set are also clearly demonstrated. Lorelei reports that Ernest Boyd, who was not a Round Table regular, came to join the party:

> So then Mr. Boyd [. . .] asked "What fellow-literatours did you meet on your trip abroad?" I mean Mr. Boyd does not know the etiquet of holding a conversation, and he kept asking questions that had very little reply.
>
> But it turned out that one of them did have a letter to a literatour called James Joyce, but he did not bother to present it, because he said, after all, James Joyce did not know who *he* was, and why bother to meet somebody who knew so little about the "Algonquin" that he probably would think it meant a tribe of uncivilized Indians. (142)

Loos's compliment to Joyce here, in combination with her evident respect for the writers attending the Jersey party, distances her from the realm of the popular and affirms the value of serious literature and high culture. In the book as a whole, however, her position cannot be so straightforwardly expressed, and her attitude to high modernism is difficult to characterize.

Various critics have attempted to characterize it. Wyndham Lewis points out numerous similarities between the prose of Stein and Loos, commenting that they both employ narrators who are "illiterate," "naïf, and engagingly childish" (55). Lewis cites this similarity only to demolish it by distinguishing between Stein as genuinely experimental and Loos as imitative. It is, however, possible to employ quite the opposite tactic, as Susan Hegeman does. She views Loos as an active participant in the modernist project: "The deliberate depthlessness of Loos's prose has some of Stein's cubist fascination with surface. Indeed, Loos's comical use of illiteracies [. . .], her repetition of words, her simple diction, suddenly seem akin to Stein's stylistic experiments, foregrounding the materiality of language" (527). Barbara Everett similarly positions Loos in relation to the modernist canon, likening the prose style of *Gentlemen Prefer Blondes* to that of T. S. Eliot's fragments of verse drama, *Sweeney Agonistes,* first published in *The Criterion* in 1926 and 1927. The dramatic "jazz-age or machine-gun-fire style" (252) on which the success of his fragment depends was, she argues, new to Eliot. Certainly, although Eliot's earlier work had been associated with jazz in several influential contemporary reviews, it was not until *Sweeney Agonistes* that he wrote extensively in an obviously "jazz age" manner.[24] Everett suggests that it may have been *Gentlemen Prefer Blondes* which "found him a glittering new set of conventions" (254). She also claims that Lorelei provided the model for Eliot's two chattering, uneducated good-time girls, with "their capacity to collapse empty cultures" (250) and their "farcically blank and yet diamond-hard address to life" (253–254). Everett locates the significance of Loos's text in its style and formal innovation, precisely the qualities which high modernists primarily valued:

> This structure of complex crudities, the "Lorelei" style, is a pure urban-pastoral medium of the 1920s, capable of seeming to sum up in its cadences—with a limpidity that hung in the air for decades—the whole difficulty of maintaining innocence at this late point in human history. Thus, sentences like "Fun is fun but no girl wants to laugh all of the time" (the one which haunted Empson) or the more famous "Kissing your hand may make you feel very very good but a diamond and safire bracelet lasts forever" manage to absorb into themselves the whole dissolution of Victorian romanticism in the anarchistic unillusioned 1920s. (255)

Brad Buchanan, taking a somewhat different line, describes *Gentlemen Prefer Blondes* as "a satire on modernist literary pretensions," commenting that Lorelei "has been encouraged to write by a 'gentleman friend' who, no doubt mindful of recent experiments in stream-of-consciousness story-telling, has informed her that if she 'put down all [her] thoughts it would make a book'" (268).

Perhaps one method of negotiating among these various assessments of Loos's relationship to high modernism is to attend to Lorelei's role as author/narrator. In this aspect, *Gentlemen Prefer Blondes* differs from better-known examples of stream-of-consciousness writing. The consciousness of Mrs. Dalloway or Stein's Melanctha is rendered, not by those characters themselves, but by a third-person narrator. In some of Stein's other work, the naïve persona apparently narrates her own story, but is given no name or identity to separate her clearly from Stein herself. Lorelei Lee, by contrast, has a distinct identity as a fictional character and narrates her own history. Further, Lorelei explicitly constructs herself as an author. She writes her diary to be read: it is a performance of herself, and it is her first step in a projected literary career: "So here I am writing a book instead of reading one [. . .] It would be strange if I turned out to be an authoress" (3–4). Indeed, Lorelei's role as author is visible not only in her act of narrating, but also in the plots she creates through her manipulation of other characters in her own story and her multivalent and creative self-presentation and self-censorship. This means that her book is counterfeit stream-of-consciousness writing, since by definition, a stream of consciousness cannot be ordered and constructed by its own subject. Thus, in a characteristically doubled maneuver, Loos uses Lorelei's prose to parody avant-garde experiment and draw attention to its artificiality, whilst directing a simultaneous attack on the best-selling fiction industry by having her heroine succeed in writing a commercially successful book despite her poor literary skills. Since Loos's texts are identical with Lorelei's own, it is only the structural device of irony which turns the satire against the character rather than the author herself.

In later years, Loos deliberately maintained the fiction of Lorelei as the author of *Gentlemen Prefer Blondes*. She published, for example, an essay entitled "Memoirs of a Best-Selling Blonde," purporting to be written by Lorelei, in which she remarks: "I wrote [a book] years ago called *Gentlemen Prefer Blondes,* and it sold like the preverbial hotcakes" (3). This kind of strategy could be read as distancing character from author by erasing Loos's name and allowing Lorelei's text to stand alone. On the other hand, by ventriloquizing through her heroine, Loos might be seen to be identifying herself more closely with her. In another instance, Effie Huntriss in *A Mouse Is Born* is told by her bookseller that the only books by sexy female authors he has in stock are "a book of poetry by an Ancient girl called Sapho and a Modren Authoress called Lorelei Lee" (81). Again, Loos could be modestly distancing herself from the "sexy" book written by Lorelei, or she could be engaging in a form of self-advertisement—inscribing her own book in a tradition of women's writing going back to Sappho and asserting its significance on the literary landscape. Here, as so often, Loos's apparently simple—even simplistic—comments prove unexpectedly complex, and her fictions resist being located in any fixed position in relation to contemporary culture.

In 1966, Anita Loos published her autobiographical volume *A Girl Like I,* which received enthusiastic reviews and led to retrospectives of her films.[25] In the same year, her tribute to Aldous Huxley appeared in a memorial volume compiled by Julian Huxley, which included pieces by a range of other famous people, among them Lord David Cecil, Stephen Spender, T. S. Eliot, Osbert Sitwell, Leonard Woolf, and Isaiah Berlin. Loos wrote: "One of my most cherished mementoes of him is a delicate bottle of Schiaparelli perfume in a fancy pink box made in the shape of a book. On the fly-leaf Aldous wrote, 'For Anita, one of the few books that doesn't stink'" (97). The name of the perfume was "Shocking." [26] In some respects, this was appropriate: her work did produce a shock, not only because of her comic treatment of sexually "immoral" heroines but because of the challenge she posed to established categories of literary value. Anita Loos's novels, in fact, are largely about cultural hierarchies. They satirize both the inanity of mass entertainment and the pretentiousness of highbrows, and even take swipes at the newly constituted category of the middlebrow. This is one reason why there is no consensus as to whether the novels themselves should be classified as literary or popular fiction.

In combination, the responses of Loos's eminent contemporaries demonstrate that the reception and literary status of *Gentlemen Prefer Blondes* during the interwar years were, to say the least, ambiguous. The contrast between the admiration of Huxley, Joyce, Wharton, Santayana, and Empson and the contempt of Lewis and Leavis indicates this clearly enough, while the equivocal remarks of Faulkner and Mencken contain this ambiguity within themselves, as does Loos's own tendency to celebrate her own intellect whilst deprecating her literary achievements. All these responses are determined not only by the personal taste of the writers involved but also by a complicated set of factors relating to literary value, mass culture, contemporary morality, and the status of women writers. There are several ironies in the hostile reactions to *Blondes:* Loos wrote about censorship and her book was deemed immoral; she wrote about the commodification of culture and her book was dismissed as a mass-market commodity; she wrote about the anxieties over authenticity and imitation in the interwar period, and her text was judged to be itself an imitation. The primary difference between the admiring and the critical readers of *Gentlemen Prefer Blondes* is that the former consider Loos as an ironic and perceptive commentator on mass culture and the latter see her as an emanation from that culture and a producer of its commodities. In fact, Loos's novels are self-consciously both products and critiques of American popular culture.

3 | "A PLUMBER'S IDEA OF CLEOPATRA"
Mae West as Author

No *fan could have been more excited than I, as I waited on the pavement for that creature who was already a legend. Hopefully, Mae would drive me off to her apartment where our conference would be held in her fabled white-and-gold drawing room, with its setup of trap drums on which Mae was said to be taking music lessons. [. . .]*

Mae's ability to overpower any surroundings was incredible, for I found her to be as tiny as I, who couldn't have dominated an anthill. But a corset that pinched her waist pushed a smallish bosom upward and outward until it gave Mae a façade that the most buxom belle might envy.

ANITA LOOS, *KISS HOLLYWOOD GOODBYE* (174)

It is something of a surprise to find Anita Loos describing herself as starstruck: after all, from the beginning of her career, she had associated with a whole procession of celebrities, from D. W. Griffith to Marion Davies, Margot Asquith to Scott Fitzgerald. The extent of Mae West's fame in 1936 can certainly be measured by Loos's unwonted excitement. Loos, though, deliberately emphasizes her inflated expectations in order to heighten the contrast between the imagined West and the woman she actually saw. The "legend" of Mae West—fueled by rumors of the "fabled" apartment, the music lessons she was "said to be" taking—is subtly undermined, and the physical image West projects on screen is revealed as a "façade." Yet the power of her presence is fully acknowledged, and her status at the top of the hierarchy of film stars is reaffirmed by Loos's remark "at a time when every other star in Hollywood would have made any sacrifice to play with Clark Gable, Mae turned him down" (174).

Herself a consummate creator of a personal legend, Loos employed some of the same strategies as West. Born within a few years of one another,[1] both worked as child actresses around the turn of the century, and in their autobiographies, each points to the determining influence of this early immersion in the entertainment business on her adult life. From a perspective of maturity, they write their lives as if they were prescripted in childhood. West and Loos present themselves as though they had appeared on the scene fully formed, in marked contrast to writers such as L. M. Montgomery or E. M. Delafield, who emphasize their long struggles to achieve success. Loos claims to have had her first movie script accepted at the age of thirteen; she was in fact eighteen, and *Gentlemen Prefer Blondes* did not appear until she was in her late thirties. Mae West likewise depicts herself as a precocious star, dwelling on her experience acting with stock companies between the ages of eight and eleven; yet she too was well into her thirties before she achieved big-time success. Both women began to conceal their true ages: it was naturally important for West, an actress who traded on her sexiness, to appear youthful, while Loos based her appeal on the image of the "girl," the term she always used to refer to herself. With her flapper dresses, bobbed hair, and carefree attitude, Loos's personal style aligned her with the good-time girls in her novels.

West's later writing clearly exhibits the influence of Loos's style. She writes in *Mae West on Sex, Health and ESP* (1975), for example: "When it comes to catching a man, she should remember that brains are an asset to the girl who is smart enough to hide them" (50), even adding, "I've always been the kind of blonde gentlemen prefer" (51). But as a writer, West has not been compared to Loos, though she has sometimes been compared to Dorothy Parker. In her introduction to the Virago reprints of Mae West's novels, Kathy Lette remarks: "It has been a real pleasure to dive between these covers and discover the real Mae West: not just the unthinking man's Dorothy Parker, and certainly not the prototype for Marilyn Monroe" (xii). Both West and Parker endure largely through quotation; as Emily Wortis Leider says of West: "As a writer of her own quips and laugh lines for the Paramount talkies of the 1930s she [. . .] infus[ed] the American language with as many quotable sayings as Dorothy Parker, Groucho Marx, or W. C. Fields" (139). West's writing, like that of Loos and Parker, is marked by a self-ironizing perspective and notable for its evocation of the idioms of colloquial American speech.

Neither Loos nor Parker, however, promoted herself on anything approaching the scale that Mae West did, or was so keenly aware of her own celebrity status. Following her immensely successful 1933 films, *I'm No Angel* and *She Done Him Wrong,* West was receiving fan letters at the rate of fifteen hundred a week (Frank Rose, 66). She had become, as Marybeth Hamilton notes, "the most famous woman in America, her persona a hot topic of controversy, her name a byword for sex" (176). The controversy she generated meant that her image, circulated globally, was invested with complex meanings in relation to sexuality, censorship, gender performance, and female autonomy. Because she was a film actress, West's celebrity was several orders of magnitude greater than that of any writer of her era, and yet her fame was partly a result of her own writing and the way it was marketed. Ramona Curry, in her study of West's iconic value in twentieth-century culture, notes that one facet of her star image is "that of the author and creative force" (2). Studio publicity, media coverage, and biographies often emphasize that West originated most of her own material and exercised creative control over her films and plays; less frequently noted is her authorship of fiction, autobiography, magazine articles, and health advice. Several recent critical studies offer productive analyses of her writing as an aspect of her performance, commenting particularly on her scripts, but none of them concentrates primarily on her writing or gives sustained attention to her books. Curry points out that "West enjoyed exceptional status as a star comedienne who acted in a self-referential comedic style, repeatedly drawing attention to herself as a known performer and celebrity. West's promotion in film publicity and the opening credits as author of her own stories further underscored her status as narrator of, as well as within, her films" (90). This analysis can be extended through consideration of West's three novels, which reflect on, as well as contributing to, her own celebrity.

"As the author, I was the Number One target"

Both West's acting and her writing were part of a larger strategy to achieve fame by creating and sustaining what has become known as "the Mae West character," a wisecracking, streetwise dame whose sex appeal is defined by her wit as well as her curvaceous figure, slow-motion walk, and extravagant costuming. As Marc O'Day notes in the only entry on West which has so far been included in a literary encyclopedia: "West's role as a writer was a rare and vital ingredient in her legendary control over her own image."[2] She may be remembered as a sex symbol, but she herself repeatedly identified writing as central to all her activity, even to her sex life. In a retrospective account of her erotic experience, she remarks, rather improbably: "I needed a lot of men because I had to find out how they thought, for my writing, you know" (Fleming and Fleming, 281). In another interview, Charlotte Chandler asked: "Are there any ways you feel you're different from the public image of Mae West?" West replied: "When people think you're funny, they start to laugh at everything you say. There was a lot of serious reflection in what I said. [. . .] You know, my head was always working. And I was always writing." She added: "I hope you're going to show me that way" (Chandler, 67). Like Anita Loos, West deliberately played on the discrepancy between her feminine, sexy appearance and her intellectual abilities. While this never won her any serious cultural authority, her self-construction as a writer certainly contributed to her image as a powerful woman. In the 1930s, her publicists at Paramount collaborated with this agenda, using publicity photographs and captions to depict her involvement in the whole process of making her films, from scriptwriting to directing to costume design.[3] Media profiles picked up on this emphasis: Maude Lathem, for example, noted in a 1934 magazine feature: "Mae has a supreme advantage in that she writes all her own stories and dialogue; and she puts on the screen what no other actress has even remotely attempted" (29). Occasionally West wrote plays in which she did not star, but she still managed to place herself centrally by emphasizing her status as author. Recalling the 1928 production of her play *Pleasure Man,* she notes: "My name was up in lights on the Biltmore's marquee as the author"; adding, "the police came onstage in droves and carrying night-sticks, and arrested the entire show. As the author, I was again the Number One target" (West, *Goodness,* 132).

West's novels are intriguing texts in their own right and relate in complex ways to her plays and films. They are: *The Constant Sinner,* originally published as *Babe Gordon* in 1930; *She Done Him Wrong,* originally published as *Diamond Lil* in 1932; and *Pleasure Man* (1975). Despite their initial success,[4] however, the two earlier novels disappeared from view for decades, and criticism of West's fiction is extremely sparse.[5] In 1995, capitalizing on the reissue of West's major films on video two years previously, Virago Press reprinted *She Done Him Wrong* and *The Constant Sinner*. West's fiction, in fact, makes for better reading than might be expected. She shared with Loos and Parker a wonderful ear for dialogue (a talent which doubtless partly explains why all three succeeded as Hollywood scriptwriters, while several of their eminent peers, notably Scott Fitzgerald and John Dos Passos, were defeated in the attempt).

West's specialism is the language of the Harlem street. This sample, from *The Constant Sinner*, is a dialogue between two prostitutes, Babe and Jenny:

> "I was up at Nigger Gert's. A guy up there busted Sing Sing, an' he sent me word he wanted a fix-up of coke with his liquor. Jackass is going to pull another job. Look, here's the dough. [. . .] Who's been blowin' around tonight?"
>
> "Saw Tiger Williams," said Babe, "breeze in with the manager of the Black and Tan Revue. I'm not so particular to-night. I'm tellin' you I ain't passin' up anything that looks like a lousy buck. I got to give that landlady somethin' besides a by-and-by smile to-morrow. Ought to be some class, though, in this bunch to-night. Maybe a bank roll." (3)

But Babe is able to abandon this method of supporting herself: she attaches herself to a series of increasingly wealthy men and soon achieves a truly luxurious way of life. This success is partly due to her ability to adapt her language and style to different social milieus. When her rich lover asks whether Jenny is still pursuing her, she says: "Why, she called up yesterday morning, Wayne, [. . .] and I told her not to bother me any more, and told her that if she thought I would come across with any money, she was just out of her mind" (161). Informed that Jenny has revealed her past as a streetwalker to Wayne's family, Babe says: "what a terrible, dangerous creature Jenny is. She thinks nothing of ruining my reputation, of destroying our happiness. But you don't believe these things!" (162). The narrative moves easily between these scenes, extending also to the high-toned home of Wayne's millionaire father, and to a flat-house in a run-down neighborhood, where Babe visits her black lover, Money Johnson. Her arrival is observed by a jealous former flame of his, Big Ida:

> "Ah knows it was dat dirty white trash! Yes, she's up dere now. She's up dere wid dat man. Lawd hab mercy on her soul, 'cause Ah'll snatch duh eyes outen her head." [. . .]

"Look yere, woman," Liza Jones said to her, "whutcha goin' on like dat fo'? Actin' lak a mad baboon! [. . .] Whutcha all talkin' on about, woman?" (171)

The juxtaposition of these varied New York scenes and dialects, ranging widely over the whole social scale, distinguishes West's work from that of most other women authors of the period.[6] *She Done Him Wrong* includes Chinese and Brazilian characters, introducing a further range of speech styles, and while it is largely set in a dance hall, there are also excursions to the opium dens of Chinatown. Whereas *The Constant Sinner* has a contemporary (1920s) setting, *She Done Him Wrong* represents the New York of the 1890s:

> Flounces and ruffles and feather boas . . . the sickish-sweet odour of cheap perfume mingled with the smell of Irish whisky . . . flying suds of mammoth schooners of beer . . . the hard bright faces of harlots . . . the bleared eyes and bloated faces of habitual drunkards . . . the bruised, swollen faces of rowdies and gangsters, killers, drug addicts . . . curses and smells and more curses . . . and underneath it all—crime, and the half-laughing, half-sneering face of lust. [. . .]
>
> Immigrants, German, Irish, Italian, and Jews from Russia, Poland and the hidden ghettos of the world poured in through Castle Garden to be woven later into the fabric and to enrich the texture of New York.
>
> Everywhere, it seemed there was an overwhelming preoccupation with the frivolities. Downtown, virtue was only extolled in sentimental song when the night grew grey and tears came easily to fall saltily among the beer-slops. Uptown, vice was toyed with in a dandified way, a toothsome concomitant of lobster à la Newburg and champagne. (12)

This impressionistic, fragmented style shows a trace of modernist influence and represents a new direction for West. *She Done Him Wrong* can be considered an advance on *The Constant Sinner* in stylistic terms, since the dialogue is more successfully imbued with West's trademark wit, and the narrator's evocation of atmosphere is more adventurous.

The quality of West's books is, however, due at least in part to the assistance of various collaborators. Although her name appears as sole author on all her books and articles, her texts were in fact produced collaboratively, with varying degrees of input from West herself. She generally provided the ideas, much of the dialogue, and all the epigrammatic lines for her novels and scripts, but her pressured lifestyle and shaky mastery of written English meant that she required assistance with her writing. Most of her plays were effectively constructed on stage: she began with the jottings she had made on scraps of paper and had typed up, and then added dialogue, including some lines suggested by the cast or supplied by other playwrights, as the rehearsals progressed. During her years in Hollywood, scriptwriters cowrote, or drafted, the screenplays attributed to her, although she always tailored them to her own requirements. Her evident skill led to invitations to work on scripts for other actresses, including Marlene Dietrich and Jean Harlow. She refused these, not wishing to contribute to the celebrity of her competitors. In any case, her talent was for writing lines to fit her own personality. John Mason Brown, reviewing a 1949 revival of *Diamond Lil,* wrote: "like *The Constant Sinner* and *Sex* before it, *Diamond Lil* is no play at all. It creates a category of its own which can only be defined as a Mae Western. If it is a drama, then so is a trip to Chinatown on a sightseeing bus. Without Mae West it would be nothing. With her it is Mae West" (259).

As for her books, *The Constant Sinner* was produced with the aid of a Dictaphone and an assistant, Howard Merling, while her autobiography, *Goodness Had Nothing to Do with It* (1959), was cowritten by Stephen Longstreet. West rarely made full acknowledgment of the contributions of these authors: Longstreet, for example, is thanked for mere "editorial assistance" on the acknowledgments page of *Goodness,* while in her novelization of *Pleasure Man,* the page containing the ISBN and copyright information also includes a half-concealed mention of a coauthor: "Mae West acknowledges the kind assistance of Lawrence Lee in preparing *Pleasure Man.*" Lee was employed as her "secretary," but it is almost certain that he did more than type the manuscript. West's insistence on taking all the credit for texts she produced collaboratively ensured that they could all be assimilated into, and subordinated to, her effectively copyrighted persona. Despite working with other authors, her style emerged as distinct and instantly recognizable. As a *Variety* reviewer said of her first film, *Night after Night* (1932): "Miss West's dialogue is always unmistakably her own. It is doubtful if anyone else could write it" (quoted in Leider, 244).

"I'VE GOT A STYLE ALL MY OWN"

Some of her remarks indicate that West considered fiction a more enduring form than drama or cinema. She notes in her autobiography:

"I was thinking of writing a novel. A play is soon finished, remembered only by its photographs and yellowing reviews. A book lasts as long as someone keeps it on a shelf" (West, *Goodness,* 143). And yet, as is so often, her maneuvers might be read as opportunistic. She wrote *She Done Him Wrong* because her other ventures were failing: her latest play had closed early and she had no performance bookings. Likewise, she only insists on the value of the written word when seeking to promote her own writing. For example, her preface to her late novel *Pleasure Man* explicitly privileges text over performance: "I could open *Pleasure Man* on Broadway tomorrow if I so desired. Instead, I prefer to offer you *Pleasure Man—as a novel*" (Preface, 8). For a woman in her eighties, fiction would perhaps seem an effective way to maintain her reputation—the novel includes a Westian character, Helen Webster, who is "sex personified" (*Pleasure Man,* 136) and projects West's remembered prime rather than her actual decrepitude.

Pleasure Man was transformed into a novel several decades after its Broadway performance, and West's preface uses the circumstances of the play's production to stimulate interest in the book: "The excitement that the play had created in its break-in weeks had saturated Broadway and theatergoers with great expectations of seeing a sensational piece of entertainment" (7); "Headlines shouted: MAE WEST BAD GIRL OF BROADWAY IN TROUBLE AGAIN" (8). Her habit of transferring her work across different genres, exploiting each character and story line to the full, makes the distinction among West's plays, film scripts, and fictions difficult to maintain. Like *Pleasure Man, Diamond Lil* began life as a play, premiered in 1928, and the film version, *She Done Him Wrong* (retitled to circumvent the censors, since the Hays Office had vetoed the filming of the original play), appeared in early 1933, a few months after the novelization was published. This pattern was reversed in the case of *The Constant Sinner,* which started as a novel, published in 1930. West's very effective marketing strategy was to use the book, and the scandal surrounding its depiction of prostitution and interracial relationships, to generate publicity for the upcoming play version (1931). She later used some of the characters and plot situations from *The Constant Sinner* for her film *Belle of the Nineties* (1934).

Capitalizing on the recent success of her national tour with *Diamond Lil,* West produced her first novel rapidly. Its publisher, Macaulay, initially launched it as *Babe Gordon,* after the central character. Under this name, it went through four printings in as many months, partly as a result of the interest created by Macaulay's unusual promotional ploy: a title competition. An advertisement was placed in *Publishers Weekly,* announcing a $100 prize for the reader who could come up with the best new title, and the judges, among them the celebrated columnist Walter Winchell, chose *The Constant Sinner,* which was then used for the Broadway version as well as later editions of the novel. Emily Wortis Leider argues that this title "invited ironic comparison with the play *The Constant Wife,* a Somerset Maugham opus in which Ethel Barrymore had starred in 1926, and perhaps with Dorothy Parker's *New Yorker* column, 'Constant Reader'" (223). Surely a more obvious connection is to Margaret Kennedy's *The Constant Nymph,* which was far better known than Maugham's play. Kennedy's title was frequently repeated or parodied and doubtless inspired the name of Parker's column. The ironic play on "constant" in the title *The Constant Sinner,* I would argue, points to the contrast between the faithful nymph of Kennedy's book and the faithless nymphomaniac of West's. This in turn exploits audience fascination with West's own scandalous sexual behavior, both on and off stage.

West remarks in her autobiography: "More people had seen me than saw Napoleon, Lincoln and Cleopatra. I was better known than Einstein, Shaw or Picasso" (*Goodness,* 164). This is an interesting list, constructing fame as largely the preserve of men, notably statesmen and artistic or scientific geniuses, and perhaps suggesting that West's invasion of this arena has challenged traditional cultural hierarchies and power structures.[7] The only woman she mentions, Cleopatra, is a figure with whom she had long felt an affinity. In the play version of *The Constant Sinner,* stage directions indicate that Babe Gordon's hotel room should be decorated with pictures of Cleopatra, Madame Du Barry, and Catherine the Great. West clearly aspired to the iconic sexual allure of these women, and probably also to their power and autonomy. W. C. Fields, however, privately described West as "a plumber's idea of Cleopatra,"[8] nicely encapsulating her ability to draw on high and low cultural referents, reinventing figures from myth as fantasies for a mass media age. West's use of Cleopatra also exploits the contemporary fascination with Egyptology which followed the discovery of King Tutankhamen's tomb in 1922. The first of her several performances in a Cleopatra costume was in *The Mimic World of 1921,* a revue in which West's turns also included a parody of film actress Alla Nazimova and two character roles, a French temptress with good business sense and "Shifty Liz" from the New York underworld. At this early stage of her career, West's success was predicated on her talent for imitation: travesties and burlesques were staples of the American variety stage in the early twentieth century. As a child performer, "Baby Mae" took off performers including Eddie Foy, Bert Williams, Texas Guinan, and Eva Tanguay. When West began to market herself in terms of her unique personal style, she did so using a song called "I've Got a Style All My Own," which directly and paradoxically evokes Tanguay's "It's All Been Done Before But Not the Way I Do It." The elements of burlesque and camp resurfaced in some of her later work; in her 1935 film *Goin' to Town*, for example, she parodies a prima donna, performing a duet from a Saint-Saëns opera.

West's plays, films, and novels reveal a continuing preoccupation with disguise, performance, and assumed identities, but while her early revue work required her to shift among a series of distinct characters, she later consolidated the best of her various roles into "the Mae West character." Her signature role, Diamond Lil, may have been—as John Kobal points out—a re-creation of "the two most celebrated symbols of self-made wealth and beauty of her era, the legendary railroad tycoon 'Diamond Jim' Brady and the beauty [. . .] Lillian Russell, the actress Brady showered with diamonds" (154). Yet West made this character so entirely her own that, eventually, it became itself the subject of imitations and spoofs by younger performers, as well as inspiring several cartoons.[9] Indeed, in the later stages of her career, as Emily Wortis Leider argues in her valuable biography, West effectively became imitative of herself:

> World-famous, a creature of myth, but underemployed for long stretches of time once she left Paramount, when she did work she compulsively repeated her own best lines and flaunted the glittering, larger-than-life personality [. . .] that she worked so hard to create and promote. She prized that persona and fought to protect it from unauthorised imitators in the same way a successful manufacturer would a company's product [. . .] In these later years Mae West became as repetitive and predictable [. . .] as the formula for Coca-Cola. (10)

Yet the formula for Coca-Cola is, famously, a closely guarded secret. Like Coca-Cola, West could be imitated but never quite equaled. In her stage career, it was West herself whom audiences clamored to see; when she made the transition to film, her signature character became increasingly detached from the living actress and increasingly fixed in

its lineaments. The endless reproducibility of this character on celluloid extended West's image through space and time, yet simultaneously made it seem manufactured and diminished its worth.

"A LITTLE BIT SPICY, BUT NOT TOO RAW"

In her play scripts and screenplays, West created a series of protagonists who were evidently vehicles for her own performance. Her novel-
ized versions of her best-known heroines, Diamond Lil and Babe Gordon, are just as obviously projections of her fantasized self, as is Helen
Webster in *Pleasure Man,* whose surname echoes West's and who
is "blond, gorgeous, and voluptuous" (135), as well as witty and self-
possessed. In the stage version of *Pleasure Man,* the character of Helen
does not appear; instead, the play features a gay female impersonator.
As Hamilton notes: "The substance of West's revision was to drop the
drag queens and throw in Mae West" (230). Indeed, this point can be
taken further: in comparison with her scripts, West's fiction reveals a
greater, and sometimes more sophisticated, awareness of the marketability of her own image. In *Pleasure Man,* reproductions of the vaudeville performer Helen Webster build up her reputation, but are ultimately no substitute for the real thing: "This was the first time Rodney
had come across her in the flesh. He had seen pictures of her, but now
he was forced to admit that they didn't do her justice" (135). Emphasis is
placed on Helen's uniqueness: "the way she could sell those song numbers and get over a personality that exuded sex in every look, gesture,
and curve was what made the difference between Helen Webster and all
the others everywhere who leaned against pianos and warbled the latest
tunes from Tin Pan Alley" (135). Helen's sexual appeal is so improbably
powerful as to become comic, and this kind of humorous exaggeration
is also found in West's other two novels.

Babe Gordon, in *The Constant Sinner,* is likewise a projection of
West's own supposedly irresistible sexual appeal: "she looked at her
glowing body with self-appreciation. The well-turned arms and legs,
the smooth contour of curving hips, her pink, curling toes, all combined to give her a thrill of sensuous pleasure and to remind her how
she might captivate any man" (30). Even when alone, Babe performs
her sexuality, and the narrator repeatedly presents her as an erotic
spectacle, as if she were on stage: "Babe sat cameo'd against a blue velvet overstuffed chair, with an amber floor lamp shedding a soft glow

on her smiling features" (56). In an assignation with her black lover, who has a bed completely surrounded with mirrors, Babe's continual awareness of her audience is emphasized: "In that great mirrored room in Strivers' Row Money Johnson appeared like an army by reflection and she was like a shimmering white quicksand ready to consume these black battalions" (115). The multiplication of Babe and Money in the mirrors emphasizes Babe's own status as a sexual commodity, but also constructs her lovers as replaceable, each of them only one in a series. Babe's ability to reproduce her performance of being in love with each new man, together with her awareness of her own marketability, allows her to retain the balance of power in all her relationships.

In *She Done Him Wrong*, the relationship between original and reproduction is explored in more detail. The most detailed and erotic descriptions of the heroine's body in the novel refer, not to Lil herself, but to pictures of her. Suicide Hall, the dance venue owned by Lil's lover, Gus Jordan, is adorned with an enormous painting:

> The subject of the painting was none other than the alabaster and gold Lil reclining in all her voluptuous nudity upon a background of purple velvet. No masculine eye could travel from the crown of that spun-gold head past those vermilion-tipped peaks of breasts down to those curling rose-petal toes without being conscious of a physical change. A visiting French artist had painted that lusty, life-like reproduction of Lil. The original had been sent to the World's Fair in Chicago. Lil's picture was soon to be seen on new calendars, and already it appeared on the band of a high-priced cigar. (14)

This "reproduction" of Lil is also a reproduction in another sense—it is not the original painting, but a copy, and thus immediately suggestive of Lil's commodification. Her image is used in the bar to arouse the lust of customers and stimulate their drinking, and also in the global market to sell calendars and cigars. (Mae West's own image likewise adorned various consumer products, including cigarette cards, fans, soap advertisements, and perfume bottles.) The association of Lil with luxury goods, "high-priced" cigars, diamonds, and champagne, reinforces her status as a commodity, as does the repeated description of her hair as "gold." At the same time, the golden, or blonde, color of her hair is suggestive of sexual availability.[10] She has, admittedly, far more power than a prostitute, since—like Lorelei Lee—she has a choice of lovers and is not paid for sex, but rather showered with gifts of diamonds. Yet both

Lil and Lorelei are, in effect, in circulation among the powerful men of New York and available to the highest bidder—that is, to the man who can provide the most comfortable lifestyle and the largest jewels. As the description of the painting reveals, Lil lures men by deliberately designing her own image and exhibiting herself to the gaze of the painter and of the male customers of the saloon. She exploits her sexuality for her own gain—to achieve power, celebrity status, and wealth—yet is herself exploited to sell alcohol and luxury items.

The reproduction of Lil within the novel mimics West's own reproduction of her in stage and film performances. West effectively converted Lil into a range of financially profitable cultural products. A comparison with one of West's other stage characters is relevant here. Her play *The Wicked Age* (1927) is about a flapper, Babe Carson, who wins a beauty competition and is gradually transformed from a fun-loving girl to a selfish and mercenary prima donna who is willing—for a large payment—to endorse a range of products from milk to liver pills. The final act, as Leider argues, "sends up Mae West, exaggerating her self-infatuated diva tendencies and defusing them with laughs. She even has fun at the expense of celebrity testimonials in advertisements, of the very sort Mae's highly glazed giveaway postcards plugging Cammeyer shoes exemplified" (181).[11] In varying degrees, all the authors considered in this study accept and profit from their own commodification, but among them, West does so with the most insouciance.

In *She Done Him Wrong,* there is a scene in which Lil exhibits a new set of photographs of herself to Jordan's business associates: "Skilfully, the photographer had included the whole of her diamond array in each picture, and she had brought to each pose the full value of her high-corseted breasts and swelling hips" (42–43). The word "value" explicitly identifies Lil's body as a commodity, and the diamonds indicate the extent of her worth in the marketplace. The picture draws on the established conventions of theater and visual art, which connect sensuality and wealth through displaying rich materials and jewels on the female body. Lil's deliberate manipulation of her own image is still more evident in this scene than in the account of the painting:

> To one print she called attention as giving her style and dignity. [. . .] Another pose displayed her hair, unbound, draped over a shoulder and spreading down to her tight waist.
>
> "That's sorta simple and unaffected, don'tcha think?" Lil inquired. There was a general murmur of approval.

"It makes you look very virginal," said Rita.

"God forbid!" retorted Lil, giving her a sharp look. (43)

As in the painting, Lil's hair is deployed to suggest a range of meanings: its loose, flowing arrangement is initially read in terms of simplicity and virginity, yet this is instantly undermined by Rita and Lil's sarcastic exchange; while the age-old association between women's hair and sexuality complicates the meaning of the photograph. (There is no indication as to whether Lil is a natural blonde. West herself was not—her hair changed from brunette to platinum over the course of her career, so that her image as a blonde is just one more artifice.) West acknowledges that Lil's "simple and unaffected" image is patently manufactured, while the contrast with an alternative, more risqué shot reveals Lil's ability to project an entire range of personae to suit different occasions:

Then she held up another photo with a pleased smile.

"Wait till you see this one. I show my legs in this."

In this pose she stood over a chair with one knee crooked and resting on its seat. Her legs, sheathed in black, lace-clocked stockings, moulded the sensuous swell of her calves before disappearing discreetly under the hem of her gown.

"A little bit spicy, but not too raw," she said. [. . .]

"Lemme look at that again, will you, Lil?" Flynn asked. [. . .]

"You can have that one, Flynn. [. . .] It's for the bedroom. It'll keep you company when you're sleepin' alone."

"You're a card, Lil," Jordan said, with an uneasy laugh. (43)

Lil titillates the customers in the bar by presenting different facets of herself, virtually transforming herself into a one-woman harem and thereby retaining a measure of control over the way she is commodified.

At the same time, the juxtaposition of the flesh-and-blood Lil with the images draws attention to the way in which the painting and photographs, whilst ostensibly designed to display her charms to the full, actually function to contain her excessive sexuality. In each picture, she can only adopt one "pose," only show off one aspect of herself. The movement of her body, which was key to West's stage rendering of Lil (and key to the legendary sex appeal of West herself), is frozen in the pictures—she is fixed in space and thereby diminished. Yet, paradoxically, she is also extended through space—her image circulates in places where Lil is not physically present. Just as she presides over the saloon through the medium of her painting, so she enters the bed-rooms of numerous men through the photographs she distributes. By giving Flynn her picture for his bedroom, Lil enacts a simulation of adultery which arouses Jordan's jealousy and Flynn's uneasiness and which draws attention to the very real power of her image.[12]

Compare the equivalent passage from West's script for the play *Diamond Lil*, in which Lil's speech runs: "There, I had them taken with all my rocks. Here, this one is great, isn't it? And this one is a pip—full length, see? Gives me style and dignity. This is my best: this is for the bedroom; you'll get one. You can have that, Flynn; a little bit spicy but not too raw."[13] This abbreviated version, with the response and "approval" of the other characters eliminated, contains fewer layers of irony than the fictional rendering and demonstrates West's perception of the different requirements of the comic stage performance and the novel. While some of the ironies carefully built into the novel could be achieved on stage by the expressive responses of the onlookers, the dramatic scene is nevertheless much more simply structured than the fictional one. This is because the novel uses a detailed verbal render-ing of Lil's impact to substitute for the physical presence of West on stage. Also, the unease generated by Lil's sexuality in *She Done Him Wrong* is much less overt in *Diamond Lil*, which may have been due to the constraints imposed by censorship. A wholly comic approach to sexuality was more likely to get past the censors than a more disturb-ing rendition. Marybeth Hamilton comments that West's script for Lil suggests "that her sexiness is a good-natured pose, that she is keenly aware of the impression she makes and vastly entertained by it" (113). The idea that her sexiness is a pose suggests that not only are the pic-tures manufactured versions of Lil, but the supposed original is herself in some sense manufactured. And Lil is being played, in the film and stage versions, by an actress, Mae West, who is famous for having cre-ated herself as an improbable, erotically excessive "character." This dizzying regression leaves us with no original for any of the images, imitations, and performances.

"Depression, repression and suppression"

West presented herself, to a certain extent, as an exemplar of the American Dream. Her autobiographical narratives construct her as a girl from a fairly ordinary family who becomes a major star through talent, determination, and continuous hard work, progressing up the scale from vaudeville to the legitimate stage to Hollywood, increasing her prestige, fame, and wealth along the way. She does not lay claim to an underprivileged upbringing or an unduly painful acting apprentice-ship: indeed, she tends to represent her family as rather better-off and higher up the social scale than they actually were. In *Goodness Had Nothing to Do with It,* she never admits to suffering any self-doubt or failure in her career; as she remarked: "Her fans don't want Mae West to have problems and to have to struggle. Mae West always triumphs" (McCorkle, 48). But since she deliberately identified herself closely with her character Diamond Lil, the patterns of Lil's career were widely associated with West herself. The rich, flamboyant Lil and her film counterpart, Lady Lou, remind audiences that they were formerly poor, and West repeats this story in her film *I'm No Angel,* whose heroine Tira starts as a lowlife circus lion tamer, but ascends via a series of increasingly wealthy suitors and eventually lands a millionaire. To coincide with the appearance of this film, the costar, Cary Grant, wrote a series of pieces about West for the British magazine *Picturegoer,* and he depicts her career as a hard struggle, requiring immense commitment. He emphasizes her long hours of work and says that she has sacrificed pleasure and personal opportunities for the sake of her career.[14] During the depressed 1930s, this kind of celebrity image—the ordinary American who has succeeded through self-discipline and survived the bad times—held a particular attraction, and *I'm No Angel* was phenomenally successful.[15] As John Kobal remarks, during this period, "Mae gave [people] back confidence and the notion of a time in America when a man's, or a woman's, get-up-and-go was all that was needed to gain fame [and] fortune" (154). In her autobiography, West reiterates the image of herself as a defiant survivor during the Depression, also taking the opportunity to reinforce her supposed sole authorship of her novels: "The world was going mad. I went on writing. Brokers leaped from windows. I wrote. The President sank his head in his high hard collar and said, 'Prosperity is *just* around the corner.' I plunged deeper into my novel. [. . .] Bankers went to jail. I wrote and finished my book" (*Goodness,* 147). This passage effectively positions West as more effective than the president in countering the problems caused by economic downturn.

Indeed, she claimed in a 1934 interview: "The very best thing I have done for the public during this depression has been the humorous manner—even ribald sometimes—in which I have treated sex. My fight has been against depression, repression and suppression" (Lathem, 93).

She addressed working-class audiences through her fantasies of success and through her humor, common touch, colloquial speech, and familiarity with popular culture. But she was also a genuine "crossover success." Her performances were admired by respected writers, critics, and artists, including David Belasco, Carl Van Vechten, Scott Fitzgerald, Colette, and John Colton; she sometimes received highly favorable reviews from serious papers such as the *New Republic* and the *New York Times,* particularly following the national tour of *Diamond Lil;* and her plays increasingly drew high-society theatergoers. Her work in film further demonstrated her ability to please a variety of audiences. Hamilton argues that West was at her most effective on screen when she achieved an open-ended performance, leaving the task of interpretation to the audience:

> In the wake of *I'm No Angel* she was praised by a diverse collection of writers who united in adoring her performance style while holding flatly contradictory opinions about what it actually meant. [. . .] That Mae West could sustain all these interpretations and more was the secret of her Hollywood success. *I'm No Angel* was West's biggest hit, with good reason: male traditionalists could delight in a full-figured sex bomb, feminists in an unabashedly autonomous heroine, homosexual men in seemingly intentional camp, and the Hays Office in seemingly intentional restraint. (174–175)

The development of her ambiguous, suggestive, yet increasingly subtle performance style was largely a response to the new climate of censorship in early-twentieth-century America. Intense controversy surrounded most of her films, books, and stage performances. Her first play, *Sex* (1926), which she wrote, directed, and starred in, was a smash hit on Broadway but was raided by police in its forty-first sell-out week. West was charged with obscenity and sentenced to ten days' imprisonment, a turn of events she naturally managed to convert into a publicity stunt: she was interviewed and reported on by numerous columnists, wrote about her experience, and repeatedly referred back to it in later interviews. But as a result of the prosecution, no New York theater would book her next play, *The Drag,* about contemporary gay culture, even though it had played successfully in provincial theaters. Its subject was too obviously (and deliberately) controversial.

West's relationship with censorship has been interpreted in several different ways by critics and biographers. Some date her emergence as a major star to the *Sex* trial (Fenton, 86), while others claim that censorship "left Mae West sadly debilitated" (Walker, 74). Still another interpretation is that "On Broadway, the relationship between Mae West and the censors was almost symbiotic. In Hollywood, the Production Code laid her low" (Doherty, 1577). Certainly, her problems with censors worsened as she moved into cinema, which was increasingly strictly regulated. Her films were decimated, with many suggestive lines and shots eliminated and endings changed to ensure that only the virtuous were rewarded. Some cuts were made by the studio in anticipation of the censors and others after the film was made. The extent of the postproduction cuts varied according to country or state, and some countries banned certain West films altogether. West therefore had to adapt her writing and performance style to work around the censors. She ensured that her scripts were free of potentially shocking material so that those inspecting them would find that there was nothing to delete, since the risqué element was all in her voice, timing, and expression. Some of her memorable quips originated this way—in *Belle of the Nineties,* for example, a maid asks Ruby (the West character) whether she was nervous when her rich admirer gave her a lot of presents. Ruby replies: "Why no. I was calm and collected."[16] This apparently innocent line takes on a new meaning, of course, when a pause is inserted after "calm." West's films contain a greater number of witty one-liners than do the original stage plays, and she suggests that these were a substitute for the kind of physical and amorous action she was no longer allowed to represent. In a 1969 interview, she remarked: "I didn't start putting in all these wisecracks till I started pictures. When I wrote *She Done Him Wrong* [. . .] the studios and censors wouldn't let me do certain things [. . .] and so with everybody weakening my drama, I figured I had to put some other element in" (Meryman, 52).

In the process of seeking to make her suggestiveness more oblique and wordless, West developed and refined her style. Later, she turned censorship to her advantage in another way, retrospectively constructing herself as the central figure in its emergence: "I brought the censors on in Hollywood, but I saved the industry" (Fleming and Fleming, 287). Both these claims are, of course, seriously exaggerated. West was indeed a major asset to Paramount for a number of years, and her image certainly became iconic in the censorship debates, through its use as media shorthand. As Curry points out: "West's aura of power, rather than her generally transgressive sexuality, had come to dominate her emblematic function within the film industry, and increasingly that in movie reform discourse" (56). But censorship did not simply result from the unorthodox performances of one particular star. Film industry reform was a far-reaching and complex phenomenon, a site of social and economic struggle over two of the dominant, if conflicted, tenets of middle-class America: family values and free enterprise.[17]

West's choice to publish novels might also be read as a response to censorship. Fiction was rarely subject to the same stringency on the part of censors as films and plays were. The system of literary censorship had come under intense pressure in the 1920s, owing to the high-profile trials of *Ulysses, The Well of Loneliness,* and *Lady Chatterley's Lover;* while the Nazi book-burnings in May 1933 heightened anticensorship feeling in America. In cinema, by contrast, censorship was just gaining momentum at this period, partly due to perceptions of the immense popularity and seductive power of the new medium and its potential to corrupt the younger generation. While many forms of publication were deemed to be protected by the First Amendment (regarding freedom of speech and of the press), a 1915 Supreme Court ruling specified that the film industry was not, since it was purely a business and not part of the press. The increased freedom offered by print publication is likely the reason why West's fiction is more detailed and explicit with regard to taboo subjects than is her work in other media. For example, *She Done Him Wrong* makes it much clearer than does the play *Diamond Lil* that the heroine has been a prostitute and is involved with white slavery. The Hays Office objected to the critique of the Salvation Army in the film version, and it had to be removed; in the novel, this is retained, and Lil's blasphemous views are freely expressed. Fiction publishing was not, however, entirely unproblematic for West. For the novel which became *The Constant Sinner,* she initially signed a publishing contract with Lowell Brentano, but she would not make the cuts he suggested, and he could not convince his editorial board to back it. It was quickly taken up, however, by Macaulay, who evidently saw that its commercial potential partly depended on its raunchy subject matter.

"HOW OLD IS MAE WEST?"

In Hollywood, West's attempts to dominate the whole process of making her films led to frequent conflicts with directors and studio bosses. Outspoken actresses were rarely tolerated in Hollywood: a comparable example is Louise Brooks, whose refusal to submit to what she saw as rude treatment by male directors led to a series of breaches and rejected roles. As Barry Paris notes of her attitude early in her film career: "there was something ominous for her future in the fact that she was so articulate and opinionated, for male studio executives tended to share Valentino's 1922 view: 'I do not like women who know too much'" (131). Declining a summons to return to Paramount after she had gone to Germany to make *Pandora's Box* (1929) was the beginning of the end of her career as an actress. Like West, Brooks created her own character on screen and resisted being molded into prescribed roles. Late in her life, she remarked: "To be a great actress, you must know what you're doing," adding, "I was simply playing myself, which is the hardest thing in the world to do."[18] West said of her own films: "I was really always the director. Nobody could tell me how to be me" (Chandler, 64). Brooks and West were, of course, performing not themselves but a fantasized version of themselves, which became the basis of their posthumous reputations. In her autobiographical writing, West reveals a clear awareness that her celebrity self was an artificial creation: she described herself as "a star seen in the third person, even by myself," and noted, "I had evolved into a symbol" (*Goodness*, 165, 44). She also suggests that she identified so fully with the fantasy self that it became the lived reality: "Diamond Lil—I'm her and she's me and we're each other"; "I was Diamond Lil off stage as well as on" (*Goodness*, 117–118, 114). This was, however, largely a strategy to ensure her ownership of the character and of the profit and prestige she generated. West's performance of Lil was imitated by several other vaudeville and nightclub performers, and West's anger over this involved her in threatened and actual lawsuits.[19] Her possessive attitude toward her character might be connected with her insistence that she could not be understudied for any of her stage roles, so that when she was ill or injured, shows had to be canceled. These were deliberate maneuvers to emphasize her uniqueness and irreplaceability. As Curry notes: "By the late 1930s, West's image exceeded every script and suffused every new character she might play" (104).

West's identification of herself with Lil was noticeably in tension with other elements of her self-presentation. While Lil presides over a saloon, becomes involved with crime and criminals, and never engages in intellectual activity, West repeatedly constructs herself as clean-living, health-conscious, and fond of staying in to read and write. Her increasing tendency to represent herself in this way seems to have resulted initially from the need to retain audience sympathy in the climate of moral reform of the interwar years. In one remarkable piece, "Apologia Pro Vita Sua," published in the *New York Times* on 4 October 1931, she claims to be "retiring by nature, in my private life, to the point of shyness," and adds: "I do not drink. I do not smoke. I have my books, my writing, my friends—that is my private life" (quoted in Leider, 231). She does not, of course, mention her string of lovers, her habit of frequenting Harlem nightclubs, or her taste for luxury in various forms. In this period, Paramount publicity material likewise promoted a whitewashed image of West in an attempt to divorce her from her screen persona. Much later in her career, she increasingly sought to bolster her reputation and income through writing, seizing the opportunity to become a health guru by capitalizing on her age-defying good looks. Her book *Mae West on Sex, Health and ESP* (1975) insists on the importance of plenty of sleep, abstention from alcohol, and a healthy diet.

Although West continued to be fairly active in acting, broadcasting, and writing through the middle decades of the twentieth century, her reputation was certainly not at its peak in these years. As early as 1935, Alfred Hitchcock's film *The 39 Steps* included the query "How old is Mae West?," shouted out in a music hall to a performer named "Mr. Memory." By the 1960s, many thought West had died. Louise Brooks, meanwhile, had completely disappeared, enduring years of a hermitlike, poverty-stricken existence. The 1970s, though, saw a rediscovery of both, during the renaissance of interest in early Hollywood. Brooks gained a cult following, largely on the basis of *Pandora's Box*, while West began to attract increasing attention from gay men and feminists, and was newly celebrated in the context of camp. Gay men had been fans and imitators of West since the 1920s, but it was not until the last years of her life that she became strongly identified with female impersonation as well as with feminist self-determination. As a result of this renewed interest, West, now in her eighties, made two further films, *Myra Breckinridge* (1970) and *Sextette* (1978). The majority response suggested that instead of demonstrating her continuing power, these films represented its final destruction, overlaying the recently rediscovered image of the glamorous star of the 1920s and 1930s with the hideous reality of an ancient and extremely deluded woman. In view of this, it is perhaps fortunate for West that these films are now largely forgotten and her reputation rests on her earlier work. However, some critics have been more receptive to the value and possible significance of these two last films. Ramona Curry, in particular, describes West's performances as "sustained self-referential pastiche" (99) and argues that her "campy role" in these films "validated and encouraged retrospective readings of the star's 1930s films as implying sexual practices and orientations other than the conventional heterosexual—if promiscuous—mode that dominated the plots" (118). In the wake of these films, feminist critics, who had previously tended to attack what they saw as West's invention of herself in the image of male fantasy, gradually came to "find common cause with gay men in understanding the sign 'Mae West' as a masquerade parodying the social construction of gender" (Curry, 114).[20]

Brooks and West are remembered largely through images. Photographs and films do not age as the woman ages, and thus, while they limit her power at the moment of their production, they also extend her sexual appeal far beyond the point of her physical decline and death. Toward the end of her life, in 1979, Louise Brooks went in a wheelchair to an exhibition of the work of Edward Steichen, and a poignant picture taken on that day shows her sitting next to Steichen's instantly recognizable portrait of her in her jazz-age prime.[21] Strangely, it is the frail lady in the wheelchair who seems unreal, not the familiar black-bobbed flapper. But Brooks tended to efface herself in her later years. She concentrated on her writing, particularly film criticism, led a reclusive life, and was received into the Catholic Church. Even in the apparently self-promoting gesture of writing a memoir, she deflected attention from herself, noting: "Now, in September, 1967, I have learned how to write my autobiography disguised as a book of essays. [. . .] The reader, assuming I am writing about other people, is told the truth about myself."[22] At the same period, Mae West, now well into her seventies, clung fiercely to her image as sex goddess, improbably claiming in *Mae West on Sex, Health and ESP* that her healthy lifestyle had enabled her to avoid all illness and even to maintain an entirely unwrinkled complexion. She too was attracted to Catholicism, in spite of the Church's condemnation of her films, and its formation in 1934 of the Catholic Legion of Decency, which policed motion pictures. West attended mass daily during her years at Paramount, donating to Catholic charities and receiving holy unction at the time of her death, but in her case, this was perhaps just another possible route to the immortality which had always been her aim. Like Brooks, she lived alone and reclusively, yet her Hollywood apartment was filled with representations of herself in earlier days: her famed nude statue, by Gladys Lewis Bush; a painting (also a nude, also by a female artist); and many framed photographs and scrapbooks.[23] These celebrations of herself, as Charlotte Chandler suggested after visiting to interview West, "signified that in her mid-eighties she was not afraid to be in competition with her younger self" (39).

Since her death in 1980, West's autonomy, rebellious behavior, and self-mocking perspective have led to her appropriation as an icon of female power: she has been "resurrected as a poster girl for all that is transgressive and subversive" (Doherty, 1577). The forms of her resurrection have been multiple. She has influenced a whole range of later performers;[24] she inspired the central character of Angela Carter's highly successful novel *Nights at the Circus* (1984);[25] several of her films were reissued on video in 1998; three of her plays and two of her novels have been republished; her play *Sex* was revived in New York in 1999,[26] while Claudia Shear's play about West, *Dirty Blonde,* premiered in the same year. Written for three actors, each playing multiple parts, it concerns two modern young people, Charlie and Jo, who are obsessed with West and first meet beside her grave. Interspersed are scenes from West's life, in which she is played by Jo, and eventually also by Charlie, in drag. While not uniformly admiring of West, the play does celebrate her courage, especially in breaking taboos relating to female sexuality. Taking a less balanced approach, Kathy Lette writes:

> By the time she died [she was] a successful comedienne, singer, dancer, playwright, director, actress, scriptwriter, producer, Sex Goddess and novelist. If this isn't enough to make any writer impale herself on her pen, Mae was also a feminist who makes Madonna look like Julie Andrews, an intellectual who rubbed shoulder pads with the Roosevelts (this woman plucked her highbrows) and a civil libertarian who went to jail in defence of freedom of expression. To cap it all, she was a brilliant business woman, who insisted on creative control: she refused to sign any Hollywood contract unless it contained a clause that the completed film must in every way be "to her satisfaction." (vi)

This is an extremely generous assessment of West. She was, in fact, far from being an intellectual, and rarely read books of any kind. The publicity she received from the raiding of her plays and her jail sentence was certainly more important to her than civil liberties, and she is open to the accusation that she exploited her acquaintance with black and homosexual culture in order to titillate a bourgeois audience. But whatever celebration or criticism she may attract, it is certain that Mae West is one of the most significant and intriguing figures in the history of celebrity. Both her open-ended, self-parodying performance style and her self-reflexive novels demonstrate her awareness of the multivalency of her own image, and of its marketability when reproduced and circulated. Whilst the uniqueness and influence of West's acting have long been recognized, the significance of her writing and its contribution to the creation of her legend should now be acknowledged. There is still truth in John Mason Brown's comment about West, made nearly fifty years ago: "More than being a person or an institution, she has entered the language and taken her place in the underworld of the present's mythology" (259).

4 | "Astronomers located her in the latitude of Prince Edward Island"
L. M. Montgomery, Anne of Green Gables, *and Early Hollywood*

Lucy Maud Montgomery is the only author considered in this study who can be compared to Mae West in terms of her impact on popular culture. Her first novel, *Anne of Green Gables* (1908), became an international best seller and spawned seven sequels, numerous screen adaptations, a series of spin-off products, and an entire tourist industry in Prince Edward Island. In their book on Canadian popular culture, *Mondo Canuck,* journalists Geoff Pevere and Greig Dymond identify *Anne of Green Gables* as "the most widely read Canadian book ever written" (13). By the 1910s and through the interwar years, Montgomery was known around the world, but her fame has always been contingent on the much greater renown of her character Anne Shirley. Anne might be considered a celebrity sign in her own right; today, even the official Prince Edward Island car license plates proclaim the province "Home of Anne of Green Gables" rather than "Birthplace of L. M. Montgomery." Anne's identity, like that of "real" celebrities, has frequently been appropriated by, or imposed upon, others. In the earliest instance, L. M. Montgomery found herself being reinvented in Anne's image: journalists and publicists projected onto the author the qualities they discerned in the heroine, notably wholesomeness, youthful modesty, and identification with a rural environment.

In 1919, Paramount released the first Hollywood adaptation of the novel, a silent film directed by William Desmond Taylor. Its success further increased the popularity of the original novel, yet in the reviews, Montgomery's name, and even Anne's, were given much less prominence than that of the starring actress, Mary Miles Minter.

Through her role in the film, Minter's celebrity image was invested with some of the same innocent, pastoral associations which the media had already attached to Anne and Montgomery. Yet Minter and Taylor effectively turned Anne into an American girl and relocated her to New England. By contrast, the media image of Montgomery-as-Anne was intimately connected with a conception of Canada, and specifically Prince Edward Island, as a refuge from the materialistic modernity of urban America.

Three years after this film was made, William Desmond Taylor was murdered. Minter, thought to be his lover, was suspected of some association with the case, which was never solved, and this ended her screen career. She later began writing for magazines, and instead of signing her work with her own, rather tainted name, she used the pen name "Anne Shirley," perhaps seeking to evoke the sweet, girlish image on which she had earlier based her screen appeal. The actress playing the lead in the next film version of *Anne of Green Gables* (1934) went one better than Minter, actually changing her screen name from Dawn O'Day to Anne Shirley for this film and all her future roles.

The relationship among Montgomery's celebrity image, that of Anne herself, and those of the actresses playing Anne on screen is fascinating and can be traced through numerous sources. Montgomery's extensive personal writings, including a journal running to two million words, provide one set of narratives of her rise to fame, while others can be traced in her novels, especially her autobiographical *Emily of New Moon* trilogy (1923, 1925, 1927). It is fascinating to compare the forms of self-mythologization discernible in Montgomery's own writing with the way she is constructed by the media. Her clipping scrapbooks attest to her interest in the way she was reviewed and profiled in newspapers and magazines,[1] and reveal that different periodicals appropriated her into different ideologies, such as cultural nationalism, regionalism, Protestant ethics, and literary idealism (including a resistance to naturalism and its perceived association with the corruption of the American city). The scrapbooks also document the reception and impact of the 1919 film, although it is impossible to offer a critique of the film itself, since no copy has survived.

Nothing has yet been written on this first screen version of Montgomery's work. Critics have, though, recently turned their attention to the later adaptations,[2] especially Kevin Sullivan's immensely popular films and miniseries for Canadian television, broadcast in the 1980s and 1990s.[3] This new attention to Montgomery's significance within popular culture has been paralleled by a growing interest in her life and her autobiographical writing, spurred by the publication of five volumes of selections from her journals. Two recent articles consider the role of her personal writings in her self-construction as celebrity, and also the way she was marketed by her publishers.[4] There has been little attention, however, to representations of her in the media, and none to the impact of Hollywood on her celebrity image.

"A LITTLE LOCAL CELEBRITY"

At the age of eleven, Emily Byrd Starr, heroine of Montgomery's 1920s trilogy, is already determined to "be a famous *authoress*" (*Emily of New Moon*, 38). Although her writing is construed as a vocation, it is also repeatedly connected with a desire for fame, which is presented as a noble aim in itself. Emily records her solemn vow to "climb the Alpine path and write my name on the scroll of fame" (290), and her teacher endorses this: "If it's *in* you to climb, you must—there are those who *must* lift their eyes to the hills" (338). Montgomery, too, aspired to literary fame from her childhood, and in her journal, she both romanticizes and satirizes this. In a March 1901 diary entry, giving an account of her early career, she comments on her "early dreams of future fame," remembering that at thirteen she submitted her first verses for publication and anticipated their acceptance: "I saw myself the wonder of my schoolmates—a little local celebrity."[5] This detached amusement is replaced by self-dramatization when she recalls that on receiving rejection slips: "Tears of disappointment *would* come in spite of myself, as I crept away to hide the poor crumpled manuscript in the depths of my trunk" (SJ I, 261). The dominant note in the account, though, is one of determination: "Down, deep down, under all discouragement and rebuff I knew I would 'arrive' some day" (261). At the point when she made this entry, Montgomery was not yet really famous. At twenty-six, she had established herself securely as a writer, yet it would be seven more years before the book which was to make her name, *Anne of Green Gables*, was published. Though she apparently came from nowhere to stardom with her first novel, this celebrity was in fact a long-term project of hers, achieved through unwavering commitment and a lengthy apprenticeship.

Media profiles of Montgomery often picked up on this, using her to exemplify an inclusive notion of fame as achievable by ordinary people with courage and energy. A short item sent in by a reader to a Canadian newspaper in 1923 affirms this democratic concept of fame:

> Some time ago, a group of Normal School students were interviewing that distinguished authoress, L. M. Montgomery. The subject of inspiration came up, and the writer declared vehemently against it. It was hard work, not inspiration, that made good stories, she declared.
>
> The authoress then told her eager listeners a story to illustrate that the road of those who would be famous is paved with hard work.
>
> In the early stages of her career, the now noted L. M. Montgomery lived in a farmhouse. One bitter cold morning, indeed more than one, she arose from a warm comfortable bed, and dressing hurriedly went downstairs. No one else was up so the fires had not been lit. But cold though it was, she resolutely pulled on a pair of woolly, red mittens, and went to work on a story.[6]

This text draws on both the Protestant work ethic and popular discourses of self-help. The Maritimes were overwhelmingly Protestant during Montgomery's lifetime, and the Protestant churches in North America tended to retain a Puritan spirit, emphasizing constructive activity and thrifty management and approving art and literature only if they were demonstrably edifying.[7] The church's work ethic was reinforced by the emergence during the early twentieth century of aspirational middlebrow culture, with its emphasis on self-improvement.[8] The author of the "red mittens" piece praises Montgomery for rising through her own efforts from her very ordinary agricultural background to a position of distinction. Montgomery is presented as a writer who succeeded against the odds, who suffered and has been duly rewarded—a version of the American Dream.

Her journal collaborates to a certain extent with this narrative, but it certainly does not reject the idea of inspiration so firmly as the account of her speech to the students suggests. Montgomery does not identify genius as a prerequisite for authorship, but does construct writers as somewhat set apart, writing of her own childhood: "I felt strongly, though inarticulately, that there was no one about me who understood or sympathized with my aspirations. I was not like the other children around and I imagine that the older people of my small world thought there was something uncanny about me" (SJ I, 258). She projects her sense of her special imaginative abilities onto her various heroines, particularly Emily—who has occasional, fleeting access to "a world of wonderful beauty," an "enchanting realm beyond" (*Emily of New Moon*, 7).[9] Yet a more persistent motif in the journal and the novels is the necessity for endless effort and unfailing self-belief in order to translate imaginative gifts into published books and fame.

Montgomery's autobiographical texts present her career as a difficult struggle, first with rejection and discouragement, and later with the exhausting effort to balance the demands of her family with those of her exigent publisher, Lewis Page. She concludes her 1917 book *The Alpine Path: The Story of My Career* by describing her ascent of the Alpine path as a journey "through bitter suffering and discouragement and darkness, through doubt and disbelief, through valleys of humiliation and over delectable hills where sweet things would lure us from our quest" (95–96). Quoting this passage, Lorraine York comments: "By framing her apprenticeship narrative in religious terms that would have been acceptably humble and labour-oriented to many of her readers, Montgomery finds a socially-sanctioned way to appease all the old jealousy and spite that she has endured as a literary celebrity" (105). In accounts of the process of composition, Montgomery lays stress on the labor of writing. She advises in a 1915 newspaper article that while the idea for a book "may come by impulse or accident," yet "it must be worked out with care and skill, or its embodiment will never partake of the essence of true art. Write—and [. . .] cut, prune, and rewrite. Repeat this process until your work seems to you as good as you can make it."[10] The heading of this piece, "The Way to Make a Book," positions writing alongside craft or cookery, something which can be learned using recipes and instructions, and this, perhaps, encodes a certain anxiety on Montgomery's part about the cultural legitimacy of her own work. Such anxiety is more clearly visible in her personal writing, although it is often disguised as appropriate modesty. In a letter informing her highbrow penfriend Ephraim Weber that her first novel had been accepted, she admonished: "Don't stick up your ears now, imagining that the great Canadian novel has been written at last. Nothing of the sort. It is merely a juvenilish story, ostensibly for girls" (*Green Gables Letters,* 51). Apparently suggesting that her work could not impress an intellectual such as him, she nevertheless, through her word "ostensibly," reveals that she hopes for an adult audience.[11] She did, in fact, achieve this. It was not until the 1930s, as Mary Rubio and Elizabeth Waterston note, that her "increasingly sentimental longing for a lost world [. . .] turned her out of favour with the literary taste-setters" and her books were "demoted to the children's shelves in book stores" (Introduction to SJ IV, xxv).

"I SIT RAPT IN INSPIRATION—APPARENTLY"

Montgomery's revision and recopying of her journal attest to her consciousness of her own growing value in the literary marketplace; she became aware at an early stage that her personal writing would become a desirable literary artifact.[12] The readership for the published diary she clearly envisaged would be an adult one, and Cecily Devereux reads the journal as Montgomery's attempt to manipulate her own celebrity image, "to manage the ways in which her public would see her, and, crucially, how they would read her published fiction in relation to that constructed figure" ("'See my Journal,'" 246). Yet while the diary was certainly part of Montgomery's social performance as famous author, it also functioned as a refuge and confidant in difficult times, a repository for details she wished to keep private, at least during her lifetime. The diary thus reveals the growing separation between Montgomery's public role as celebrity author and her private life.

Montgomery could never have embraced the kind of luxurious celebrity lifestyle enjoyed by certain other Canadian women writers: Martha Ostenso, for example, or Mazo de la Roche.[13] As a young woman, Montgomery was the sole carer for her aged grandmother; subsequently she became the wife of a Presbyterian minister (who suffered from melancholia) and the mother of two sons. While she never sought to escape her domestic and parish duties, they frequently conflicted with the demands of her literary work, and both her diary and fiction thematize such tensions.[14] She notes in February 1920:

> A letter from some pathetic ten-year-old in New York who implores me to send her my photo because she lies awake wondering what I look like. Well, if she had a picture of me in my old dress, wrestling with the furnace this morning, "cussing" ashes and clinkers, she would die of disillusionment. However, I shall send her a reprint of my last photo in which I sit rapt in inspiration—apparently—at my desk, with pen in hand, in gown of lace and silk with hair just-so—Amen. A quite passable looking woman, of no kin whatever to the dusty, ash-covered Cinderella of the furnace-cellar. (SJ II, 374)

Montgomery here emphasizes the radical split between the two elements of her identity: they are "of no kin whatever." Her word "apparently" indicates the highly fabricated nature of the image of herself as an elegant, rather high-class novelist. Yet the picture was probably not wholly the creation of the publisher's portrait photographer. As Elizabeth R. Epperly notes, Montgomery had a "dramatic sense of self" and "usually posed very carefully for a camera." She also "always dressed meticulously and prided herself on the image she created for the public, whether she was the famous author or the minister's helpful wife" (96). Both visually and textually, she shaped her own image, allowing only selected details to reach the public; and she was evidently complicit in the invention of herself as a genteel lady writer. As early as March 1909, she recorded in her journal that Page had asked for a new publicity photo, which he considered was "urgent and important" to get before the "American public" (SJ I, 348). Holly Pike explains: "The urgent need, of course, was to begin to create the persona of the author." She adds that "advertising surrounding Montgomery consistently focused on the pastoral aspects of her work and life, her dainty physical appearance, and her domesticity. The marketing strategy was to present her as a suitable companion and guide for the young women and girls who were her readers" ("Mass Marketing," 243, 245).

The marketing of authors through images dates back to the mid-nineteenth century. The origins of the modern star system can likewise be traced to this period, and, as Joshua Gamson explains, its early development resulted from improvements in communications, printing, and photographic technology combined with the rapid expansion of media financed through advertising (19–20). The primacy of print media in this era before cinema and broadcasting meant that writers were especially important as public figures. Interest in them was fueled through author photographs on book jackets and in magazines; personality journalism was beginning to dominate periodical publishing and was sponsored in particular by the illustrated weeklies. In America, the lecture circuit—another forum for the public display of the author—contributed significantly to the emergence of literary celebrity. Joe Moran notes in *Star Authors* that as the circuit developed in the later nineteenth century, "the lectures became less obviously educative and took on more and more of the qualities of mass entertainment, a shift which encouraged an emphasis on the idiosyncrasies of the speaker rather than the content of the speech" (17). In the early twentieth century, the arrival of radio and cinema produced new kinds of stars, whose images were circulated through entertainment papers and on posters, postcards, and advertisements, as well as on the cinema screen itself. In terms of literary celebrity, however, lectures and other forms of public appearance retained their importance; indeed, the circulation of author photographs on book jackets or in magazines intensified the reader's desire for an encounter with the author "in the flesh."

Montgomery was in great demand as a speaker. She could command very large audiences: during the first Canadian Book Week in November 1921, for example, she gave talks at various Toronto schools and bookshops to overflowing audiences of up to 1,500. Yet at this period, when her fame was at its height, she continued to accept invitations to local community gatherings. The clipping scrapbook reveals that she gave numerous readings to church groups near her home, which suggests an attempt to reconcile professional and private or religious duties. In the same month that she spoke to audiences of thousands during Canadian Book Week, she also attended a much less prestigious event in Whitby, Ontario, which was reported in a local paper:

> It was a rare treat which the Ladies' Bible Class of the Methodist Tabernacle provided for all lovers of Canadian books and authors in Whitby last Thursday evening, when Mrs. MacDonald [*sic*], well-known by her pen-name "L. M. Montgomery," gave one of her delightful evenings of readings.
>
> The Rev. F. H. Howard, who acted as chairman, said in introduction that it was a very great pleasure to have Mrs. MacDonald come to Whitby for this purpose. He stated that it was especially appropriate, in view of the coming Canadian Authors' Week, November 19–26, which was for the purpose of "displaying our Canadian authors, and increasing the sale and circulation of Canadian books. More and more as Canada progresses will there be authors of note in this Dominion."[15]

The journalist insists on prioritizing Montgomery's married name (actually Mrs. Macdonald) over her "pen-name," thus anchoring her to a domestic identity. But the minister designates her as an element in the "progress of Canada," due to her success in taking Canadian cultural products to an international audience. He quotes approvingly from the Canadian Book Week publicity material, demonstrating that the powerful Protestant churches, along with other elements of the Anglo-Canadian establishment, cooperated with nationalist agendas. Indeed, the Methodist Church during this period was particularly committed to a conservative nationalism and was also "much concerned with providing a 'wholesome' alternative to popular, sensational fiction" (Neijmann, 142).

Canadian Book Week was organized by the Canadian Authors' Association, which was founded in 1921 and became an important element in the first flowering of cultural nationalism following the First World War. Through such nation-building projects, celebrity authors were deployed in narratives of Canada's progress, and cultural nationalism is perhaps the most obviously political formation into which L. M. Montgomery as celebrity was appropriated during her lifetime. She collaborated with this agenda, both through her fiction (her writer-heroine Emily resists the lure of a literary career in New York, choosing instead to remain in PEI and inscribe its social and geographical landscapes into her novels) and through her participation in public celebrations of Canadian literature. By promoting the CAA, Montgomery received a substantial amount of publicity herself. The organization was, however, scorned by a younger group of more experimental writers, including F. P. Grove, F. R. Scott, Raymond Knister, and Morley Callaghan. As Daisy Neijmann explains, these authors published mainly in the progressive *Canadian Forum*, which "carried many snobbish complaints of the CAA's perceived crass commercialism, its uncritical boosterism of anything and everything Canadian, and its largely female membership." She adds: "The polemic between the two factions is instructive, however, for it represents in many ways a debate between writers of a more popular Canadian literature, much of it written by women, and those of intellectual, cosmopolitan, and experimental writing" (144).

The Authors' Association, and its best-selling celebrity members such as Ralph Connor, Nellie McClung, and Montgomery, thus became the focus of interwar debates about the relationship of literature to commerce.[16] Montgomery's work was sometimes attacked for its idealism and traditional aesthetic and, in effect, for its commercial success. Laura Goodman Salverson, for example, writing to Callaghan, deplored the "sentimental" quality of "Green Gables and all that crew of cheery songbirds pour out at so much per word" [*sic*].[17] Other critics and readers, by contrast, considered Montgomery's work as serious, high-quality literature. The poet and essayist James Laughlin Hughes told her in 1921 that *Anne of Green Gables* was "the finest piece of literature we had in Canada." Recording this in her journal, Montgomery notes that it is "an absurd statement," but adds, "at least he meant

it for he is a terribly outspoken old fellow and pays no compliments"
(SJ III, 25). Robert W. Douglas of the Carnegie Library, Vancouver,
wrote to her that in *Rilla of Ingleside* (1920), she had written "a book
that will live, I think, when most of the ephemeral literature of the time
will be forgotten. You have visualized the soul of the Canadian people
in the war [. . .] and you have lighted up the canvas with gleams of
humor which no other living writer could have excelled" (SJ III, 27).
Early-twentieth-century readers such as Douglas often attributed to
Montgomery's work the kind of national symbolic value which was
later denied her precisely because of her popularity.[18]

"ENTIRELY UNSPOILED BY HER UNEXPECTED STROKE OF FAME AND FORTUNE"

In the English-Canadian news media during the early twentieth
century, L. M. Montgomery was credited with raising the profile of
Canadian literature, and she was also hailed—especially by local
journals—as the writer who put Prince Edward Island on the literary
map. Canadian papers based outside the Maritimes used the geography of Montgomery's books and the traditional, isolated society depicted in *Anne of Green Gables* as a way of injecting "local color" and
"quaintness" into their copy. Such accounts tended to marginalize the
Island by suggesting it to be outdated and slow-moving in comparison with the rest of Canada, even as they constructed it as a cherished
retreat from the modern world. These patterns are reproduced on a
larger scale in the American media, where not only PEI but by extension the whole of Canada is at once idealized and relegated to an insig-
nificant status in comparison to the United States.

A 1911 profile of Montgomery, published in a Boston newspaper, is
worth analyzing in detail, since it exemplifies the multiple and sometimes contradictory meanings which Americans invested in Montgomery's celebrity image. It begins:

> Recently a new and exceedingly brilliant star arose above the literary
> horizon in the person of a previously unknown writer of "heart inter-
> est" stories, Miss L. M. Montgomery; and presently the astronomers
> located her in the latitude of Prince Edward Island. No one [. . .] had
> ever imagined that such a remote and unassertive speck on the map as
> Prince Edward Island would ever produce a writer whose first three

books should one and all be included in the "six best sellers." But it was in this unemotional little island that "Anne of Green Gables" was born [. . .] The story was the work of a modest young woman school teacher, who doubtless was as greatly surprised as any of her neighbors when she found that the sweetly simple tale of the childish joys and sorrows of a diminutive red-haired girl had made the literary hit of the season with the entire American public.[19]

L. M. Montgomery, Anne, and the island itself are all strongly associated with the feminine and the childlike through the vocabulary of the report: "unassertive," "unemotional little island," "modest young woman," "sweetly simple tale," and "diminutive." (These terms are not particularly accurate: in the novel Anne is rather tall, and Montgomery's age was then thirty-seven.) The author and her native country are thus treated reductively in an article purporting to celebrate them, and this becomes still more obvious as her visit to Boston is described:

> Miss Montgomery, who is entirely unspoiled by her unexpected stroke of fame and fortune, made her first visit to Boston last winter and was lionized to quite an extent, her pleasing personality making a decidedly favorable impression on all who met her. [. . .] It was all very nice and novel, but the young lady confided to her friends that she would be more than glad to get back to her quiet and uneventful country life and that she would far prefer it as a regular thing even to a residence in Boston. One of the most delightful of her Boston experiences was a lunch that was given her by the local publishing house that issues her books, a thoroughly Bostonian idea as well as a most creditable one.

Montgomery here becomes representative of an idealized woman writer who remains in a rural and/or domestic environment and does not aspire to publicity and notice. The emphasis on her modest and retiring nature refers to fears that women's professional aspirations entailed the sacrifice of femininity and the neglect of womanly duties. In implicit dialogue with the unattractive stereotypes of women writers which circulated in popular discourse, the Boston journalist uses the figure of L. M. Montgomery to suggest a more acceptable model of female authorship, associating her unassuming personality with the perceived purity of a rural environment.

At the same time, the piece reveals a curious city-dweller's blend of nostalgia for rural life with a patronizing attitude toward country people. Montgomery's "unspoiled" nature provides a useful foil for the sophistication of her American hosts, just as Canada's unspoiled landscape and traditional ways of life offer a focus for the nostalgic longings of urban Americans. Montgomery's place of birth is described in highly sentimentalized terms:

> Britain possesses, as a cherished literary shrine, the Isle of Man, but on this side of the ocean we have our Isle St. Jean, where, in the good old summer time, as Anne Shirley found it on the day of her arrival, the gulf-cooled air is "sweet with the breath of many apple orchards" and the meadows slope away in the romantic distance to "horizon mists of pearl and purple."

The deliberately archaic use of the earlier name of PEI,[20] together with the reference to a "shrine" and the evocation of a misty, romantic landscape, constructs the Island as an otherworldly fantasy space.

In this and other media texts, the Island is associated with the simple life lived close to nature, something with an undoubted appeal, since the increasing movement of the Canadian population into cities during this period fed the desire to enjoy outdoor recreation and discover pristine rural landscapes (Edwardson, 86). Before the advent of Anne, Prince Edward Island was already a holiday destination for wealthy East Coast families; in 1899, for instance, seven thousand Americans visited the province (Pike, "Mass Marketing," 247). But Montgomery's popularity has greatly increased the scale of the tourist industry centered on her native place, a process which has impacted significantly on the island's economy.[21] The items in her scrapbook demonstrate that this process began almost as soon as *Anne of Green Gables* was published: a great many early reviews of the book and the film versions comment on the idyllic setting and the attractive, traditional lifestyle depicted. As Graham Huggan points out, "tourism tends to nourish itself on the invented reminiscences of pastoral" (179), and this is precisely how Montgomery's "Avonlea" has become a destination for both literal and imaginary tourism.

Although the Boston article acknowledges the best-selling status of Montgomery's books, it simultaneously manages to suggest that her "sweetly simple" writing is somehow removed from market economics and uncorrupted by commerce. This exemplifies a broader cultural phenomenon; as Moran explains, literary celebrities are

> complex cultural signifiers who are repositories for all kinds of meanings, the most significant of which is perhaps the nostalgia for some kind of transcendent, anti-economic, creative element in a secular, debased, commercialized culture. They thus reproduce a notion, popular since the Romantic era, of authors and their work as a kind of recuperated "other," a haven for those creative values which an increasingly rationalistic, utilitarian society cannot otherwise accommodate. (9)

Thus, the representation of authors and other kinds of artists becomes a way of channeling human impulses and desires which do not fit the patterns of capitalism and rationalism, so that authors acquire an almost priestlike status; and thus it is essential to maintain the myth of their separateness from mainstream society. Authors such as Loos, Parker, and West were so closely identified with commercialized and fashionable culture that they could never be "recuperated" in this way. Montgomery, by contrast, despite achieving far higher sales than any of them, was identified (and identified herself) so differently in terms of geography, career, lifestyle, and literary aesthetic that she could be celebrated in Romantic and nostalgic terms.

By the same token, since her work was associated with childhood and with the low-status genre of the girls' series, as well as embodying both a geographical and a gendered marginality, she was less easily assimilated into nationalist conceptions of *greatness* than were her male peers. During the nationalist Twenties, many newspapers drew up lists of great Canadians. In 1924, for example, a list of the ten greatest living Canadians was compiled by the *Maple Leaf Magazine,* the journal of the Canadian Clubs, which were founded from 1893 onwards in order to foster an interest in public affairs and an attachment to Canadian institutions. The final selection, based on a reader survey, was composed entirely of men: scientists, politicians, military leaders, and writers. (It is worth noting that eighty years later, in November 2004, CBC Television launched a search for the ten greatest Canadians. One hundred forty thousand votes were cast, and the winners were all men.) In the 1924 list, a further fourteen names were appended as runners-up, among them two women: L. M. Montgomery and the singer Mme. Emma Albani.[22] The survey was taken up in national newspapers, and one report commented that "all who have gained a place have become conspicuous for some form of public service," adding: "Money making ability alone does not open the way to the highest esteem of the Canadian people."[23]

The construction of literature and the arts as public service contrasts strikingly with the emerging tendency to categorize literature—and especially fiction—as commercial entertainment, by classing it with film and the mass media. In the 1920s, the incompatibility between these two conceptions of literature was legible in the conflicted discourses of both popular journalism and serious critical writing. Quests for great Canadians aligned literature with institutional forms of public service, which meant they favored authors whose work conformed to dominant political ideologies. Unsurprisingly, the writers included in the *Maple Leaf Magazine*'s pantheon are Sir Gilbert Parker, who was also a Conservative politician and a recruit to Britain's War Propaganda Bureau; Bliss Carman, highly respected nature poet of United Empire Loyalist descent; and Ralph Connor, who was senior Protestant chaplain to the Canadian forces during the First World War and whose novels concern the triumph of muscular Christianity.

When the category of great Canadians was delimited by gender, however, Montgomery did usually gain a place. In 1923, *The Border Cities Star* of Windsor, Ontario, ran a feature on the twelve greatest Canadian women. This list, too, includes several women noted for public service, among them the judge Emily Murphy, the doctor and social service worker Helen MacMurchy, and the Red Cross worker Lady Drummond. An artist, a historian, and two writers (Montgomery and McClung) also figure. But alongside these appear an opera singer and two actresses. In the accompanying article, it is these three who are picked out: "How many people in Canada ordinarily think of Mme. Albani, Margaret Anglin and Mary Pickford as Canadians? Yet this is the fact."[24] According to stereotype, Canadians are perceived as unassuming and possibly dull, and thus it is the glamorous and internationally famous women on the list, rather than the worthy public-servant types, who might be supposed not to be Canadian. An American paper, reporting on the greatest Canadian women story, remarked: "Mary Pickford is chosen as one of them, however much such a choice may jar upon the ideas of the United States movie fan who has been taught to regard the young lady as the 'best beloved American movie actress.'"[25]

Among the most well-known women in the world during the early twentieth century, Mary Pickford was one of the four "pioneers of film celebrity" (Schickel, 46), along with D. W. Griffith, Douglas Fairbanks, and Charlie Chaplin. Their wartime tour in the Liberty Loan drives, designed to raise money and promote participation in the war effort, ended in Washington, where Fairbanks, Pickford, and Chaplin were photographed with President Roosevelt. Pickford also acted in propagandist wartime films such as *The Little American* (1917). Like L. M. Montgomery, then, she was co-opted into politicized narratives, but while in Montgomery's case, this process depended on the assertion of her Canadianness, in Pickford's, it was predicated on the obliteration of her earlier identity as Gladys Smith from Toronto. The occasional Canadian attempts to claim Mary Pickford went largely unnoticed; she was marketed as an American patriot and gained the nickname "America's sweetheart."

"THE PERSONIFICATION OF ALL THAT IS PURE AND TENDER IN LIFE"

Given her many recent adolescent roles in films such as *Rebecca of Sunnybrook Farm* (1917) and *A Little Princess* (1917), Pickford would have been an obvious choice for William Desmond Taylor's *Anne of Green Gables*. But the actress who actually appeared was the one Paramount had hired—on Pickford's recommendation—to replace her, the American Mary Miles Minter. Ten years younger than Pickford, she was born in 1902 and became a child star on Broadway at six. Her four last films were released after the scandal about Taylor's murder had broken in 1922, but Paramount executives were convinced that in the future, Minter's typical role as a demure innocent would be unsustainable, and despite receiving offers from other studios, she never made another film (see Wagenknecht, 237).

Montgomery's publisher, Lewis Page, used the images of both actresses to sell books, producing early examples of the film tie-in edition. In 1920, he brought out a Mary Miles Minter edition of *Anne of Green Gables* and a Mary Pickford edition of Eleanor H. Porter's *Pollyanna* (1913), which had also just been filmed. Paradoxically, the practice of basing a film on a popular novel, and promoting the two in conjunction, can both augment and diminish the status of the author. L. M. Montgomery was mentioned widely in the international news media when the film came out, yet reviews which included her name invariably relegated it to third place, after those of Minter and Anne Shirley. In one review, she was even transformed into "Mr. Montgomery."

This particular piece reports on the Los Angeles premiere and presents Montgomery, along with William Desmond Taylor and the cinema's owner, Roy Miller, as the three "men" who facilitated the appearance of "the lovely little star" and are definitely subordinate to her in importance. The article is titled "Enter Mary Minter," and neither Montgomery's nor Taylor's name appears until two-thirds of the way down.[26] This promotion of named stars was a very recent development in Hollywood: during the early 1910s, studios did not credit creative personnel, in order to control salary costs. It was not long, though, before IMP began luring stars such as Florence Lawrence and Mary Pickford from Biograph with the promise of screen credits and larger salaries, and actors soon held the balance of power in Hollywood.

Some reviews of Taylor's *Anne of Green Gables* imply that Minter's fame and Anne's were equally responsible for raising the film's profile. *Photoplay,* for example, wrote: "Mary Miles Minter is a bit of established popularity. So are L. M. Montgomery's 'Anne' books. The combination, ergo, was a well-advised one."[27] *Harrison's Reports,* by contrast, locates the entire appeal of the picture in the star: "Miss Minter is a beaming, radiant 'eyeful' of youthful charm, and 'Anne of Green Gables' [. . .] is by all means an attractive setting. Miss Minter is, of course, the whole show. The beginning, middle and end of 'Anne of Green Gables' depends upon her for whatever appeal there is contained in the play."[28] Just as Montgomery's own celebrity image was invested with meanings relating to her supposed youth and modesty and to the virtues of a secluded country lifestyle, so Minter, through her portrayal of Anne, becomes a focus for the idealization of youthful purity. The *Harrison's Reports* review asserts that " 'Anne of Green Gables' is one of the cleanest, sweetest, most human pictures the screen can boast of. It is the personification of all that is pure and tender in life." The *Variety* reviewer similarly noted: "there's a wholesome charm to it," while *Moving Picture World* wrote:

> The whole story is sweet and wholesome [. . .] and the different stages of [Anne's] development from pigtails and knee dresses to young womanhood are followed with every attention to beauty and truthfulness of background [. . .]. A simple, clean story which is just what it claims to be, the merit of "Anne of Green Gables" is the fidelity with which it brings out the better side of humanity [. . .]. Mary Miles Minter has the youth and personal charm required for the part of Anne.[29]

This account attempts to reconcile the competing claims of realism and idealism by yoking beauty to truthfulness and emphasizing that the film *faithfully* represents "the better side of humanity."

Almost all reviews of the film draw on this vocabulary of sentimental idealism, which also marked the contemporary response to Montgomery's novels. Both her books and the adaptations are valued for their sweetness, pathos, charm, heart appeal, cleanliness, purity, and tenderness; while the adjective "wholesome" recurs endlessly through the newspaper clippings. These words are part of a larger discourse of resistance to naturalism and social realism, and to the supposedly degenerate, immoral urban culture which was thought to have produced them. A similar critical resistance was in evidence in the States, but it was more marked in Canada and became inflected by a hostility to America. In early-twentieth-century Canada, creative and critical texts repeatedly associated modernity itself, especially in its threatening aspects, with America.[30] It seemed to many Canadian commentators that American writers had abandoned the romantic idealism to which a large proportion of Canadian readers and writers were still committed.

The major turn-of-the-century U.S. naturalists, Theodore Dreiser, Stephen Crane, and Frank Harris, focus on urban environments and reject the exclusively white middle-class subject matter of the nineteenth-century realists. American literary critics initially evinced distaste for the apparently reductive, deterministic philosophy of naturalist writing and its preoccupation with sexuality and violence. A few texts, including Dreiser's *The Genius* (1915), were suppressed because of their sexual content. By the 1920s, however, naturalism and social realism had gained more acceptance in America. In Canada, a significant minority of progressive writers and critics welcomed the first Canadian efforts at social realism and naturalism as a sign of the growing maturity of the national literature, but the more general response was a marked hostility. E. D. Blodgett quotes from 1930s literary critics' "warnings that the new literature of realism is 'corruption'" and characterizes this position as "'normal' for the time" (80), and E. L. Bobak points out that Canadian readers in the 1920s refused "to believe that social discontent and human distress are suitable subject matter for the novel" (87).

American taste in this period was significantly broader than Canadian, but in both countries there was a large audience for regional fiction of all descriptions, evidenced by the high sales of such varied writers as Edna Ferber, Willa Cather, Hugh Walpole, Booth Tarkington, Mazo de la Roche, and Martha Ostenso, as well as Montgomery herself. The popularity of regional fiction in North America, as in Britain, was part of the interwar nostalgia for disappearing rural ways of life, and many regional novels catered to fantasies of an escape from encroaching industrialization, urbanization, and new technologies. England was often the setting for such fantasies, but for Americans, English Canada was also suitable, because of its large areas of rural and forest land, and because it retained strong links with its British heritage and traditions. Taylor's *Anne of Green Gables* film, however, reveals an eagerness to locate this rural idyll within America itself, since it is set in New England. A reviewer in *Moving Picture World* mistakenly referred to "the genuine New England atmosphere called for by the story," adding that "William D. Taylor, the director, chose a wonderful old place for the home where Anne finds love and happiness, and many of the locations are rare examples of rural landscape effects."[31] The age of the house used to represent Green Gables situates it in an idealized past, while the landscape effects indicate Taylor's effort to cash in on the vogue for rural fictions. The pastoral nostalgia of early-twentieth-century literary and filmic texts arose from a perception that rural life is in some sense more authentic than urban life. Graham Huggan defines authenticity, in this sense, as "the symbolic representation of what is felt to be missing from one's own [life-experiences]—the simulacrum of loss, the manufactured nostalgic moment" (172).[32] It appears, then, that the attraction of *Anne of Green Gables* for the cinema audiences of 1919 was only minimally related to the specific landscape of the Canadian Maritimes. This has also proved true in later decades; as Janice Fiamengo points out: "Whether or not Montgomery's descriptions represent Prince Edward Island faithfully, geographical fidelity seems to have little to do with her popularity" ("Theory of," 227). Images of Anne and Avonlea, largely detached from geographical context, are circulated globally through films, spin-off products, and Internet sites, and many readers have little idea where the novels are set.

Montgomery herself was horrified by the film's Americanization of her books. She saw it in February 1920 and recorded in her journal:

> It was a pretty little play well photographed but I think if I hadn't already known it was from my book, that I would never have recognized it. The landscape and folks were "New England," never PE Island. [. . .] A skunk and an American flag were introduced—both equally unknown in PE Island. I could have shrieked with rage over the latter. Such crass, blatant Yankeeism! (SJ II, 373)

This, of course, is consistent with virtually all Hollywood representations of Canada. Pierre Berton, in *Hollywood's Canada: The Americanization of Our National Image* (1975), analyzes around six hundred Hollywood films referring to Canada, made from 1907 onwards, and points to the misinformation, distorted geography, and insulting stereotypes to be found in nearly every one.

Just as PEI was turned into New England by William Desmond Taylor, so Anne of Green Gables was turned into an American girl by Mary Miles Minter. Montgomery found her "a sweet, sugary heroine utterly unlike my gingery Anne" (SJ II, 373), and the screen character was also shaped by some other Hollywood stereotypes. As Montgomery noted in a 1935 article, Minter's Anne was seen at one point "at the door of her school, a shotgun in hand, standing off a crowd of infuriated villagers who were bent on mobbing her, because she had whipped one of her pupils" ("Is This My *Anne*," 333). Minter contributed to the Americanization of Anne by publicly identifying herself with the character, probably because this was her most successful film. Asked in 1922 what her favorite role was, she replied: *"Anne of Green Gables.* I loved Anne. Played it when I was seventeen and have never forgotten it. I write sometimes for magazines and when I do, I always use the name Anne, and sometimes Anne Shirley, the heroine of Green Gables." [33]

"THERE WAS SCOPE FOR IMAGINATION HERE"

The next film version, in 1934, starred Dawn O'Day, who still more determinedly sought to reinvent herself as Anne by changing her name to "Anne Shirley." Another Hollywood production, the 1934 *Anne* was directed by George Nichols Jr. for RKO studios. The advent of sound had removed one of Montgomery's objections to the first film—when the silent version was in production, she wrote in her journal that the book's emphasis on language would be replaced by a filmic stress on action, noting that several of her characters "do little in the books but *talk* and unluckily talk can't be reproduced on the screen. Only the characters who *do* something can appear there" (SJ II, 358). Another improvement was that Nichols filmed two of the scenes on Prince Edward Island, although the rest were described by Montgomery as "pure California" (Montgomery, *My Dear Mr. M.,* 179). In general, Montgomery thought Nichols's *Anne of Green Gables* "a thousand-fold better than the silent film" (SJ IV, 326) and saw it four times, but she also commented that it "was so entirely different from *my* vision of the scenes and the people that it did not seem *my* book at all" (SJ IV, 326). Theodore F. Sheckels explains this apparent contradiction by pointing out that in the early years of cinema, viewers—including Montgomery herself—were "enthralled by the [. . .] magic of film," so that the screen version of *Anne* could be enjoyed on its own terms, quite apart from the issue of its fidelity to the novel.

Sheckels argues, though, that in the 1934 film: "The critical elements that made the novel a distinctly Canadian and feminist work were sacrificed" (191). Certainly, Anne's subversiveness is contained and diminished through the conventions of a romance plot, and the novel's emphasis on female community is eliminated. As Montgomery observed, the film has "a silly, sentimental commonplace end tacked on for the sake of rounding it up as a love story" (SJ IV, 325), and when Nichols's sequel film, *Anne of Windy Poplars* (1940), was being planned, she remarked that RKO would "murder the book as per usual" (*L. M. Montgomery's Ephraim Weber*, 190). Later adaptations of Montgomery's work have also tended to blunt the feminism of the books and remove darker episodes from the stories. Montgomery had no hand in the making of any of the three films produced during her lifetime, since Lewis Page refused to sell the adaptation rights to her novels until after her contract with him was ended, so that she would not receive any of the profits. This was of a piece with his exploitation of her throughout their association, which eventually led to a bitter copyright lawsuit (see Gerson, "Dragged"). More recently, other court cases relating to copyright, profits, and resulting charges of libel have pitted the heirs of Lucy Maud Montgomery and the Province of PEI against the film director Kevin Sullivan.

As well as becoming the focus of a legal dispute, Sullivan's Anne films and *Road to Avonlea* television series have inspired heated debate among Anne fans and Montgomery critics. The decision to film *Road to Avonlea* in Ontario because the film industry tax incentives were more attractive there than in PEI was contentious, and the politics of the films and series in relation to gender, race, region, and nation has been the focus of both journalistic and academic attention. As Irene Gammel comments: "Avonlea, far from being an idyllic and innocent pastoral space, is a highly contested and litigated arena in which passions about the appropriate representation of Montgomery's name and legacy run high" ("Making Avonlea," 6). Yet the supposedly "idyllic and innocent" vision which the passionate battles over Montgomery's legacy seek to protect is itself a popular cultural invention, a "spin-off" rather than part of Montgomery's published texts. Her novels are not uniformly sunny, and her heroines have to use their imaginations to escape from the painful experiences of bereavement, injustice, disappointment, poverty, and loneliness. In *Anne of Green Gables,* Anne tells Matthew Cuthbert:

> This morning when I left the asylum I felt so ashamed because I had to wear this horrid old wincey dress. All the orphans had to wear them, you know. A merchant in Hopetown last winter donated three hundred yards of wincey to the asylum. Some people said it was because he couldn't sell it, but I'd rather believe that it was out of the kindness of his heart, wouldn't you? When we got on the train I felt as if everybody must be looking at me and pitying me. But I just went to work and imagined that I had on the most beautiful pale blue silk dress [. . .] and a gold watch, and kid gloves and boots. (66)

In her book *Under Eastern Eyes,* Janice Kulyk Keefer says of a group of Maritime writers, including Montgomery: "Death, the bloody laws of nature, the tyranny of adults, violence—all poison the sweetness of these writers' Arcadia." She argues further that "the idyllic vision is also undercut by what we might call 'meta-idylls,' realized through the forces of magic, fantasy, mass-cultural cliché, and language itself. Together, 'menace' and 'meta-idyll' produce subversive subtexts to each idyll" (188). In *Anne of Green Gables,* Anne uses fantasy and play to escape from the harsher experiences of her life, and her stories and games actually emphasize the existence of "non-idyllic, even ugly and malicious aspects of life in Avonlea" (Keefer, 194). She draws on her reading to construct her own stories and imagined worlds, and the novel is highly allusive throughout. The quotations and allusions mostly refer to religious texts and to the classics of English literature, especially Shakespeare and the Romantic and Victorian poets. As Devereux notes, most of the texts Anne quotes appeared in school readers and indicate the educational context of the Maritimes in the late nineteenth century ("Introduction," 34); many of them additionally reveal Anne's taste for romance and idealism.

Anne also finds refuge in the landscape, and her first sight of the view from her window at Green Gables is described as follows:

> A huge cherry-tree grew outside, so close that its boughs tapped against the house, and it was so thick-set with blossoms that hardly

a leaf was to be seen. On both sides of the house was a big orchard, one of apple trees and one of cherry trees, also showered over with blossoms; and their grass was all sprinkled with dandelions. In the garden below were lilac-trees purple with flowers, and their dizzily sweet fragrance drifted up to the window on the morning wind.

Below the garden a green field lush with clover sloped down to the hollow where the brook ran and where scores of white birches grew, upspringing airily out of an undergrowth suggestive of delightful possibilities in ferns and mosses and woodsy things generally. Beyond it was a hill, green and feathery with spruce and fir; there was a gap in it where the gray gable end of the little house she had seen from the other side of the Lake of Shining Waters was visible.

Off to the left were the big barns and beyond them, away down over green, low-sloping fields, was a sparkling blue glimpse of sea. (81–82)

The description is, to some extent, local and specific—it clearly corresponds to aspects of the island's scenery and flora (orchards, lakes, seashore, fir, birches, and so on). But it is also an idealized landscape, colored by Anne's imaginative projections and excessive in its fertile luxuriance.

The extended, loving re-creation of the scene demonstrates that the narrator endorses Anne's romantic vision of Prince Edward Island, yet the idyll is counteracted in several ways. First, the description is preceded by Anne's fear of expulsion from the newfound paradise: "Anne dropped on her knees and gazed out into the June morning, her eyes glistening with delight. Oh, wasn't it beautiful? Wasn't it a lovely place? Suppose she wasn't really going to stay here! She would imagine she was. There was scope for imagination here" (81). Also, the narrator points out that Anne's rapturous response is partly due to her previous confinement among scenes of poverty and ugliness: "Anne's beauty-loving eyes lingered on it all, taking everything greedily in; she had looked on so many unlovely places in her life, poor child; but this was as lovely as anything she had ever dreamed" (82). Finally, her reverie is interrupted by Marilla Cuthbert, the very person who is threatening to send Anne away. Speaking to the child "curtly," Marilla startles her, and recalls her attention to the chores. Marilla's perspective on the view from the window is then juxtaposed with Anne's, foreshadowing the way in which Marilla will repeatedly puncture Anne's bubbles of fancy later in the novel:

"Oh, isn't it wonderful?" [Anne] said, waving her hand comprehensively at the world outside.

"It's a big tree," said Marilla, "and it blooms great, but the fruit don't amount to much never—small and wormy." (82)

The novel frequently returns to themes of loneliness and poverty (emotional or financial) and continually balances Marilla's resolutely literal, practical outlook on life against Anne's melodramatic and romanticized visions. By contrast, in many popular culture re-creations of Avonlea, including the early Anne films, romantic landscapes, stories, and forms of play become the primary reality, and ugly or prosaic aspects are relegated to the margins or eliminated.

In nonliterary visions of Avonlea, the ascendance of fantasy is intimately connected to the rhetorical practice of nostalgia. Aspasia Kotsopoulos's comment on Sullivan's *Road to Avonlea* might be applied more widely to adaptations of Montgomery's work. The series, she argues, "contributes to a sense of continuity with the past which renders these fantasies safe and appealing, particularly in times of economic insecurity and social instability" (101–102). It is true that a certain amount of the nostalgia inherent in popular culture projections of Avonlea can be traced back to Montgomery's original texts. Her best-known girl heroines both grow up in the late nineteenth century, so that while *Anne of Green Gables* evokes a society belonging to the recent past, *Emily of New Moon*—published fifteen years later—re-creates a prewar world which would by then have seemed distant to adolescent audiences. In comparison with the Anne books, the Emily series also exhibits a much greater preoccupation with preserving tradition. Emily's aunt refuses to replace her candles with oil lamps, for example, and she rejects patent cleaners, retaining the old methods of sanding her floors in a herring-bone pattern. The extra labor which these methods entail also evokes the Protestant work ethic. More broadly, the New Moon traditions which Emily strives to live up to are an expression of particular moral values, notably dignity, rectitude, courage, and duty, and even the house itself is imbued with these ideas: "What charm and dignity and fineness the old rooms had, with their candles and their ladder-backed chairs and their braided rugs," thinks Emily (*Emily Climbs*, 317). In recent popular re-visions, though, these values are no longer central, and Avonlea and New Moon offer instead a "sanitized vision of pastness" (Kotsopoulos, 101), in which traditions are presented in terms of fairly superficial lifestyle choices. Yet as Montgomery's scrapbook demonstrates, this process began as soon as *Anne of Green Gables* was published, while the reception of the 1919 film reveals how "sugary" Avonlea had already become in the first ten years of its existence in the popular imagination.

Lucy Maud Montgomery's celebrity image has always been invested with complex and various meanings. Her fiction and her personal writings negotiate between the democratic notion of celebrity as meritocratic and the rather aristocratic idea of an elite being naturally set apart. During her lifetime, she was deployed in the media—with varying degrees of willingness and complicity—in numerous discourses and value systems, including those of national and regional pride, the Protestant work ethic and self-help, as well as democratic notions of cultural participation, a gendered conception of privacy and domesticity, pastoral nostalgia, and romantic idealism. Yet her secluded lifestyle, and the concealment of her identity beneath the genderless designation L. M. Montgomery, meant that her personal fame was readily eclipsed both by the more knowable Anne, whose interior life was available to the reader, and by the visual appeal of the actresses playing Anne on film. Indeed, following the silent film, even Anne herself, already an internationally recognized character, became subordinated to the celebrity of Mary Miles Minter.

Today, the positions have shifted. Minter has been largely forgotten, while Anne is Canada's most successful cultural icon and international export. Montgomery's celebrity is still largely dependent on, and sometimes effaced by, that of her fictional heroine. This is visible in many ways, most obviously in the Prince Edward Island tourist sites. The so-called Green Gables House, on which the house in the book was based, was never Montgomery's own home, but has now become Anne's.[34] Reconstructed to reflect the novel, its rooms are labeled— "Anne's Room," "Matthew's Room," and so on—and items supposed to belong to the characters, such as Marilla's amethyst brooch and Anne's brown silk dress, are on display. The ever-increasing global circulation of Anne's name and image has, though, also ensured that Montgomery's own name has remained in the public view. In recent decades, her cultural and academic capital has grown rapidly, and she is now acknowledged as Canada's most important celebrity author.

5 | "THE BEST PRODUCT OF THIS CENTURY"
Margaret Kennedy's The Constant Nymph

Among the novels discussed in this study, *Anne of Green Gables* and *The Constant Nymph* (1924) are the most romantic in their vision. Kennedy, like Montgomery, places much emphasis on imagination and creativity, imbues her texts with literary allusiveness (particularly in reference to Shakespeare), and creates a pastoral idyll. But the romantic qualities are not straightforward. Both authors undercut the pastoral fantasy, and also refuse "romantic" endings in the love-story sense. In *Anne of Green Gables* and also in *Emily of New Moon*, Montgomery ensures that her teenage heroines' relationships with the leading males remain on the level of friendship. Whilst the reader is aware that Dean Priest, in his thirties, has fallen in love with Emily, aged twelve, Emily herself is protected from this knowledge. Kennedy, whilst more daring in her depiction of a love affair between a fourteen-year-old girl and an adult man, takes care that the affair shall not be consummated, and her novel ends in tragedy. Some have judged Kennedy's work as "excessively romantic" (Harold Bloom, 167), yet while she certainly does work partly in the genre of romance, her texts also include ironic critiques of romantic excess.

The role of female protagonist in *The Constant Nymph* is split between Teresa (or Tessa) Sanger and her older cousin Florence Churchill. Tessa's father, Albert Sanger, is a composer who lives in the Austrian Alps with his children, so numerous and unruly that they are known as "Sanger's circus." This family, representative of artistic genius, is pitted against Florence, who is identified with civilized culture. On the death of Albert Sanger, Florence travels to Austria to take charge of her orphaned cousins, but her entanglement with them changes her from a benevolent, if interfering, woman into a cruel and uncontrollable one. The real heroine of the novel is Tessa, whose instinctive taste and natural distinction are ranked far higher than Florence's carefully acquired cultivation and polish.

The Constant Nymph appeared in the same year as Michael Arlen's *The Green Hat,* and these were the most notable international best sellers of the 1920s. Arlen's novel was immediately identified as a popular culture product and was not, on the whole, taken very seriously, but *The Constant Nymph* was a great critical success. Across the spectrum of British periodicals, reviews were almost all admiring: repeated terms included "brilliant," "work of genius," "moving," "masterpiece," and "dazzling." Dozens of eminent writers, from Thomas Hardy to Antonio Gramsci, bestowed great accolades upon the novel. Its appeal crossed the Atlantic; by October 1926, it was reportedly selling a thousand copies a day in the States.[1] The same year it became a successful stage play, cowritten by Kennedy and Basil Dean and starring Noël Coward and, later, John Gielgud. Two years later, Dean directed the first film adaptation, starring Ivor Novello and again cowritten by Kennedy. Already extremely famous on her own account, her renown was increased through association with these theater and film celebrities.

The Constant Nymph was the classic "crossover success," and Kennedy became, as Billie Melman puts it, "the writers' bestseller" (77). Readers and reviewers reiterated the paradox that the book had "achieved the remarkable success of being the admiration of the 'highbrows,' a 'best-seller' and a box office triumph."[2] High sales, however, threatened its literary status, and dissident voices began to emerge, expressing distaste at the novel's eroticizing of young girls or branding it as a deliberately commercial undertaking. The text anticipates these issues in that it is much preoccupied with cultural hierarchy, and the debates about its literary value and possible sensationalism often seem to be inscribed on its own pages. Several of Kennedy's later books, notably *Return I Dare Not* (1931), *A Long Time Ago* (1932), *Together and Apart* (1936), and *The Heroes of Clone* (1957), continue the exploration of romance and sensationalism and also of cultural value, as well as reflecting on the nature of celebrity. These little-known but intriguing fictions can productively be compared with their celebrated predecessor.

It is perhaps because of the ambiguous literary status of Kennedy's work, and her complex attitudes toward cultural value, that later generations of critics have apparently not known what to make of her.

Very few have engaged with her books in any detail,[3] and many survey studies simply omit to mention her surprise best seller. It is a measure of the extent to which Kennedy's career has been neglected that the large collection of personal papers held at Somerville College, Oxford (where she studied), has not been consulted by scholars. It contains a wealth of material which will contribute significantly to this reassessment of Kennedy's work.

"The desarts of Bohemia"

In *The Constant Nymph*, Florence is entranced by the bohemian atmosphere she finds at the Sangers' Alpine home, the Karindehütte. Her uncle Robert, who accompanies her there, is "appalled" by the disreputable appearance and forthright manners of the children, but Florence finds them "charming" (100). The first morning of her stay, she awakes "in a mood of remote, impregnable happiness and, while she dressed, she looked out, in the pocket Shakespeare which always travelled with her, that passage in *A Winter's Tale* [sic] beginning: 'Thou'rt perfect then our ship hath touched upon / The desarts of Bohemia?'" Florence feels that "The desarts of Bohemia was an apt description of the place as seen by poor Uncle Robert. For herself the wilderness was flowering like a garden" (101). She interprets the scene before her according to the literary paradigms she has learned, and the fact that she is never without her Shakespeare reveals her inability to abandon her cultured frames of reference in order to observe new scenes more directly.

The Winter's Tale (1611) is a key intertext for *The Constant Nymph*. The name of one of Sanger's daughters, Paulina, is taken from the play, adolescence is significant in both texts,[4] and unjustified sexual jealousy is central to the plots. The most significant thematic parallels relate to the literal or figurative setting in "Bohemia." Bohemia in Shakespeare's play is both a threatening and a deceptive place. In the opening scene, the Bohemian Lord Archidamus, visiting Sicily, laments the comparative inferiority of Bohemia and its hospitality. Anticipating the Sicilians' return visit, he tells them: "We will give you sleepy drinks, that your senses (unintelligent of our insufficience) may, though they cannot praise us, as little accuse us" (1.1.13–1.1.16). In Act Three, Antigonus, arriving in Bohemia to deposit Perdita, the Sicilian king's daughter, is warned by a mariner: "We have landed in ill time: the skies look grimly / And threaten present blusters" (3.3.3–3.3.4). The mariner adds: "this place is famous for the creatures / Of prey that keep upon't" (3.3.12–3.3.13). Antigonus is then devoured by a bear. Despite her familiarity with *The Winter's Tale,* Florence takes no heed of its warnings. She quotes, indeed, the line about creatures of prey, but misidentifies them as three relatively harmless characters at the Karindehütte:

> The mysterious lady who lurked in her room with a headache was very possibly a creature of prey. Nor did the term sit badly upon the two fat youths, the Jew and the Russian. But these amusing, pathetic children, this mild and bashful young peasant, with his wonderful talent and his gentle voice, were [. . .] with her inside the magic circle where all the world was gay and innocent and funny. (102)

Her perceptions are affected by the "sleepy drinks" of her pastoral fantasy, and she sees the Karindehütte purely in terms of the picturesque, even mistaking the Sangers' upper-class friend Lewis Dodd (also a composer) for a peasant. Lacking the clear-sighted detachment of Gibbons's Flora Poste, who is bored by bohemian styles, Florence is taken in by Lewis's masquerade. She does not notice that he has no affinity with genuine peasants, something which is clearly signaled to the reader (at one point, he refers to a cowherd as "it" [12]).

Lewis adopts peasant manners and clothes in order to disaffiliate himself from the world of culture and social display he detests. Sanger's sons and daughters also have a peasant appearance and lifestyle, but this is no masquerade, for—like the princess Perdita, brought up by a shepherd—they have never known any other life. Nevertheless, they too are differentiated from actual peasants by their natural distinction and talent. For Florence they represent an idealized vision of a life close to nature, but her naïveté is satirized, and Lewis and the children exceed her limiting view of them, proving to be far more perceptive, determined, and dangerously charming than she had suspected. Curiously, though, while the novel harshly criticizes Florence, the narrator participates in her nostalgia for the simple life and in her tendency to romanticize. Indeed, Florence's fantasy is also the novel's fantasy; as Phyllis Lassner points out, "*The Constant Nymph* begins in the Austrian Alps, a timeless, pristine setting that suggests denial of the war as well as recuperation" ("Objects," 253). Also, the novel's gradual rejection of Florence is contingent upon an idealization of her rival, Tessa, and this replicates Florence's initial tendency to see the Sangers as pure children of nature. The narrator characterizes Tessa in terms of "innocence," "intensity of mind," and "wild, imaginative solitude of spirit" (68). Her portrayal invites the reader's full sympathy, and the pathos and emotional charge of the novel depend entirely on scenes concerning her. She is also, however, amusing and unpretentious, and thus, though idealized, she is not simply a sentimental creation. From the start, she was responsible for the book's success, and she inhabited the imaginative worlds of many readers. William Gerhardie wrote to Kennedy: "I've fallen in love with your Tessa."[5] Cyril Connolly found her so compelling that he referred to her continually in his correspondence, describing her as possessing "the cruel purity of the unattainable," and admiring the generous, diffuse quality of her love for Lewis.[6]

Although only fourteen when the story opens, Tessa has always been in love with Lewis, but he is barely conscious of this or of his reciprocal attachment to her. Florence knows nothing of it, and determines on marrying Lewis, which enables her to enact her fantasies. Her discerning taste is, she considers, validated by her marriage to a musical genius. While his actual family background represents social capital to Florence, the fact that he is ostensibly an outsider with no visible means of support allows her to construct herself as independent and slightly rebellious. She fetishizes Lewis's unconventionality. In the Chiswick house she buys for them, she seeks to re-create the atmosphere of the Karindehütte whilst containing its unruly elements. Even people are used as props: she brings Roberto, the Sangers' servant, to London, telling the puzzled Lewis: "He goes so well with the sort of effect I want to produce [. . .] I want this house to look like us . . . pleasantly Bohemian . . . a sort of civilized Sanger's circus, don't you know, with all its charm and not quite so much . . . disorder" (178–179). Unfortunately for Florence, the serious bohemianism of the early twentieth century was not very compatible with being "pleasant" and, as Melman points out in her reading of *The Constant Nymph:* "Bohemia in a suburb is pitiful" (86). (This point is also clearly demonstrated in Stella Gibbons's portrayal of the suburban setup of the would-be bohemian Mr. Mybug and his new wife Rennet.) Broadly speaking, true "bohemianism," in the context of this period, demanded rigorous commitment to art and a revolt against convention, both aesthetic and social. In the 1920s, Western European and American bohemians were not usually associated with egalitarianism (as they were in the 1960s). Much bohemian thinking was closer to an elitist rebellion against democracy and emphasized independent thought, rejection of consumerism, and contempt for the conformity of the "mass." It is this form which is espoused by Lewis and Sanger, whereas Florence imagines the bohemian in terms of an interest in the arts and some "alternative" styles of décor. Through Florence, Kennedy destabilizes the opposition between bohemian and conventional styles, in a maneuver similar to that enacted in *Cold Comfort Farm*. Yet while Gibbons renders bohemianism entirely as superficial style, Kennedy does acknowledge the genuine difference of outlook, and the subversive potential, of serious bohemianism.

Florence attempts to invent Lewis as a celebrity. Enchanted by the romance of "discovering" him in the Austrian mountains, she resolves to take him to London, display him at concerts and parties, and introduce him to influential people. Lewis fiercely resists these maneuvers. His own method of distinguishing himself is to refuse opportunities for advancement, disclaim any desire to give pleasure through his music, and hold to his convictions that "beauty and danger are inseparable; that ideas are best conceived in a world of violence; that any civilization must of necessity end by quenching the riotous flame of art for the sake of civic order" (209). This explicitly Romantic position is set against Florence's advocacy of the social justifications of art. She approves of schemes to take "really good music [to the] proletariat" (206) and argues that music is not an end in itself, but "only part of the supreme art, the business of living beautifully" (209). Florence's view is stated quite convincingly, but it is expressed through dialogue, in her rather tiresomely superior idiom, whereas the narrator articulates Lewis's thoughts about beauty and violence for him, since he "could not say what he meant" (209). This aligns the narrator with Lewis and in opposition to Florence. As a reviewer in *The New Republic* perceived: "An author who can so clearly state one cause [Florence's], and yet throw her sympathy and hero worship to the other has [. . .] securely pinioned her subject to the wall for all to laugh at, and yet she has lured a public composed largely of such subjects to read her book and thus to laugh at themselves" (Opdycke, 169). Lewis, with his impassioned commitment to music, even though it leads to selfish behavior, is made to seem far more admirable than Florence, whose fairly enlightened, sensible perspectives weigh little in the balance against her hardness, social climbing, and condescension.

The novel sets up an opposition between art, as represented by Lewis and Sanger, and culture, represented by Florence and her father, Charles Churchill. Tessa is caught between the two. Her early allegiance to art is strong enough to withstand her realization of the cruelty of Lewis and her father. But her acceptance of the supremacy of art is challenged when Florence teaches her to appreciate courtesy, considerateness, and other civilized practices. Charles, a more persuasive advocate for culture than his daughter, begins to convince Tessa of the value of education. The change in her is shown when Lewis asks her to run away with him. She says this is unfair to Florence, and that she will endure another year of school for her sake. Tessa's vocabulary noticeably alters as she seeks to express new ideas. She tells Lewis: "I must, what do you call it, compromise! That's a useful thing to do, Lewis. It shows you've got a regulated mind" (245).

Realizing that she has lost her husband's affection, Florence turns on Tessa and unjustly accuses her of being Lewis's lover. This cruelty destroys Tessa's newfound faith in culture: she feels that if her cousin can seem so beautiful and refined but behave so appallingly, then there is "no safety" in "a civilized life" (286). She therefore decides to elope with Lewis, but dies on the same day. While modern readers may identify this denouement as sentimental pathos, Kennedy's contemporaries considered it tragedy.[7] The continual emphasis on Tessa's innocence indicates that the novel is laying claim to the tragic by culminating with her death; indeed, this ending is necessary precisely because her sexual purity must not be compromised. But the death of the constant nymph is also significant as a resolution to the conflict between Florence and Lewis. Tessa dies partly because of Lewis's lack of care—inattentive to her increasing weakness and unaware of the seriousness of her heart condition, he is absorbed in justifying himself for running away with her. Yet Tessa only consents to go in the first place because Florence drives her to it. While Lewis's cruelty to Tessa is inadvertent, Florence's is deliberate, and the worse for being concealed beneath an appearance of kindness. The narrative thus blames Florence for her cousin's death. According to the logic of the novel, the deceptiveness of a cultured, well-mannered surface poses a greater danger than does the self-absorption of the artistic genius.

In her reading of *The Constant Nymph,* Susan J. Leonardi argues: "The text's attempt to contrast art and culture fails, in part because art and culture are strange opponents and art and nature strange allies. Neither the opposition nor the alliance can be logically or philosophically sustained. Even for those 'natural' geniuses Sanger and Dodd, musical education and the musical world itself, such an obvious product of civilization, have made their work possible" (157). Lewis and Sanger, however, disdain the audiences which provide them with both income and recognition. Lewis's attitude to the musical world and the reception of his work is revealed with particular clarity in his encounter with Trigorin, a ballet choreographer: [8]

> He learnt that Mr. Trigorin had watched his career with attention; that he was, of all the younger men, the most promising and the most likely to stand by Sanger's side; that his least popular work, the "Revolutionary Songs" for choir and orchestra, was indisputably the finest and showed a great advance upon his better-known Symphony in Three Keys; and that he must not be depressed because the public was taking a long time to discover him. With all original work, said Mr. Trigorin, this must be the case. The critics have always persecuted young genius. The plaudits of the herd are as nothing to the discerning appreciation of a small circle. Lewis found that his hand was seized and that he was being tearfully besought to rise above his own unpopularity. [. . .]
>
> Lewis was not as grateful for this encouragement as he should have been. He disengaged his hand with a venomous look. It was not for the appreciation of people like this fat Slav that he had written the "Revolutionary Songs." (8–9)

Trigorin attempts to distinguish himself through his appreciation of work which does not have a widespread appeal, but his tribute is merely an amalgam of predictable sentiments and journalistic cliché ("the younger men," "the plaudits of the herd," et cetera). Lewis is disgusted, yet supports his own claim to distinction by expressing contempt for popular acclaim. He is amused by an exchange between Sanger and a man who tells him, following a concert, that it has given great pleasure "to a poor working man." Sanger retorts: "I suppose you think I ought to want to please every son of a bitch who can pay for a sixpenny ticket." Florence, horrified, declares: "It was particularly odious to say that to a poor man." But though she is seemingly in the right, the narrative challenges her position when Lewis replies: "He'd have said it, just the same, to a grand duke. [. . .] That's how Sanger felt about pleasing people" (207). Sanger's dismissal of social hierarchy and refusal to pander to popular taste suddenly seem admirable, even as his unattractive elitism is criticized.

The music written by Sanger and Lewis is "revolutionary" in the sense that it is apparently a form of modernist composition, intended for a select audience. But the novel does not adopt a clear perspective on the exclusionary logic of modernism, any more than it does on the supposed conflict between art and culture, or on the popularization of art. The characters are all defined through their relationship to concepts of genius, art, culture, and civilization, and the narrative negotiates among them, but—despite its biases—does not finally affirm a particular position. Lewis's and Sanger's elitism and lack of humanity, Trigorin's sycophancy, and Florence's attempt to enlist art in the service of social display are all satirized, and the only character who escapes ironic treatment is the constant nymph herself. Tessa's innocence and faithfulness are the only stable, enduring, and fully celebrated qualities in the novel.

"THEIR VULGARITY, THEIR CONSPICUOUS BRILLIANCE"

The term "vulgar" is perhaps the most slippery value judgment in *The Constant Nymph*. Initially it is applied to the children, "Sanger's circus," whose nickname was inspired by "their wandering existence, their vulgarity, their conspicuous brilliance, the noise they made, and the kind of naphtha-flare genius which illuminated everything they said or did" (3). The owners of the real Sanger's Circus (founded by the self-styled "Lord" George Sanger in the mid-nineteenth century) threatened a libel case against Kennedy's publisher Heinemann. They objected to the word "vulgarity" in this passage, considering that it damaged their reputation for refined entertainment.[9] In relation to Sanger's children, "vulgar" implies a lack of polish and manners. Yet the same adjective is applied to the eminently well-mannered Trigorin, who is regarded by "musicianly people [. . .] as something of a mountebank and undeniably vulgar. They were deceived by his air of metropolitan prosperity; he looked too much like the proprietor of an Opera House. They could not see into the humble, disappointed heart beneath his magnificent waistcoats" (13). Vulgarity, in relation to Trigorin, indicates commercial-mindedness and showmanship. The multivalency of "vulgar" arises from the varied perspectives which are combined and recombined by Kennedy's narrative. In both the passages quoted, the emphasis is on the opinion of society at large, which resorts to the term "vulgar" as a catchall condemnation for that which appears showy, but is not properly understood. Sanger's children playfully use the adjective against one another: Tessa describes her sister's new hat as "rather vulgar," adding "it suits you" (38). When the word is applied to their talentless, pushy half sister, Susan, however, it suggests a far harsher criticism: "Her facility, self-confidence and inaccuracy were on a level with the amazing vulgarity of her performance. She paraded every cheap effect, every little trick, most likely to outrage the pure taste of her relations" (57). The more the word is used in the novel, the more it is deconstructed as a category, until it finally loses its meaning altogether, and functions only to draw attention to the disparity between the different characters' conceptions of taste and brilliance and attractiveness.

Vulgarity is also a key term in Kennedy's later novel *Together and Apart,* which concerns the marital problems of Betsy and Alec Canning. Betsy disapproves of her husband's working as a lyric writer:

> I do think he is inspired when he writes words for Johnnie's music. But I never imagined that they were going to turn into the Gilbert and Sullivan of this generation, and, when they got their first operetta produced, I was always against it. I would so much rather it had just been a hobby. [. . .] there was something just a little vulgar about it all. [. . .] It isn't as if he and Johnnie were producing great works of art. They don't pretend to be; they say themselves that they are only out to provide entertainment. I cannot respect Alec as much as I did when he was at the Ministry doing an obscure, dull, but useful job. (5)

Betsy's letter affects a highbrow disdain for the professional artist, implicitly affirming the traditional ideal of the gentleman amateur, and the vulgarity she perceives in her husband's work arises entirely from its saleability. The novel as a whole neither endorses nor entirely rejects her view, but such passages could be read as dramatizing the anxiety of the amateur writer who has achieved unexpected popularity and turned professional. For Alec, too, there is "something indecent [. . .] about the labour involved" in producing his librettos; it is implied that he considers true art to be produced spontaneously, as the overflow of creative genius. The narrator describes his working processes fancifully:

> Deep below the surface of his thought, in some obscene tarn, lay the words, the ideas, that he wanted. He would send down a line and haul them up [. . .] For hours together his line would come up empty. Sometimes it brought up rubbish [. . .] But, if he persisted, the right object would come up in the end. [. . .] He could shape and polish the

bright treasure and assign it to its proper place. There were days [. . .] when the exertion of hauling became too intolerable and he fell back upon the rubbish, faking it as he had learnt to do and incorporating chunks of it into his fabric. (32)

Kennedy frequently renders the process of writing by means of analogies such as these, and thus subtly demeans the literary work performed by her characters. Fishing and weaving, the passage suggests, are fairly prosaic, practical activities, requiring a limited degree of skill, and this may reveal the cultural embarrassment of the commercially successful writer. In a 1937 essay on the origin of *The Constant Nymph*, Kennedy's analogies for creating literature accumulate rather dizzyingly: fishing, cellaring wine, laboratory science, alchemy, metalwork, cooking ("The Constant Nymph," 41). The displacement of creativity into this series of more tangible activities reduces its singularity or specialness, yet simultaneously accords it a certain status through association with other, more conventionally professional kinds of work.

This tendency of Kennedy's is replicated in reviews of her work from the 1930s onwards. Clara Smith commented in a review of *Return I Dare Not*: "Miss Kennedy's craftsmanship is dazzling, and this is a beautifully-made novel." She describes the book as "a triumphant *soufflé*," adding: "And that delicious romantic ending is a happy echo of *The Constant Nymph*" (1134). This is the vocabulary of the middlebrow appreciator: analogies are drawn between writing and craft or cookery—activities associated with skill rather than genius. But Kennedy only started to be constructed as middlebrow at this somewhat later stage of her career, when it became evident she was not going to write the "great book" which several reviewers of her first two novels confidently predicted.[10] Since *The Constant Nymph* itself had been widely hailed as a work of genius, it is difficult to know how these reviewers conceived of Kennedy's supposed future masterpiece. They perhaps hoped for greater originality, since her dependence on a romantic literary heritage had been noted. Rebecca West, for example, wrote that *The Constant Nymph* "is based on certain romantic traditions that are the crystallization of the discoveries made by preceding artists." West described the book as "a masterpiece of decadent art," explaining: "For when an artist makes no discoveries, adds nothing to the stuff of tradition, then his art, so far as he is concerned, is on the way towards decay" (209). Whatever it was that was expected of

Kennedy, she apparently did not provide it. Following her third novel, critics began to trace a narrative of decline,[11] and by the 1930s, they had accepted that *The Constant Nymph* represented the height of her achievement.[12]

At first, however, *The Constant Nymph* was considered to herald a very significant literary career. One critic wrote in *The Saturday Review of Literature:* "there are literary virtues in *The Constant Nymph* which, to my mind, remove it entirely from the ranks of ephemeral best-sellerdom," and added that Kennedy "neither caricatures nor sentimentalizes the human scene," and "she has a pervading humor and also a dangerous wit which she holds severely in check" (Dodd). Similarly, Hugh Walpole asked in 1928: "What new writers with promise of lasting reputations have appeared since 1920?" His own opinion was that in terms of novelists, "I think only three: Mr. Mottram, Mr. O'Flaherty, and Margaret Kennedy" (297). This is not a comment of particular prescience, but it does emphasize that *The Constant Nymph* was initially received as a significant contribution to high culture.

Reviews were particularly glowing in the first few weeks, before sales belatedly took off, and the novel was repeatedly identified as a work of "genius" and "brilliance."[13] The influential critic Augustine Birrell reviewed *The Constant Nymph* enthusiastically in the *New Statesman*, describing it as "one of the best novels old or new, that had ever absorbed a reader's attention during the still hours."[14] The reviewer for *Punch* noted its "originality" and "perception of stark truth" ("Our Booking Office"). Its high-profile admirers, several of whom sent congratulatory letters to Kennedy or asked to meet her, included J. M. Barrie, Arnold Bennett, Cyril Connolly, John Galsworthy, William Gerhardie, Jean Giraudoux, Antonio Gramsci, Thomas Hardy, L. P. Hartley, A. E. Housman, Walter de la Mare, A. A. Milne, and George Moore.[15] These, it will be noticed, are all men, most of them belonging to an older generation. *The Constant Nymph* was placed, somewhat uneasily, in a tradition of male-authored writing, and Kennedy was compared variously to Meredith, Galsworthy, Masefield, Forster, and Shakespeare.[16] Galsworthy himself claimed that *The Constant Nymph* was "The best novel by a woman for many years" (241). Gramsci was reminded of Dostoyevsky's *The Idiot* and considered the book "remarkable, both because it's written by a woman and because of the psychological atmosphere and the world that it describes."[17] Housman recommended the novel to Junior Fellows at Trinity high table, describing it rather ambiguously as "the best product of this century" and lamenting that it had been written by a woman.[18] These comments reveal the continuing belief in the mental inferiority of women, as well as the perception of women's writing as being confined to the minor genres, or to comedy, and to domestic or feminist subjects. Kennedy's novel, however, is not greatly preoccupied with the domestic, it is tragic more than comic, it contains intellectual and allusive passages, and it cannot be described as a feminist text. These may be some of the reasons why it was inscribed into a masculine tradition and dissociated from the realm of the middlebrow, which tended to be gendered feminine.

Once it made the best seller lists, however, the debate about the relationship between popularity and artistic value which is enacted within *The Constant Nymph* began to be replicated in its reception. Notices of the 1926 stage production frequently reflect on the puzzling status of the original novel. The drama critic for the *Sunday Times* enumerates several categories of best seller, classing Kennedy's book as a "best-seller by inadvertence," and suggesting two explanations for this phenomenon. First, "the public will sometimes buy the highest when it is for sale," and second, "the writer, having given his story the sentimental core beloved of the multitude, has had the supreme luck not to offend with the artistry with which he has surrounded that core" (Agate). The review in *The Queen* remarks: "There are two types of people who dislike *The Constant Nymph*. There is the person who dislikes the subject—that of a schoolgirl's love for a man—and describes it with that queasiest of all adjectives, 'unsavoury'; and there are those who [. . .] dislike any book as soon as its sales touch two thousand." And yet, the reviewer continues, "Miss Margaret Kennedy has a spark of genius which no amount of abuse, on the one hand, and no amount of publicity, on the other, can help to dim" ("A Best Seller on the Stage").

The level of publicity certainly was astonishing. *The Constant Nymph* was turned into a highly profitable commodity, and yet the method by which it was claimed for popular culture depended on an assertion of its literary value and uniqueness. American newspapers reported in May 1925 that "Mr. Heywood Broun [. . .] is quoted from billboards, street car placards, motion picture screens, newspaper columns, magazine covers, handbills, window placards, theater programs, rear tires of automobiles and all the other advertising mediums, as saying: '*The Constant Nymph* is the best book I have read in ten years'" (Schwinn). Kennedy's name, and still more the title of her book, were circulating extremely widely, yet her cultural capital was decreasing in proportion to the increase in her economic capital.

"THAT ENORMOUS MASS OF PEOPLE WHO HAVE BEEN TAUGHT TO READ"

Kennedy's rather complex attitude toward commercially successful art is legible in her letters. In April 1925, she wrote to her friend Flora Forster: "The sales of the book go well. I had a funny, furious letter from my young friend Richard Hughes who is in America, complaining that it is being sold on the Pullman sleeping cars along with peanuts and the *Saturday Evening Post*. He can't bear anything so vulgar, and what he will say when he hears I've sold the film rights I can't think." She added: "I can't get used to making money." [19] Her amusement at the highbrow posturing of her friend was intensified when Hughes's own novel, *High Wind in Jamaica* (1929), became a best seller. She wrote again to Forster:

> *High Wind in Jamaica* is as good as a stunt can be—but it has the fundamental sterility of a stunt. [. . .] Richard Hughes is very funny about it; fearfully self conscious and afraid lest success shall interfere with his inspiration. He keeps asking "What shall I do," "will all the publicity hurt me." I teased him dreadfully and told him that success is invariably fatal and that it has killed my art. He hopes that it is marriage not success which has probably killed my art and urges me to leave David! It will be amusing to see what he does next. [20]

This is a curious letter; she seems to dismiss the idea that commercial success will "kill" art, and at the same time exhibits contempt for the deliberately commercial nature of *High Wind*, almost echoing Hughes's own perception of popularity and large sales as "vulgar."

This ambivalence is repeatedly evident in Kennedy's self-positioning in relation to cultural hierarchy. She disclaimed any pretensions to being intellectual, writing in a 1928 letter: "I'm no highbrow—and am so far from being one that all true highbrows are extremely offensive to me on sight." [21] The following year, she commented: "there's too much intellect about [. . .] it freezes the current of the soul," and protested against "the amount of poppycock that's talked!" [22] Yet she could also be critical of mass audiences and uncritical readers, as the unresolved tensions surrounding the value and reception of Lewis's and Sanger's music in *The Constant Nymph* reveal. In later life she was more forceful about this: her paper "The Novelist and His Public," read in 1961 to the Royal Society of Literature (which had made her a fellow), disdains the popular readership she had herself acquired: "Occasionally some novel will capture so many readers that they approximate to *the public*—to that enormous mass of people who have been taught to read and who do sometimes under some unusual stimulus, read a book" (72). She also argues, though, that while a writer needs to be aware of "his *own* public, 'an audience fit though few,' capable of giving him, should he deserve it, the response that he desires," nevertheless he should not conceive of this ideal audience as limited to his friends, since "Novels written for the approval of a small, choice circle are sometimes distinguished but seldom very robust" (82). In the various texts just cited, then, Kennedy rejects ordinary readers and mass popularity on the one hand, and highbrow exclusivity on the other.

Her balancing between these two positions is broadly characteristic of a middlebrow perspective, and yet—like some of the other writers considered in this study—she resisted fully identifying herself with middlebrow culture. When the Book Society invited her onto its committee in 1932, she commented in a letter:

> It is rather fun for a short time and gives me an opportunity to make up my mind if I approve of the Book Society or not. At present I feel that it's all right but that it ought to have rivals. It makes people buy books—and very often better books than they would have bought unaided, but not the best books. [. . . It] caters for old ladies in the country. I find the Committee awfully fair and efficient and conscientious—but . . . but . . . but . . .[23]

Her commitment to "the best books" positions her in an Arnoldian critical tradition and connects her with some of the male agents of consecration who celebrated her own novel in the late 1920s. In her defense of the novel *The Outlaws on Parnassus* (1958), she works in this same tradition, which had by then been reinforced by F. R. Leavis. Seeking to rehabilitate fiction in comparison with other art forms, *The Outlaws on Parnassus* moves confidently among the classics and a whole range of modern European novels, analyzing narrative voice, ethics, the nature of plot, realism, and modernism. Many of the books discussed belong to "the great tradition," as defined by Leavis ten years earlier. Kennedy maintains a definite distinction between "the novel written out of creative impulse [and] the potboiler" (91), arguing that art, even if bad, addresses itself to an intelligent audience, whereas the potboiler, however technically proficient, assumes that its audience will not understand its meaning without clear directions.

Kennedy applies this same distinction to her own work, separating her serious fiction from the potboilers she wrote during the 1930s, a period when the family finances were at a low ebb. Although she always published under the name Margaret Kennedy, in her personal correspondence she began referring to herself using two sets of initials, M. K. and also M. D., which stood for her married name, Margaret Davies. Her married self was identified as the one who wrote potboilers, because the money was required to support her children. In 1931 she wrote to Flora Forster about the success of her latest novel, a sequel to *The Constant Nymph:* "*The Fool of the Family* sold badly and the Davies have financial [pause?]. MD is just looking into short stories. The new book is *finished* and is gone to publishers who do *not* hang out flags about it: but MK considers herself justified in the sight of 'one above' and MD continues to potboil."[24] Kennedy's commitment to family life, like that of some of her peers (including L. M. Montgomery and E. M. Delafield), meant that her concurrent role as celebrity author became, in some ways, split off from her domestic self. As with the other authors, this split was symbolized through an alternation between her married and maiden names, according to context.

Her wider family did not always approve of her career, however. When *The Constant Nymph* appeared, some of Kennedy's relatives became incensed, since the story featured illegitimacy, infidelity, and the near-seduction of a minor. She wrote in a letter in October 1924 that her aunt "is so deeply outraged by the book that it can't be mentioned in her home. [. . .] She took the line that I had made it improper on purpose to be in the fashion, a very insulting attitude."[25] This was certainly unjust, as both author and publisher were much surprised by the success of the novel, and Kennedy's work as a whole shows little evidence of being shaped either by fashion or by commercial requirements—with the exceptions of her scriptwriting and the "potboiling" fiction of the 1930s. She did not become an author of repeat best sellers, as—for example—L. M. Montgomery or Daphne du Maurier did. Kennedy maintained that the unexpected hit she scored with *The Constant Nymph* had established her so well, both financially and in terms of reputation, that in later years she had more freedom to write what she liked.

The Constant Nymph apparently influenced several subsequent texts by women writers, such as Rose Macaulay's *Crewe Train* (1926) and Nancy Mitford's *The Pursuit of Love* (1945).[26] But it has never been critically recuperated into a canon of women's writing. It is true that it was Virago Press which brought several of Kennedy's novels back into print during the 1980s,[27] yet critical assessments continue to connect her to male writers.[28] She is rarely placed with the other authors considered in this study, and Nicola Humble is the only critic to read her in relation to other successful female novelists of her era. One explanation might be the somewhat regressive gender politics of *The Constant Nymph*. Leonardi argues persuasively that Kennedy—despite her Oxford degree—seems hostile to the educated woman and her potentially emasculating effect. "Florence's hard, monstrous rationality triumphs over Tessa's fragility, but by such hardness the educated, civilized Florence loses the sympathy of every character in the novel" (156). While some of Kennedy's later work explores female artists,[29] in her best-known book, as Leonardi notes, art is a male preserve. The small number of other late-twentieth-century critics who have addressed *The Constant Nymph* likewise tend to resist the romance plot and read oppositionally, finding the ideologies of race, gender, and class problematic. Humble observes that Sanger's children "are characterized by the novel in positively eugenic terms according to the class of their respective mothers," and that "there is absolutely no irony in the novel's establishment of a class system within the family, or in its assignment of moral worth according to this system" (153). Phyllis Lassner argues that postwar dislocation is evident in the novel, despite its prewar setting. She notes that, paradoxically, "Recovery and danger are represented in the novel by a Jew. Although Jacob Birnbaum is stereotyped as a garish dabbler in international finance, he is also the novel's one stable male presence" ("Objects," 253).

The Constant Nymph has always been acknowledged to have a "sentimental core" (Agate), but while early readers and critics considered this compatible with tragedy, the book was later reinterpreted in the more debasing terms of pathos. Ethel Mannin, in her memoir *Young in the Twenties* (1971), writes of her peers: "with all our Jazz Age sophistication we were sentimental at heart. We were moved by *If Winter Comes* in 1922 as we were by Margaret Kennedy's *The Constant Nymph* in 1924 [. . . and] Michael Arlen's *The Green Hat*" (86). The continuing perception of the novel as sentimental owes something to the fact that, for modern audiences, it is easy to associate it with *The Sound of Music* (1965), likewise set in the Tyrol and featuring a large family of musical children. The three film versions of *The Constant Nymph* (1928, 1933, 1943)[30] have also influenced modern readings of the novel. The 1943 film in particular was excessively romantic and altered the story in various ways. In this version, Lewis's final concert presents a piece written especially for Tessa, while Sanger tells Lewis that he must love and suffer in order to become a successful musician. This comment is totally contrary to the outlook of the Sanger of the novel. Kennedy disliked this film so much that when the rights reverted to her estate, it was withdrawn from circulation and is now unavailable for general viewing.

"THE VERY LAST PERSON I SHOULD HAVE EXPECTED TO HAVE BECOME FAMOUS!"

In the mid-1930s, a former neighbor of Kennedy's parents, remarking on the amount of publicity devoted to her as author of plays running in the West End, said: "When I see your name written on a 'bus I go into fits of laughter. [. . .] Margaret, I say! Margaret Kennedy! The very last person I should have expected to have become famous!"[31] Certainly, the available evidence suggests that she was not given to self-promotion or attention-seeking. John Galsworthy, meeting her in 1925, described her as "a nice unspoiled creature, quite young,"[32] while Cyril Connolly wrote the following year: "I met Margaret Kennedy but could not fathom her much."[33] A 1928 *Time and Tide* feature on women novelists at Oxford describes Kennedy's "unobtrusive" personality and "quietly observing eyes" (GREC, 1271), while the profile in *The Queen* is titled "The Mysterious Margaret Kennedy" (Ryan, 26). A cover feature in *T.P.'s and Cassell's Weekly* notes that she is "reserved, diffident, even shy" (Evans). Yet the image of her as a retiring, private person, which was built up through media and personal accounts, may have owed something to a deliberate strategy on Kennedy's part. Her biographer Violet Powell, who knew Kennedy, refers to her "self-effacing policy," attributing it to her determination "not to let literary and financial success go to her head" and "to avoid making friends [. . .] who might leave her stranded on the beach of outdated popularity" (*Constant Novelist*, 123).

In fact, her reticence often increased—rather than limited—public speculation. As Joe Moran explains in his discussion of reclusive celebrities, "disappearance from public life [can] itself become an inverted form of self-promotion" (123). He argues that in some cases, "an all-consuming culture of publicity has simply packaged and marketed the author-recluse for consumption like other kinds of celebrity" (124). Moran's comments relate to 1990s celebrity culture; nevertheless, this kind of process was evidently at work earlier in the century. The feature on Kennedy in *The Queen* begins:

> Surely very few young writers have been more discussed than Miss Margaret Kennedy. [. . .] Anyone who could contribute some knowledge of her was welcomed in literary circles. [. . .] There were people who told you she belonged to a Sussex County family and was a dashing society belle. Others who assured you she was very demure and quiet, lived in Cornwall, had never been abroad, and knew nothing of music and musicians. Others who said her family so disapproved of her literary work that she had taken a flat in London all by herself. She has been a mystery, an enigma, and no one is more surprised by all the reports about her than she is herself. (Ryan, 26)

Similarly, a paragraphist in *The Outlook* remarked in June 1925: "The announcement of the engagement of Miss Margaret Kennedy has put a fresh edge on public curiosity about the personality of the author of *The Constant Nymph*." He adds: "Few best sellers are so anxious to avoid the limelight: with the result that many personal paragraphists have had to rely largely on their imaginations" (Over). Kennedy certainly sought to avoid undue publicity; indeed, she got married very suddenly because "we wanted to avoid publicity and the papers were already being a little tiresome about the engagement—and reporters kept ringing up and pestering us to know when the wedding was to be."[34] Nevertheless, *The Outlook*'s comment is somewhat exaggerated; Kennedy did, albeit unwillingly, grant interviews to many periodicals, and most articles on her were reasonably well informed.

The media elaborated a narrative of Kennedy's rise to fame which roughly echoed those constructed for Delafield, Gibbons, and Montgomery, but contrasted strikingly with the legends created around Loos, West, and Parker. The typical periodical feature on Kennedy notes the conventional respectability of her family background, her undramatic life story, and her early dedication to a literary career. Also, she is frequently said to be modest, not corrupted by her astonishing success, and committed to her family above her profession. A 1926 interview by Roy Cumberland, published in *The Schoolmistress,* is fairly representative. It begins: "Even if you have not been to see the play of *The Constant Nymph* at the New Theater, you will have read the brilliant and searching novel which has brought fame to its modest author, Margaret Kennedy (or, to give her real name now, Mrs. David Davies)" (91). Modesty, rather than brilliance, is the keynote of the piece. Cumberland's insistence on detaching Kennedy from her celebrity image, and affirming her domestic, private identity as her "real" self, is reinforced by his description of her as a reluctant celebrity, "not fond of being interviewed" (91). He also parallels the work of authorship with the work of wifehood, but privileges the latter: "She works hard in the time she can spare from the duties in her home in Kensington. *The Constant Nymph* [. . .] involved the most painstaking labour as well as considerable erudition" (92).

Many early profiles of Kennedy exhibit a clearly gendered discourse endorsing conventional female roles and retaining traces of the Victorian ideology of separate spheres. In the interwar years, the writers who were praised for their ordinary lives, modesty, and avoidance of publicity, and for fitting their work around their domestic commitments, were generally female. The construction of Kennedy as an overtly feminine writer is, however, in tension with critics' inscription of her into a male literary tradition. Also, the media emphasis on her domestic existence and unobtrusive personality was somewhat counteracted by aspects of her lifestyle (especially her social and professional association with theatrical and literary celebrities),[35] as well as by her publishers' strategies for marketing her through her appearance. As she was under thirty and attractive, Macmillan circulated numerous publicity photographs, and most articles on her were illustrated. She was even invited to sit for a bust by the well-known sculptor Frank Dobson, which was first exhibited in 1926. But these visual images could themselves contribute to her reputation as remote and private. One journalist commented that the Dobson bust had "admirably caught the secretive charm of her personality" (Evans).

Kennedy's style in dress was used to construct her as an ordinary woman, an accidental celebrity, rather than an outlandish bluestocking or genius. Marion Ryan remarks that when she met Kennedy for an interview in 1925, she was wearing a dress which "showed she is not too clever to add a *flair* for clothes to her other gifts" (26), a comment which invokes an implied opposite: the deliberately eccentric clothing of a flamboyant, self-publicizing intellectual woman, such as, perhaps,

Lady Ottoline Morrell or Edith Sitwell. Beverley Nichols, including Kennedy in his series of celebrity portrait articles for *The Sketch,* likewise remarks that the "ultra-Bohemian individuals" in *The Constant Nymph* might lead to the assumption that the author "was brought up by the oddest relations, and lived exclusively on seps [*sic*] and pimentos, and had straws in her hair." In fact, he explains, "She dresses with the utmost severity. Her conversation is sober and restrained." These adjectives dissociate Kennedy from any hint of frivolity, deliberate eccentricity, or excess, align her with middlebrow common sense, and locate her within acceptable frameworks of female behavior.

Despite being presented as the very reverse of bohemian, Kennedy had, in fact, a certain familiarity with bohemian circles and was clearly rather intrigued by them. The portrayal of the Karindehütte ménage was probably informed by Kennedy's acquaintance with the bohemian painter Henry Lamb, a favorite of Ottoline Morrell's. Lamb, whose affinities with Lewis were recognized by some readers (Melman, 79), lived for a time at the artists' colony established by the painter Augustus John at Alderney Manor, Dorset. John moved there in 1911, taking his five legitimate children, his mistress Dorelia McNeill, and his two children by her; and they remained until 1927, in the company of numerous long-term guests. Many readers of *The Constant Nymph* would have heard of this setup. Augustus John, although a painter rather than a composer, was easily recognized as a likely model for Albert Sanger, who lives with his mistress, his various visitors, and his brood of unkempt children by several different women. Ryan, however, records that Kennedy told her: "Sanger and his family were not drawn from any musician's family in particular [. . .]. They are a compound of Shelley and Wagner and other artistic and temperamental geniuses and their families" (26). In explaining this, Kennedy was perhaps seeking to protect herself against recrimination; nevertheless, it is important to remember that Sanger is not a direct portrait of John. Rather, he stands for a broad concept of genius, not limited to music but extending into art and literature.

"I ALWAYS SEEM TO BE LEADING A PUBLIC LIFE, EVEN WHEN I'M ALONE"

Kennedy's acquaintance with musicians and artists was limited, but she had a more extensive knowledge of theatrical celebrities, which she drew on for her 1931 novel *Return I Dare Not.* It features an immensely successful playwright who breaks down under the pressure of his own fame. This story, as Kennedy's contemporaries recognized,[36] was probably inspired by the collapse of Noël Coward during the first stage production of *The Constant Nymph.* In his autobiography, Coward gives an account of this episode. His description of Kennedy is both defensive and patronizing: "Margaret Kennedy, the authoress, twittered in and out endeavouring, with sudden bursts of the most obvious tact, to persuade me how good I was going to be" (168). Coward recalls his exhaustion, and reluctance to take this "heavy part" (167), and he lists its difficulties: he "hated Lewis Dodd wholeheartedly" (167); the structure of the production was complex due to the large cast and minutely orchestrated ensemble scenes; and Coward had to manage multiple, rapid changes of clothing. Yet these seem insufficient reasons for his handing over the role to Gielgud. More revealingly, Coward explains that the role was

> utterly unlike anything I had ever played before. Basil [Dean] adamantly refused to allow me to use any of myself in it at all. I wasn't even permitted to smoke cigarettes, but had, with bitter distaste, to manoeuvre a pipe. I had grown my hair long and put no grease on it for a month [. . .] I wore purposely ill-fitting suits, and spectacles through which I peered short-sightedly. (167)

In short, the role of Lewis did not allow Coward to consolidate his own polished, sophisticated celebrity image.

The pressure of maintaining an established image is the primary theme of *Return I Dare Not,* whose protagonist, Hugo Pott, feels obliged to lunch every day at the same table in a particular London restaurant: "Hugo, who was at the summit of his career, who had three plays running simultaneously in London, whose very shoelaces had news value, could scarcely be expected to escape from the bondage of a Favourite Table and a Special Dish" (1). The restaurant is always half full of well-known people, and the rest of the customers are "people who had come up from the country for the day to watch Hugo and the other half behaving in character." Obligingly, Hugo "was conspicuously popular and modest and unassuming. He laughed at every joke, [. . .] sympathized, congratulated, was very much astonished, asked advice, gave it, and promised to ring up in the morning" (3). His whole existence, seemingly, depends for validation on his ritualized behavior.

The most interesting aspect of this analysis of literary fame is Kennedy's demonstration that celebrities are effectively commodities, generated through the logic of the marketplace. The narrator's comments on this sound remarkably modern, anticipating late-twentieth-century commentaries on the nature of celebrity in a postmodern era: [37]

> To smile at them and hurry past would never have done. That might have looked as if all this success was going to his head. He had his reputation for Modesty to keep up.
>
> This reputation had been acquired by Hugo along with the Table and the Dish. It carried all the hall marks of mass production. He was known to be quite consistently unspoilt and simple. [. . .] Honesty and simplicity were natural to him until they became so much the expected thing as to be no longer entirely spontaneous. And if, under the pressure of a world publicity, he gradually ceased to be himself, the reproduction which he was at last obliged to supply resembled the genuine article so closely that even his [relatives] would not have been able to tell the difference. (2–3)

Hugo's obligation to maintain his reputation for modesty and simplicity resonates with Kennedy's own experience of fame; the image imposed on her by the media was very similar to that attributed to Hugo. Therefore, the novel might initially seem to be a protest against the demands made by the public on famous writers. But the exaggerated version of the celebrity lifestyle offered in *Return I Dare Not,* together with its satiric tone, invalidates such a reading. Hugo, though a fairly sympathetic character, is mocked for being so entirely determined by his celebrity image and for his assiduity in maintaining it. While he complains about the necessity of performing his established part, he is evidently far more afraid of the cessation of the public's attention to him than of its increase. He is intensely annoyed by the relentless gossip-column discourse which comprises his inner life: "He lay quite still on the cushions with his eyes shut and thought: 'Here is the amazingly successful Hugo Pott lying quite still with his eyes shut.' The thing was like an orchestra in a restaurant. He did not always listen to it, but it was always there" (31). Yet without this reflected image of himself, both in the media and in the eyes of those around him, he would evidently have no self-respect or identity at all. The word "success" recurs throughout the novel, its iteration demonstrating that it is

Hugo's only actual characteristic. Even his writing has no substance. We learn virtually nothing of the nature of his plays; the one extract which is quoted is clichéd and artificial.

Rather like Lewis in *The Constant Nymph,* Hugo eventually rejects the worldly, sophisticated woman he has been attached to in favor of a very young girl who instinctively understands him. Marianne has long been in love with Hugo, despite seeing him as a "King Toad" and evincing a certain contempt as she watches him "being ever so boyish and charming over the strawberries" (54). Hugo explains to her: "I haven't got a private life any more. I always seem to be leading a public life, even when I'm alone. [. . .] My mind is simply an enormous reverberator for other people's thoughts" (281). Marianne tells him that, as he does not enjoy success, he should disappear from the public view and live on his amassed profits, and Hugo—rather improbably—takes this advice. Unlike Tessa, Marianne declines to accompany her lover in his flight, but agrees to marry him at a later point. This upbeat ending, which contrasts markedly with the tragic conclusion to *The Constant Nymph,* is permitted by the fact that Hugo is not "cursed by genius," as Kennedy said of Lewis (Dyke, 49). He has no compulsion to write and only does it to maintain his public image.

In subsequent novels, Kennedy reverted more than once to the topic of celebrity. In 1932, she published *A Long Time Ago,* in which a woman named Hope reads the newly published autobiography of an opera diva, Elissa Koebel. The text of the novel includes sections of the autobiography, which constitute an entertaining parody of the celebrity memoir. Elissa's book reveals that twenty-five years earlier, she had an affair with Hope's father, Dick. Hope then consults family letters written during that summer and eventually concludes that the affair did not really take place. Her uncle Kerran, however, is convinced that it did, and the narrative does not finally endorse either view. This indeterminacy is necessary, since the novel is precisely about the various family members' conflicting views of Elissa. Dramatizing herself in many different ways, she is variously perceived as alluring, innocent and otherworldly, a priestess, and an evil temptress. Yet despite her performances, in her autobiography, she seeks to establish the continuity of her public self with a supposed inner essence: "All my life I have been happy only in giving. Just as I give of my art, so I give of myself. To go into society, to grimace and to speak politenesses where no genuine current of sympathy is flowing, this is as impossible to me as to sing badly" (14). She also determinedly retains control over her own image:

> Elissa had always refused to be photographed, just as she never al-
> lowed any records to be taken of her voice. It was possible, as one of
> the critics hinted, that she had been wise. Neither her features nor
> her voice had the qualities which survive mechanical reproduction.
> It was a question of the indwelling soul. Both her beauty and her art
> were articles of faith, to herself and to her admirers. (8)

The subtext here is, of course, that neither Elissa's features nor her voice is really beautiful, and that her fame depends on the personal legend she has created, largely by means of withholding herself from public circulation in order to achieve rarity value. She presents herself as uncontaminated by the marketplace, not desiring the profit which might accrue from recordings and publicity. Evidently, though, she actually fears the exposure of her inadequacies through public scrutiny.

Kennedy's 1957 novel *The Heroes of Clone* is also partly concerned with celebrity. It is about the literary afterlife of a Victorian spinster, Dorothea Harding, known as an author of didactic juvenile fiction. Long after her death, her diaries and some impassioned poems are discovered, and this leads to a popular biography. Its author, Alec Mundy, interprets the renunciation and pain legible in the poems and diaries as evidence that Dorothea had a love affair with her sister's husband and was persuaded by the parish vicar to end it. A sensational film is to be made from this material, but the research for it reveals that, rather than renouncing a lover, Dorothea sacrificed her desire to write poetry. The vicar, tormented by desire for her, enjoined her to write moral stories instead and sought to gain control over her and her writing. Violet Powell suggests that this plot was inspired by the life of the novelist Charlotte M. Yonge (*Constant Novelist,* 194). Yonge's parish priest was John Keble, and he cautioned her about the dangers of publicity and acclaim. As Kennedy herself notes in *The Outlaws on Parnassus,* Yonge "conscientiously refrained from taking too much trouble over her work since she had been told that this might tempt her to pride and vanity" (156). Kennedy's indignation about this carries over into *The Heroes of Clone,* in which not only Dorothea, but two modern characters—her great-niece Cecilia, and a woman named Adelaide, author of a play about Dorothea—suffer from the restrictions imposed by patriarchal ideologies. Cecilia is unable to study at Oxford because her parents have spent all their money on marrying off their older daughter and promoting their sons' careers, while Adelaide, as a woman writer and a spinster, receives as little respect in the 1950s as Dorothea did in the Victorian era.

Leonardi persuasively reads *The Heroes of Clone* as a feminist text which works against the perspectives on gender and art offered in *The Constant Nymph:*

> The multiple points of view, the frames, the starts and stops, the multiple readings and misreadings of the woman artist's life, make room in this text for the educated woman. The conditions of a woman's life, assumed to be inevitable and rather trivial in the earlier novels, in this flexible text acquire economic and social bases and assume great importance. Here women have risen from the status of servants and helpmates of male artist-heroes to the rank of artist-hero. (173)

All the characters in the novel reinvent Dorothea, revealing their own selfish agendas in the process. Among the modern characters, the young filmmaker Roy is at first contemptuous of her but on learning more about her life, reimagines her in his own image and identifies with her struggle. Cecilia, too, starts to equate her great-aunt's frustrations with her own. Adelaide initially shapes Dorothea's life to fit the patterns of romance, but on discovering she was celibate, converts her into a literary foremother. Some sections of the narrative are set in the nineteenth century, but we gain no access to Dorothea's thoughts; she is known only through her letters and through the distorting vision of her cousin, her sister-in-law, and the vicar. While *Return I Dare Not* is directly focused on the perils of fame, *A Long Time Ago* and *The Heroes of Clone* approach the subject more obliquely. Yet in effect, both Elissa Koebel and Dorothea Harding are case studies in celebrity, existing only in the perceptions of those who surround them, and perpetually reinvented according to the needs and fantasies of others.

Margaret Kennedy herself was speculated about and imagined into being by some of her readers, yet her uneventful life and unassuming public demeanor meant that there was little to feed such speculation. In 1926, a profile in *Time and Tide* stated: "Miss Kennedy, up to the present time, has shown but little consideration for her [. . .] biographers; her youth has been distressingly unsensational. No doubt in time a legend will be created" ("Personalities and Powers," 1100). In fact, a legend was not created. Kennedy was certainly constituted as a literary celebrity during the interwar years, but she did not come to stand for any ideas, longings, or values which could endure in the later twentieth century. In contrast to authors such as L. M. Montgomery, Mae West, or Dorothy Parker, whose iconic value has generated a large number of biographical books, articles, and Web sites over recent years, Kennedy's life has remained largely uninvestigated by later generations. Yet while she herself, and most of her work, may have been forgotten, the name of her most famous book continues to circulate within popular and literary culture.

Although none of Kennedy's later work had an impact at all comparable to that of *The Constant Nymph,* she sustained her reputation throughout her life and retained a reasonably large readership. In total, she wrote fifteen novels, as well as plays, works of criticism, and biographies. As Powell notes: "Until the Second World War Margaret Kennedy's novels and plays were received as those of an author whose name needed no introduction" (*Constant Novelist,* 11). In 1946, the title of her most famous book still had sufficient currency for a new hybrid plant to be named after it (Streptocarpus Constant Nymph), and even in the 1950s, she remained both respected and widely read. Her novels *The Feast* (1950) and *Lucy Carmichael* (1951) were Literary Guild and Book Society choices, while her historical fiction *Troy Chimneys* (1952) won the James Tait Black Memorial Prize. The stage version of *The Constant Nymph* was successfully revived in 1954 at the Q Theatre, Richmond, with Petula Clark playing Tessa.

On Kennedy's death, in 1967, obituaries did not construct her as a writer belonging to a past era. The *Daily Telegraph* noted that *The Constant Nymph* "is still in great demand at libraries and bookshops" and that her more recent books had also been "in the best-sellers lists for years." This obituary describes Kennedy's significance entirely in terms of her popularity and sales, commenting that she "earned a fortune from her best-selling book" and that it sold more than a thousand copies a day for several weeks ("Author of *The Constant Nymph* Dies"). The *Times,* by contrast, seeks to detach her from best-sellerdom and consecrate her work into the canon: "The overwhelming success of the novel *The Constant Nymph* in 1924 almost obscured the quality of Margaret Kennedy's personality and intellectual character." Instead of taking *The Constant Nymph* as representative of Kennedy's work, as the other papers did, the *Times* obituarist substitutes one of her least-known books: "She lived in a world of intellectual austerity and this was amply demonstrated in a book she published in 1958 called *The Outlaws on Parnassus.* This was a serious study in the art of fiction and its degeneration in public esteem during the twentieth century." The obituarist describes this book as "abnormally brilliant" ("Margaret Kennedy: Noted Novelist"). *The Outlaws on Parnassus* is, indeed, a most impressive piece of literary criticism, yet it had no impact on Kennedy's reputation. It is the *Telegraph*'s assessment, rather than the *Times*'s, which has been accepted by later generations of readers, and Kennedy is remembered only as the author of a notable middlebrow best seller.

In an April 1925 letter, Kennedy speculated on the future reputation of *The Constant Nymph:*

> It's funny how all these very clever people will fasten onto Lewis as the centre and theme of the book. People who aren't so busy being literary know that it's not. Because, if I get a hearing with any generation other than my own, it will be Teresa who will live for people [. . .] and Lewis will be rather a figure of fun, a sort of Mr. Rochester. He is a creature of the moment, Lewis, and so he's taken seriously, just as Charlotte Brontë's day took Rochester seriously, tho' they were shocked at him. But he will lose his conviction.[38]

This letter shows a certain prescience. Certainly, Lewis belongs to the moment of serious, twenties bohemianism, something which did not last, although it was later reinvented in a series of altered forms (notably in 1960s hippy culture). And if any character has endured from the novel, it is indeed Tessa. Anita Brookner, writing in 1983, suggests that "we recognize, in the brilliant Tessa, who has always, and easily, possessed Lewis's love, the three tremendous forces which give the novel its power: the mercilessness of the privileged, the subversive appeal of the wrecker, and the fatality of the wound inflicted by passion" (xi). The very fact that Brookner was writing a new introduction to the novel sixty years after its publication demonstrates that Margaret Kennedy did gain a hearing with later generations. *The Constant Nymph* has always remained in print, while the film versions have served to consolidate the novel's afterlife. Yet Kennedy deserves to be remembered for more than a single book and a single character. Her critical and creative texts offer intriguing analyses of celebrity, genius, taste, and art. Her writing explores cultural value, and at the same time, her best-selling yet critically acclaimed novels pose a serious challenge to cultural hierarchy and to the metanarratives of literary history.

6 | "LITERATURE OR JUST SHEER FLAPDOODLE?"
Stella Gibbons's Cold Comfort Farm

The narrative modes of *Cold Comfort Farm* and *The Constant Nymph* contrast strikingly, yet the two books have important similarities. Like Margaret Kennedy's Florence, Stella Gibbons's protagonist, Flora, is a confident but somewhat officious young woman, committed to ideals of civilization, good manners, pleasant domestic surroundings, and the moral benefits of culture. Both narratives are structured by the protagonist's journey away from a center of civilization (Cambridge or London) and into an unknown rural environment, where she encounters a large, genealogically complex, and entirely uncivilized family who are her cousins. In *The Constant Nymph,* Florence inhabits a romance narrative, with dimensions of tragedy and satire, and her painful involvement with her Sanger cousins transforms her personally. But since *Cold Comfort Farm* is pure comedy, Flora is in no way changed by her encounter with her Starkadder relatives, who remain on the level of caricature.

The gender economy of each text is puzzling. Florence is intelligent and enterprising, yet has no thoughts of any work or creative endeavor of her own, instead embracing the roles of supportive daughter and wife to intellectual and artistic men. She also seeks to mould her artless, undisciplined cousin Teresa—the nymph of the title—into a conventional, orderly schoolgirl. In *Cold Comfort Farm,* Flora's autonomy, refusal to be shocked, and advocacy of contraception and new technologies construct her as a thoroughly modern woman, yet she refuses to work, choosing to be dependent on relatives until she marries. She, too, trains a younger cousin, enforcing matrimony and appropriately feminine behavior on her young protégée, Elfine, previously an aspiring poet with bohemian tastes. Flora, like Florence, is the representative of civilization and culture, but while civilization is defeated in *The Constant Nymph*, in *Cold Comfort Farm* Flora and her civilized values prevail.

During the late 1920s, before she became famous for her highly successful first novel, *Cold Comfort Farm* (1932), Stella Gibbons's literary output was remarkably varied. She was developing as a poet and publishing her accomplished verse in journals including the *London Mercury, The Queen, Country Life*, the *Saturday Review*, and the *New Adelphi*. Her poem "The Giraffes," which appeared in T. S. Eliot's *Criterion* in 1927, was admired by Elizabeth Bowen and Virginia Woolf, and Woolf wrote inviting Gibbons to submit some poetry to the Hogarth Press.[1] During the same period, Gibbons was employed by the London *Evening Standard* and subsequently by *The Lady*, and her contributions to these papers included fashion articles, shopping guides, drama criticism, book reviews, and plot summaries of the regional novels being serialized (for the benefit of readers joining the serialization late). This bifurcation between serious poetry and lighthearted journalism epitomizes Stella Gibbons's ambivalent relationship to the literary. It prefigures *Cold Comfort Farm*, whose narrator, heroine, and implied reader all combine high intelligence and wide reading experience with a broadly middlebrow perspective, a preference for an elegant but conventional style of dress and speech, and an ingrained contempt for intellectual pretentiousness. Gibbons's work challenges the boundaries between journalism and literature, between elite and popular. As her nephew and biographer Reggie Oliver notes, in reviews of *Cold Comfort Farm*, there was "some incredulity expressed that a mere journalist, and a woman at that, could have produced such an accomplished work" (111). Journalism also has a certain class connotation: as Kristin Bluemel argues, the interwar writers she describes as "intermodern," who are from working-class or "working middle-class" cultures, often exhibit a "realist bias" which she suggests "may be a symptom of the journalist skills" they developed while seeking to earn a living (2, 5).

The middlebrow status of *Cold Comfort Farm* is affirmed not only through Gibbons's choice of a comic genre, an explicitly feminine perspective, and a style which might be associated with the lower end of the middle class, but also through the novel's positioning in relation to cultural hierarchy.[2] Skeptical toward intellectual as well as popular culture, it parodies both art house and Hollywood cinema, both

Bloomsbury modernism and best-selling fiction. This may partly explain its low standing within the academically defined literary canon. Yet *Cold Comfort Farm* is a fascinating and intricate text, which amply repays detailed analysis. A sophisticated parody, its meaning is partly produced through its relationship with the literary culture of its day, and also through intertextual connections with the work of a range of canonical and popular regional authors. The novel is preoccupied with social performance and satirizes various trends in interwar culture, including psychoanalysis and sexology, as well as the fascination with speed and new technology and the concomitant nostalgia for the pastoral. The pleasure of this text derives primarily from its mockery of the fashionable. Entirely of its moment, *Cold Comfort Farm* has nevertheless proved enduringly popular.

But *Cold Comfort Farm* was, perhaps, too freakish a success to be repeated. Gibbons went on to publish twenty-three more novels and several collections of short stories and poetry. But although most of these books were well received, none was notably popular or acclaimed, and all are now out of print. Gibbons refused to capitalize on her celebrity status in order to achieve either continued commercial success or consecration in the literary canon. This choice, it seems, resulted partly from her intensely private nature and partly from her distrust of the institutions of literary culture. Her objection to self-aggrandizing male intellectuals and their undervaluing of female intelligence is a major factor in her antipathy toward the literary establishment; it is also one cause of her neglect by that establishment.[3]

"SHE KNEW THAT INTELLECTUALS ALWAYS TALKED LIKE THIS"

Cold Comfort Farm is prefaced with a tongue-in-cheek foreword, dedicating it to one "Anthony Pookworthy, Esq., ABS, LLR" (7). Pookworthy represents the novelist Hugh Walpole, whom Gibbons once interviewed. As she recalled many years later, she found "poor Hugh Walpole" to be "pompous, and very vain" (Purves, "The Road"). According to Oliver, she saw in Walpole "the representative of a smug, self-congratulatory literary establishment" (76). Gibbons's foreword parodies a pompous dedication with which Walpole prefaced one of his books, and her acronyms stand for Associate Back Scratcher and Licensed Log Roller. Distancing herself from the exclusivity and corruption represented by Walpole, she takes journalism, and not "Literature," as the model for her own book, writing in the foreword: "I found, after spending ten years as a journalist, learning to say exactly what I meant in short sentences, that I must learn, if I was to achieve literature and favourable reviews, to write as though I were not quite sure about what I meant but was jolly well going to say something all the same in sentences as long as possible" (7). The English Studies Group at the Birmingham Centre for Contemporary Cultural Studies argues that Gibbons "ironically disclaims any pretensions to 'literary' status—a disclaimer entirely characteristic of middlebrow writing" (14–15). This is true, and yet middlebrow texts such as *Cold Comfort Farm* also frequently satirize popular culture, and even at times the middlebrow itself. In the complex attitudes it evinces toward cultural hierarchy, the novel reflects on its own status.

Gibbons's foreword questions the right of critics and highbrows to discriminate between the literary and the nonliterary on the basis of their own current preferences:

> it is only because I have in mind all those thousands of persons, not unlike myself, who work in the vulgar and meaningless bustle of offices, shops and homes, and who are not always sure whether a sentence is Literature or whether it is just sheer flapdoodle, that I have adopted the method perfected by the late Herr Baedeker, and firmly marked what I consider the finer passages with one, two or three stars. In such a manner did the good man deal with cathedrals, hotels and paintings by men of genius. There seems no reason why it should not be applied to passages in novels. It ought to help the reviewers too. (7–8)

Critics of middlebrow culture in this period were contemptuous of Baedeker's tourist guides, which were seen to epitomize the middlebrow project of supplying "culture" in digestible chunks to an aspiring but semieducated public. For example, in a 1925 poem, "memorabilia," e. e. cummings wrote of Americans in Venice: "particularly the / brand of marriageable nymph which is / armed with large legs rancid / voices Baedekers Mothers and kodaks" (cummings, 254). Gibbons subverts such attitudes by connecting the elite tendency to construct hierarchies of literary value with the Baedeker system of rating works of art and tourist attractions. The foreword has multiple satiric targets: it ridicules, first, the consumer-oriented Baedeker star notation, which makes no distinction between hotels and paintings; second, the elitism of avant-garde writers and critics, who exclude the ordinary reader by developing difficult, experimental styles; and third, the aspirations of second-rate writers such as Walpole who imitate stylistic innovation and succeed only in producing humorless flapdoodle. Gibbons's implied reader, intelligent but commonsensical, is flattered by the implication that s/he, unlike the average reviewer, is in fact able to recognize flapdoodle and avoid being taken in by literary fashions masquerading as artistic breakthroughs.

In the body of the novel, Gibbons's asterisk system works on several levels. It is part of her parody of popular regional writers: the asterisks draw attention to the way these writers isolate passages of "fine writing" from the rest of the text. The representations of regional speech in their books contrast sharply with the lyric landscape descriptions in the educated voice of the narrator. This inevitably constructs the characters as far less cultured and articulate than the author, an attitude that Gibbons apparently found patronizing.[4] Gibbons also uses her asterisks to stage conflicts between different literary discourses, notably between Austenian realism and the colorful, heightened style of the regional novel, which partakes both of Victorian gothic melodrama and of the modernist obsession with pattern and rhythm. I have discussed the authors Gibbons parodies at length elsewhere (Hammill, "*Cold Comfort*"); the most obvious is D. H. Lawrence, and others include Victorian regional writers (especially the Brontës and Thomas Hardy), and authors popular between the wars, particularly Sheila Kaye-Smith, Mary Webb, and their numerous imitators, and to a lesser extent Constance Holme and the Powys brothers.

Gibbons's heroine, Flora Poste, is clearly marked as belonging to the fictional world of Jane Austen; as Avril Horner and Sue Zlosnik note, Flora is "intent on resurrecting Austenian values in a world prey to the degeneracy of late Romanticism and clichéd Gothic" (168). Comparable to Emma Woodhouse in terms of her matchmaking and interfering,[5] Flora is, however, far more successful than Emma. Orphaned at nineteen, she decides to pay an extended visit to her unknown Sussex cousins, the Starkadders, and she rewrites the plots of their lives, arranging each character's destiny exactly as a novelist would. On leaving London and traveling to Cold Comfort Farm, Flora enters into an alien fictional world and remarks that she hopes to collect material for a novel while she is there. Her entirely accurate preconceptions about her cousins are derived from her reading of novels very different from those of Jane Austen. She is excited at the prospect of meeting a doomed family and discovering a "gloomy mystery" (58), and she expects her second cousins to be named Seth and Reuben, because "highly sexed young men living on farms are always called Seth or Reuben, [. . .] and my cousin's name, remember, is Judith. That in itself is most ominous. Her husband is almost certain to be called Amos, and if he *is*, it will be a typical farm" (23). She makes explicit her literary source for these ideas when she remarks on discovering the tyranny of her great-aunt Ada Doom, otherwise Mrs. Starkadder: "So that was what it was. Mrs. Starkadder was the curse of Cold Comfort. Mrs. Starkadder was the Dominant Grandmother Theme, which was found in all typical novels of agricultural life. It was, of course, right and proper that Mrs. Starkadder should be in possession at Cold Comfort; Flora should have suspected her existence from the beginning" (57). Flora, then, functions as a novelist-within-the-novel, and also a reader-in-the-text, commenting on the story as it progresses and relating it to the patterns and conventions of the books she has read.

Her first meeting with her cousin Reuben demonstrates that they are characters from two entirely different kinds of novel:

> "Hullo," said Flora, getting her blow in first. "I feel sure you must be Reuben. I'm Flora Poste, your cousin, you know. How do you do? I'm so glad to see somebody has come in for some tea. Do sit down. Do you take milk?"
>
> * * * The man's big body, etched menacingly against the bleak light that stabbed in from the low windows, did not move. His thoughts swirled like a beck in spate behind the sodden grey furrows of his face. A woman . . . Blast! Blast! Come to wrest away from him the land whose love fermented in his veins, like slow yeast. [. . .] Break her. Break. Keep and hold and hold fast the land. The land, the iron furrows of frosted earth under the rain-lust, the fecund spears of rain, the swelling, slow burst of seed-sheaths, the slow smell of cows and cry of cows, the trampling bride-path of the bull in his hour. All his, his . . .
>
> "Will you have some bread and butter?" asked Flora, handing him a cup of tea. "Oh, never mind your boots. Adam can sweep the mud up afterwards. Do come in."
>
> Defeated, Reuben came in. (77)

At first sight, this passage simply juxtaposes the conventional phrases of ordinary social intercourse with a contrasting, highly metaphorical and colorful style. But as the book unfolds, it becomes clear that this second style is, in itself, conventional. The three-star passage is a very obvious evocation of D. H. Lawrence's rhythmic prose, repetitive phrasing, and frequent use of sexual imagery, and the imitation is so little exaggerated that it is only marked as parodic by its incongruity with the register used in the rest of the extract. Compare, for example, the opening description of the Brangwens in Lawrence's *The Rainbow* (1915):

> Their life and inter-relations were such; feeling the pulse and body of the soil, that opened to their furrow for the grain, and became smooth and supple after their ploughing, and clung to their feet with a weight that pulled like desire, lying hard and unresponsive when the crops were to be shorn away. [. . .] They took the udder of the cows, the cows yielded milk and pulse against the hands of the men, the pulse of the blood of the teats of the cows beat into the pulse of the hands of the men. (10)

Lawrence was a stylistic innovator, although of course he drew on a range of literary models, most notably the Bible. Once he had established his own idiom, with its recognizable conventions, it was imitated by many lesser writers. The majority of these came nowhere near the standard of the original—most were far less skillful than Gibbons. It is possible to detect, in her rather good Lawrentian pastiche, that she did in fact admire the poetic qualities of his writing, in spite of her keen awareness of its excesses.

The target of her satire is, perhaps, not so much Lawrence as those who copied his writing and his personal style. Such people are represented in the novel by the writer Mr. Mybug, whose opinions and remarks reveal his adulation of Lawrence—he uses phrases such as "demonaic vitality" (103), describes himself as a "queer moody brute" (107), and exclaims, "God! Those rhododendron buds had a phallic, urgent look" (121). Stella Gibbons said in a 1981 radio interview that during the late 1920s "I got in with a rather intellectual set [. . . in London]. The men used occasionally to try to kiss me and also to talk to me about sex, like Mr. Mybug does. [. . .] Lawrence was just beginning to be a cult with these people" (Purves, "Interview"). Lawrence's emphasis on following the instincts of the flesh provided Stella Gibbons's male acquaintances with a rationale for seducing women and accusing those who rejected their advances of being sexually repressed. The gendered dimension of the Lawrence cult also included an identification of genius with masculinity, and this, too, is espoused by Mr. Mybug. On hearing that he is preparing a biography of Branwell Brontë, Flora correctly predicts that it will claim Branwell wrote the novels attributed to his sisters. She comments: "There has been increasing discontent among the male intellectuals for some time at the thought that a woman wrote *Wuthering Heights*" (76). (Mr. Mybug's attempted defense of the literary canon against feminization is, ironically, replicated in the exclusion of *Cold Comfort Farm* itself.)

Mr. Mybug, of course, lives in Bloomsbury, but Flora unluckily encounters him sojourning in Sussex:

> "Hullo, Flora Poste. Do you believe that women have souls?" And there he was standing above her and looking down at her with a bold yet whimsical smile.
>
> Flora was not surprised at being asked this question. She knew that intellectuals, like Mr. Kipling's Bi-coloured-Python-Rock-Snake, always talked like this. So she replied, pleasantly, but from her heart: "I am afraid I'm not very interested." [. . .]
>
> "Aren't you? Good girl . . . we shall be all right if only you'll be frank with me. As a matter of fact, I'm not very interested in whether they have souls either. Bodies matter more than souls." (100–101)

Kipling, in "The Elephant's Child" from *Just So Stories* (1902), indicates that the snake's long-winded and overcomplicated style of speaking, although peculiar in comparison to the straightforward speech of the other characters in the story, belongs to a recognizable sociolect: "That is the way all Bi-Coloured-Python-Rock-Snakes always talk" (64). In her reference to this story, Gibbons points to the conventional nature of intellectual conversation, something intellectuals themselves seek to conceal. Mr. Mybug's conversation and personal style are highly derivative, but he is an unsuccessful imitator. He overdoes his attempt to appear bohemian: Flora sees him at one point "accompanied by another gentleman of disordered dress and wild appearance, whom she judged to be one of his intellectual peers" (156). More significantly, he eventually settles for marriage and domesticity with the hare-faced Rennet, misappropriating his idol, Lawrence, in order to justify his life choices: "He said that, by God, D. H. Lawrence was right when he had said there must be a dumb, dark, dull, bitter belly-tension between a man and a woman, and how else could this be achieved save in the long monotony of marriage?" (206). As Oliver remarks: "The splendid irony is that he is using Lawrence to excuse his lapse into a very unbohemian respectability" (119).

"YOU SHALL NOT FIND ME PLUCKING MY EYEBROWS, NOR DIETING"

Flora, as Nicola Humble notes, "expresses no shock at the antics of the free-living highbrows, rather a weary contempt, produced partly by over-familiarity" (31). Flora's preference for more traditional modes of relationship between men and women, as well as for clear, comprehensible English, and ordinary, tidy clothing, constitutes a rejection of bogus bohemian styles and of the calculated performance they represent. Her teenage cousin Elfine has to be rescued from such errors. Flora identifies her strange manners as arising less from shyness than from a deliberate act: "the tall girl in the green cloak [. . .] stopped as though shot at the sight of Flora, and stood poised as though for instant flight. 'Doing the startled bird stunt,' thought Flora" (61). When Flora enquires into the origins of her peculiar clothes, Elfine explains:

> "I wanted to be like Miss Ashford. She kept the Blue Bird's Cage down in Howling. [. . .] She used to have lovely clothes—that is, I mean, they weren't what you would call lovely, but I used to like them. She had a smock—"
>
> "Embroidered with hollyhocks," said Flora, resignedly. "And I'll bet she wore her hair in shells round her ears and a pendant made of hammered silver with a bit of blue enamel in the middle. And did she try to grow herbs?"
>
> "How did you know?" (135–136)

The point is, once again, that unconventionality has its own predictable conventions: Miss Ashford's supposedly "alternative" style is as much a performance as the respectable, upper-middle-class femininity which Flora induces Elfine to embrace instead. She insists that her young cousin wear court shoes and have her hair cut in a flattering style, and counsels her to "confess that she was not brainy" (130). Elfine's reward is marriage to the local squire, a prospect she initially rejected, considering an engagement as "definite and binding" and therefore "horrible" (124). Flora explains that "it is a good thing for you to be bound down" (124), yet she ensures that Elfine is not entirely identified with her performance of a County wife, telling her that when she meets upper-class people, she can "secretly despise them" (137). Flora wishes her protégée to have "some standards, within [herself], with which secretly to compare the many new facts and people" she will encounter (137), and therefore teaches Elfine to admire the kind of elegant and delicate style which she considers to be epitomized in expensive embroidered lingerie and in "the style of Jane Austen, or a painting by Marie Laurencin" (136). Laurencin is an intriguing choice. A somewhat ambiguous artistic figure, she is described by one critic as having "cultivated a graceful, restrained Cubism in beautiful colours" (Haftmann, 111). Her combination of a lovely feminine delicacy with an engagement with the sophisticated ideas of Cubism developed by her male peers might well appeal to Flora, whose own feminine style coexists with an intellectual ability which makes her a match for all the men she meets. Flora's interaction with Elfine, in constructing both bohemian and conventional styles as superficial, but showing the social advantages to be gained from the latter, effectively deconstructs the opposition between these two identities.

As well as reinventing Elfine, Flora persuades her great-aunt Ada Doom to abandon her role as a stock eccentric character (the Dominant Grandmother of the popular regional novels, a figure deriving from the madwoman in the attic of Victorian gothic). Claiming that ever since a mysterious shed experience which befell her as a small girl, she has not been quite right in the head, Aunt Ada exploits her supposed madness, never leaving her room yet keeping the enormous Starkadder family under her control and attempting to counter Flora's modernizing plans. Flora discovers, however, that Ada is simply impersonating a madwoman and recognizes in her a degree of astuteness that makes her a possible ally:

> "I saw something nasty in the woodshed," said Aunt Ada Doom [. . .]
> "'Twas a burnin' noonday . . . sixty-nine years ago. And me no bigger than a titty-wren. And I saw something na—"
> "Well, perhaps she likes it better that way," said Flora soothingly. She had been observing Aunt Ada's firm chin, clear eyes, tight little mouth, and close grip upon the *Milk Producers' Weekly Bulletin and Cowkeepers' Guide,* and she came to the conclusion that if Aunt Ada was mad, then she, Flora, was one of the Marx Brothers. (171–172)

But before Aunt Ada can become Flora's ally, she must relinquish the kind of power which she holds and accept her niece's version of self-fulfillment. The Birmingham English Studies Group points out that "Flora's [. . .] struggle against Aunt Ada Doom [. . .] can be seen as a conflict between two forms of female power: Aunt Ada, representing the power which accrues to the female within the traditional extended family, is opposed by the power of the newly independent woman" (16–17). This is true to an extent, yet Flora makes Ada over in the image of conventional femininity. She tempts her away from the farm with a Paris hotel brochure, an issue of *Vogue,* and some photographs of the ageing yet still glamorous actress Fanny Ward.

The substitution of *Vogue* for the *Milk Producers' Weekly Bulletin and Cowkeepers' Guide* represents the translation of Ada from an agricultural, production-based economy to a consumer economy.[6] But as she did with Elfine, Flora encourages her aunt to retain her independent spirit and resist being confined by a new but equally restrictive female stereotype—that is, by the model of femininity purveyed in glamor magazines and based on an idealization of youth: "And I will remember, my dear," Ada says to Flora as she leaves the farm, "to preserve my personality as you advise. You shall not find me plucking my eyebrows, nor dieting, nor doting on a boy of twenty-five" (222). Indeed, Ada's final departure, dressed in a leather flying suit and traveling to Paris in a private aircraft, evokes a very unconventional—though still glamorous—feminine image: that of the aviatrix. Flying licenses were first issued to women in 1910, and during the following decades, female aviators achieved a series of "firsts." To mention just a few, in 1928, Lady Mary Bailey was the first woman to fly solo from England to South Africa, and in the same year Amelia Earhart became the first woman to cross the Atlantic by air. Amy Johnson flew solo from England to Australia in 1930. The celebrity of women such as Johnson and Earhart reached its peak in the years immediately preceding the publication of Gibbons's novel, and the high profile of women's aviation probably informs the closing scenes, in which not only Ada but also Elfine and Flora leave the farm by plane.[7] *Cold Comfort Farm,* then, draws on a range of contemporary images of the feminine, and as Horner and Zlosnik note, it "alerts us to social constructions of femininity in the 1930s as contemporary fictions that need to be read with cynical detachment" (170).

Flora appeals, not to the committed feminist but to the ordinary woman reader, and the ground of her appeal is the pleasure that a woman with a degree of autonomy can gain for herself. She shows Elfine how to escape her tortured life on the farm and establish her own family in a wealthy, upper-class milieu, and she teaches her great-aunt "what a pleasant life could be had in this world by a handsome, sensible old lady of good fortune, blessed with a sound constitution and a firm will" (222). Flora's version of feminism is, perhaps, one particularly designed to appeal to a middlebrow reader, because it is not based on political idealism or radicalism, but can coexist with a fairly conventional lifestyle. Yet Flora's emphasis on proper feminine behavior exists in a curious tension with her seizing of power within the Starkadder family; in this latter respect, she presents a clear image of female ascendance and defiance. She also firmly resists the antifeminist ideas of Mr. Mybug, which are based on his reading of Lawrence. Mr. Mybug contends that "a woman's success could only be estimated by the success of her sexual life" (122), but Flora rejects this view. She urges the passive Sussex women, who say that pregnancy is "the hand of Nature, and we women cannot escape it" (64), to take control of their bodies, and she introduces Meriam, a servant who becomes pregnant by Seth every spring, to the benefits of contraception. It seems that the disguise of conventionality can allow for genuine autonomy and independence. Under cover of her court shoes, tidy hair, and smart dresses, Flora behaves in ways which would be most unusual for an unmarried woman of her class.

"VARIOUS FILMS OF A FRIVOLOUS NATURE WHICH THEY HAD SEEN AND ENJOYED"

It is, ironically, Flora's bohemian acquaintances who are the most shocked by her bold behavior. Accepting an invitation to tea from an unknown man after a film showing, "Flora disregarded the raised eyebrows of her friend (who, like all loose-living persons, was extremely conventional)" (94). The film is an experimental production, "called 'Yes,' made by a Norwegian film company in 1915 with Japanese actors, which lasted an hour and three-quarters and contained twelve close-ups of water lilies lying perfectly still on a scummy pond and four suicides, all done extremely slowly" (93). This corresponds to a model of avant-garde cinema proposed in 1915 by Vachel Lindsay, a poet who once fell in love with Anita Loos. Lindsay wrote in his book *The Art of the Moving Picture:* "Imagist photoplays would be Japanese prints taking on life, animated Japanese paintings, Pompeian mosaics in kaleidoscopic but logical succession" (268). The cinemagoers in Gibbons's novel are enthusiastic about *Yes,* whispering about "how lovely were its rhythmic patterns" and "how abstract was its formal decorative shaping" (93). These empty phrases, together with the meaningless stylization of the film itself, function as analogies for some of the more ludicrous three-star passages in Gibbons's text, in which pattern and rhythm entirely obscure meaning. The cinema audience has adopted outward trappings suitable to the occasion—"beards and magenta shirts and original ways of arranging its neckwear" (93)—the supposed originality of these people has in fact made them rather a homogenous group. Flora and the stranger next to her are drawn to each other by their sense of difference from the rest of the audience: "Flora had observed with pleasure that the little man was properly and conventionally dressed; and, for his part, his gaze had dwelt upon her neat hair and well-cut coat with incredulous joy, as of one who should say: 'Dr. Livingstone, I presume?'" (93). Once again, civilization is associated with ordinary or unmarked behavior; bohemianism and self-display are coded as barbaric or primitive. The approving usage of "conventional" here contrasts with its derogatory use in reference to Flora's loose-living friend. This points to the fact that, while Flora is conventional in her manners and appearance but underneath very individual, the bohemians she meets are quite the reverse.

The properly dressed little man turns out to be Mr. Neck, a Hollywood film producer, and he and Flora discuss "various films of a frivolous nature which they had seen and enjoyed" (94). The novel's examination of divergences between mainstream and experimental art is consistently represented as a dichotomy between pleasurable and nonpleasurable experiences for the audience. In London, Flora and Elfine consider attending a dire-sounding "Neo-Expressionist" play, with only one actor but seventeen scenes including "a pest-house, a laundry, a lavatory, a court of law, a room in a lepers' settlement, and the middle of Piccadilly Circus" (147), but instead they "went to see Mr. Dan Langham in 'On Your Toes!' at the New Hippodrome [. . .] and had a nice time instead of a nasty one" (147). When Mr. Neck visits Cold Comfort and encounters Mr. Mybug, the conflict between commercial and avant-garde art is explicitly dramatized. Mr. Mybug enthusiastically describes a French film, *La Plume de Ma Tante,* whose title—a famously meaningless phrase which used to appear in textbooks for English students of French grammar—seems appropriate for a film in which, as Mr. Mybug observes: "They all wore glass clothes, you know, and moved in time to a metronome" (183). His uncritical enthusiasm for experiment is countered by Mr. Neck's comment that this film taught him a lot about what not to do. Mr. Mybug protests: "Then your interest in the cinema, Mr. Neck, is *entirely* commercial? I mean, you think nothing of its aesthetic possibilities?" (184), to which Mr. Neck replies: "I gotta responsibility. If your frog friend had to fill fifteen thousand dollars' worth of movie seats every day, he'd have to think of a better stunt than a lot of guys wearin' glass pants" (184). But although this passage once again mocks the pretentiousness of experimental art, it also exposes the mercenary motivations of Hollywood filmmaking and, in the next paragraph, even reveals the way in which American popular culture appropriates and distorts the material developed by avant-garde artists. Mr. Neck reflects: "Say, though, that's an idea. A guy buys a new tuxedo, see? Then he offends some ritzy old egg, see? A magician, or something, and this old egg puts a curse on him. Well, this egg (the guy in the tuxedo) goes off to a swell party, and when he comes in all the girls scream. [. . .] Well, he can't see his pants is turned into glass by this other old egg" (184). This ridiculous plot, expressed in Mr. Neck's semiliterate idiom, is itself mocked, which demonstrates that Gibbons's double-edged satire is directed against mainstream as well as elite culture.

The novel's satirical presentation of American popular culture includes the Hollywood star system. Seth Starkadder, a cinema addict, is entirely immersed in celebrity culture: "'I've got seventy-four photographs o' Lotta Funchal,' confided Seth [. . .] 'Aye, an' forty o' Jenny Carrol, and fifty-five o' Laura Vallee'" (83). Seth's desire for endless replications of the images of his favorite actresses parallels the behavior of his mother, Judith, who is a parodic version of Mrs. Morel in Lawrence's *Sons and Lovers* (1913). Judith decorates her bedroom with two hundred photographs of her son, prefiguring his own career as a cinema star. Seth has always been adept at striking poses. When Mr. Neck first sees Seth and recognizes his potential for film stardom, he instructs him to "Hold it!," and the narrator adds: "And Seth was so soaked in movie slang that he held it, for another second or so in silence" (185). The gossip magazines which sustain the Hollywood celebrity system are also referred to. Mr. Neck

had told Flora all about his slim, expensive mistress, Lily, who made boring scenes and took up the time and energy he would much sooner have spent with his wife, but he had to have Lily, because in Beverly Hills, if you did not have a mistress, people thought you were rather queer, and if, on the other hand, you spent all your time with your wife, and [. . .] said that you liked your wife, and, anyway, why the hell shouldn't you, the papers came out with repulsive articles headed "Hollywood Czar's Domestic Bliss," and you had to supply them with pictures of your wife pouring out your morning chocolate and watering the ferns. (94)

Entertainment papers and movie magazines, while purporting to represent Hollywood as an earthly paradise of sunshine and clean living, in fact throve on the many stories of scandal, adultery, and even murder which circulated there. This passage from *Cold Comfort Farm* has connections with Anita Loos's comic dissection of Hollywood's hypocrisy in her novels *A Mouse Is Born* and *No Mother to Guide Her.*

For Gibbons, as for Loos, Hollywood is only one element of the larger culture of performance and imposture she satirizes. At one point she explicitly links film with another form of spectacle, that mounted by Flora's cousin Amos, preacher at the chapel of the Quivering Brethren: "She was reminded of Mr. Neck, as she stood pensively watching the Brethren going into the chapel, by the spectacle of the Majestic Cinema immediately opposite. It was showing a stupendous drama of sophisticated passion called 'Other Wives' Sins'" (95). This mockery of the promotional language used to work on the emotions of cinema viewers subtly influences our reading of the next scene, in which Amos preaches:

> For some three minutes he slowly surveyed the Brethren, his face wearing an expression of the most profound loathing and contempt, mingled with a divine sorrow and pity. [. . .] Flora had never seen anything to touch it except the face of Sir Henry Wood when pausing to contemplate some late-comers into the stalls at the Queen's Hall just as his baton was raised to conduct the first bar of the "Eroica." Her heart warmed to Amos. The man was an artist.
>
> At last he spoke. [. . .] "Ye miserable crawling worms, are ye here again, then? Have ye come like Nimishi, son of Rehoboam, secretly out of yer doomed houses to hear what's comin' to ye? Have ye come, old and young, sick and well [. . .] to hear me tellin' o' the great crimson lickin' flames o' hell fire?" (97)

The comparison with Sir Henry Wood, founder of the Proms and promoter of classical music, emphasizes the theatricality of Amos's evangelism. Wood was not religious, and angered some Christian groups by pioneering the Sunday Orchestral Concerts; Amos's "imitation of Sir

Henry" (97) perhaps subtly hints that he is not genuinely motivated by religious feeling, but rather by an instinct for power and display. Amos is subsequently connected with American evangelicals—Flora persuades him to embark on a preaching tour and he sends her a postcard: "Praise the Lord! I go to spread the Lord's Word among the heathen Americans, with the Rev. Elderberry Shiftglass, of Chicago" (196). In the early 1930s, conservative Christians in America were placing renewed emphasis on evangelism, establishing mission organizations outside the mainstream churches, preaching over the radio, and centering their movement on powerful, engaging personalities. At the same time, Protestant reformers within the churches were insisting on the public authority of the pulpit, using sermons and lectures to crusade against the sins of the modern era—especially smoking, drinking, dancing, and sexual license. These developments combined to produce the celebrity preacher, precursor of the televangelist. One of the most successful was Aimee Semple McPherson, who founded her own church, while the Methodist Clarence True Wilson and the Presbyterian Billy Sunday drew large crowds with their combination of rhetorical performance and fairly orthodox theology. Sunday achieved large-scale fame and extensive media exposure, and since he was based in Chicago, Gibbons may have had him in mind when she referred to the Rev. Elderberry Shiftglass.

"Suburban uneasiness"

Mr. Mybug's Bloomsbury poses, Amos's preaching tour, and Seth's obsession with the cinema demonstrate that metropolitan culture, and also American culture, have permeated English rural areas. While *Cold Comfort Farm,* like the regional novels it parodies, is structured by an opposition between urban and pastoral, it continually deconstructs that opposition. Gibbons juxtaposes Flora's ultrasophisticated London milieu with the extremely old-fashioned life of the Sussex farm, and exaggerates the contrast by setting the story "in the near future" (6), which means that Flora is able to travel in private planes and use video telephones, while the Starkadders have no bathroom and wash dishes using a thorn twig. As Wendy Parkins argues:

The force of the parody in *Cold Comfort Farm* lies in its awareness that representations of the "unspoiled" countryside found in regional novels were simply a deliberate exclusion of new social relations and practices that bound the country and the city, an exclusion, that is, of changes that were already historical by the 1930s. It may be Flora's machinations that bring a film producer to the farm and enable him to "discover" Seth, but Seth is already devoted to the cinema before Flora's arrival. (87)

Gibbons challenges the conventional literary representation of the countryside as the location of authenticity and naturalness, in opposition to the supposed artifice and corruption of the city, and also suggests that English rural life cannot exclude American modernity.

The characterization of regional novels in terms of their representation of "unspoiled" countryside is, though, a little simplistic. It is true, as Diana Wallace notes in her study of women's historical fiction, that some of the novels written by regional authors such as Kaye-Smith, Webb, and Holme *"appear* to be historical because they are set in a countryside untouched by the industrial revolution, let alone postwar modernity" (*The Woman's,* 30). But the major regional authors, by contrast, laid emphasis on the process of decay and decline which rural England was experiencing in the face of industrialization and modernization. In Lawrence's *Lady Chatterley's Lover* (1928), Constance is driven through the remnants of the Midland countryside: "in the wide rolling region of the castles, smoke waved against steam, and patch after patch of raw reddish brick showed the newer mining settlements, sometimes in the hollows, sometimes gruesomely ugly along the skyline of the slopes. And between, in between, were the tattered remnants of the old coaching and cottage England, even the England of Robin Hood, where the miners prowled with the dismalness of suppressed sporting instincts" (162). In *The Woodlanders* (1887), Hardy expresses rural decline in Darwinian terms, but also draws on pseudo-scientific discourses of degeneracy: "Here, as everywhere, the Unfulfilled Intention, which makes life what it is, was as obvious as it could be among the depraved crowds of a city slum. The leaf was deformed, the curve was crippled, the taper was interrupted; the lichen ate the vigour of the stalk, and the ivy slowly strangled to death the promising sapling" (54). In Gibbons's exaggerated version, the degeneration of the farm's livestock is so extreme that a leg falls off one of the cows, and Reuben laments that he will be unable to sell her: "Cold Comfort stock ne'r finds a buyer. Wi' the Queen's Bane blighting our corn, and the King's Evil laying waste the clover, and the Prince's Forfeit bringin' black ruin on the hay, and the sows as barren as come-ask-it—aye, 'tes the same tale iverywhere all over the farm" (51). Gibbons's parody speeds up the processes of decline traced in Hardy and Lawrence: the normally cheerful Flora finds that "the distressing manner in which the farm-house and its attendant buildings seemed sinking into decay before her eyes, and the appearance and character of her relatives, had produced in her a feeling of gloom" (73).

By the end of the novel, the farm is beginning to prosper again, as Reuben takes over from his father Amos, institutes new working methods, and purchases the latest agricultural equipment recommended in the *Internationally Progressive Farmers' Guide and Helpmeet,* supplied by Flora (195). The final wedding scene shows Cold Comfort as the pastoral idyll constructed in the more nostalgic of the popular regional novels, a "cool, flower-garlanded, sweet-smelling farm" (215) with a kitchen full of "cool, delicious-looking food" (215), and outside "long, fresh grass" and "leaves dazzling against the pure sky" (231). Ironically, this has been achieved through the intervention of a modernizing visitor from the metropolis. Thus Gibbons counters Hardy and Lawrence by suggesting that modernization can reverse, rather than exacerbate, rural decay. At the same time, the final scenes of the novel are explicitly marked as fantasy by the insistent repetition of the key elements (flowers, coolness, clear skies, sweet smells) and by the deliberately clichéd love scene between Flora and her cousin Charles, who arrives by plane to take her back to London.

Gibbons's later novel, *Conference at Cold Comfort Farm* (1949), clearly demonstrates that the transformed, idyllic version of Cold Comfort is as improbable and fantastic as the original, rapidly decaying version with its endlessly blighted crops and three-legged cows. In this sequel, published in 1949 but set—like its predecessor—in the near future, the farm has again become unprofitable, and the Starkadders have all left, with the exception of Reuben. His operations have been interfered with by the Ministry of Agriculture, and he has been forced to sell the buildings to a trust, renting back a small area to farm on a subsistence basis. The farm buildings have been requisitioned for meetings and events, and the livestock for scientific experiment. The influence of America is even more visible than it was in the earlier novel, reflecting the new dominance of the States in world affairs. Amos's preaching, from his U.S. church, is heard over the wireless at Cold Comfort; Mr. Mybug is now dressed in "an imitation camelhair coat sent from America by *Throw-Outs for Britain*" (19), and proclaims that New York has become "Art Centre of the world" (86); while Phoebe Starkadder is advised to sell her quilting work to the rich Americans (45). The farm itself has been reinvented to match what seems like an American concept of British country life: "There were typical farmhouse grandfather clocks ticking all over the place, and [. . .] a Welsh dresser all over peasant pottery. In the Lytel Scullerie there were fifteen scythes arranged in a half-moon over the sink; there were horse-brasses all round the Great Inglenooke and all round the Lytel Fire-places" (46). This excessive and fraudulent "reconstruction" appropriates formerly practical items as decoration. It draws attention to the invention of rurality as style, something to be marketed by the heritage industry to gullible foreigners, or indeed to tourists from British cities.

Urban Britain's fetishizing of an imagined version of the country-side is also briefly satirized in Gibbons's novel *Bassett* (1946), which mocks a particular form of interwar popular literature, the ramble book. These books explored disappearing rural ways of life or sought to uncover the history beneath the expanding suburban terrain.[8] *Bassett* includes a writer character, modeled on the avuncular narrators of the ramble books, who styles himself Mohican, "because he was, he said, the last of the English: the last man left alive who knew the lost downland paths, the ancient sites of gipsy camps, the fairs and highways, the lore of tramp and thatcher, about which everybody in England, of course, used to know by instinct. And oh! what a fat piece he made out of being the last man to know these things" (189). In his magazine pieces and "his yearly novel about fairs or circuses" (189), Mohican deliberately trades on the town-dweller's nostalgia for old-fashioned rural ways, creating saleable, escapist texts by denying the reality of modern life: "To read Mohican's essays, you wouldn't think there was an idle colliery, a cinema, or an unmarried mother in the length and breadth of England" (190). There is a very clear contrast here between this conception of popular rural writing and Gibbons's own novel, which refuses to idealize rural England and prominently features both a cinema and an unmarried mother in the remote reaches of Sussex. Gibbons did have a great love for the countryside, and her ecological concerns and dismay at industrialization are evident in some of her poetry. But since Cold Comfort is only attractive once Flora has tidied it up, and since the modern lifestyle choices and technologies that she advocates are presented as ameliorating rather than damaging, Gibbons cannot be said to share fully the nostalgic attitude of writers such as Webb, who laments the estrangement between man and nature, and celebrates characters who still live in harmony with the natural world. Just as Gibbons deconstructs oppositions between bohemian and conventional, so she also challenges the standard polarity between urban and rural. As Raymond Williams observes, there is a "suburban uneasiness, a tension of attraction and repulsion" (253), in the novel's attitude toward the countryside and toward the literature which celebrates it.

The relationship between *Cold Comfort Farm* and the texts it parodies can be interpreted in numerous ways, and has had a significant impact on the literary standing of Gibbons's novel. According to Gladys Mary Coles, biographer of Mary Webb: *"Cold Comfort Farm* dealt a severe blow to the genre [of the rural novel]: and it effectively damaged Mary Webb's reputation (but not immediately the sales of her books), since it helped to reinforce among academic critics and intellectuals [an] antipathy towards her work" (326). In view of Coles's argument, it is somewhat ironic that critics and intellectuals also seem to have an antipathy toward Gibbons. It is possible that this attitude derives in part from the low critical standing of some of the authors she parodies: Webb is not widely read or studied today, nor are Kaye-Smith, the Powys brothers, or Walpole. Certain commentators have argued that the canonical status of a parody is largely dependent on the status of its target works, and W. J. Keith applies this to Gibbons's novel: *"Cold Comfort Farm* was an immense success in its time [. . .] Inevitably, however, its point has been blunted by the decline of the genre that it helped to dislodge. [. . .] many of its finer points will be lost on modern readers, and some of its implications need to be spelled out in detail" (175). This may be partially true, but there are two counterarguments to be advanced. First, the most recognizable target of *Cold Comfort Farm*, Lawrence, still holds a central position in the canon of English fiction, as of course do Hardy and the Brontës. Second, it is demonstrable that Gibbons's parody still functions effectively even though the fashion for regional fiction is so far behind us. It is certainly true that few readers today will be able to put a name to all of Gibbons's sources, or recognize the specificity of her jokes as they apply to individual authors. However, the parody is ultimately directed at a fashionable genre rather than a particular writer, and as Margaret Rose explains: "The dual structure of parody allows it to keep both its target and its own parodic function alive. Stella Gibbons's *Cold Comfort Farm*, for instance, is still comic even if one does not know the specific works it parodies, because its parody of those works has evoked them for the reader while making fun of them by exaggerating their peculiarities" (122). In parodying the highly metaphorical prose and Victorian-style melodramatic and mystery plots found in popular rural fiction, Gibbons necessarily reinscribes these conventions in her own text.

Cold Comfort Farm, then, situates itself in a somewhat contradictory manner, both in the tradition of rural writing and also outside that tradition, commenting on it from a perspective of ordinary common sense. This positioning is typical of parodic texts. Gibbons depends on the traditional structures of the agricultural novel—the family feuds, the isolated setting, the landscape description, the gloomy mysteries—but she also mocks the predictability of these motifs. Many of her jokes can only be fully appreciated by a reader familiar with a number of novels by half a dozen rural writers, and in this way, Gibbons seems to be addressing a reader who is an avid consumer of rural fictions, yet through her mockery of those fictions, she constructs a reader who shares her skepticism about primitivist writing.

The regional fiction she parodies provides the most obvious literary context for *Cold Comfort Farm;* only Evelyn Waugh, among her contemporaries, furnishes anything like an analogue for Gibbons's approach. One contemporary reviewer of *Cold Comfort Farm* speculated that Stella Gibbons might be a pen name of Waugh's, and later critics have occasionally connected the two authors. Crispin Jackson, in a brief profile of Gibbons's work published in 1995, compares "the savagery of her satire" to Waugh's, and also notes, with reference to the incidents of the video phone and the succession of planes arriving at the farm, that "the narrative includes sudden wild passages of what might almost be called science fiction. [. . .] These moments are reminiscent of similar excesses in the novels of Evelyn Waugh" (22). Waugh's writing is currently taken more seriously as cultural criticism than Gibbons's, but both authors deploy eccentricity as a form of subversion, which aligns them with what Bluemel calls "intermodernism."[9]

Among Waugh's novels, the most apt comparison for *Cold Comfort Farm* is *Vile Bodies* (1930). Like Gibbons's novel, *Vile Bodies* is prefaced by an author's note specifying that the action takes place "in the near future." Waugh adds that "existing social tendencies have become more marked" and "a certain speeding up" has taken place (7), a description which applies equally to Gibbons's fictional universe. Both authors engage with representations of speed and technology in modernist art and also in popular forms, notably cinema and regional fiction. Waugh's parody of Futurist art on the one hand and cinema

Westerns on the other is comparable to Gibbons's double-edged and broadly middlebrow parodic strategy. Yet while mocking the philosophy of Futurism, Waugh also uses its style to great effect (see Allen), just as Gibbons, while mocking the regional novel, also depends on its idiom and structures. Speed permeates the two novels: the pace of action and dialogue in the two novels is comically rapid; fashions change with dizzying rapidity; and the motif of transport, in modes ranging from horses and carts to trains, cars, and aeroplanes, recurs throughout. In these respects, the two authors are responding to one of the dominant features of contemporary art; as Hugh Kenner says of the 1920s, "kinesis was the rhetoric of that decade" (44). Gibbons and Waugh exaggerate the city-country divide which preoccupied interwar writers and artists, contrasting the manic excesses and rapid displacements of London life with the ponderous, old-fashioned rituals at the inaccessible country houses, Cold Comfort and Doubting Hall, respectively. This opposition is complicated by the evident and rapid degeneration of the country houses and by the invasion of new technologies into the rural locations. In both *Cold Comfort Farm* and *Vile Bodies,* the inhabitants of the rural houses are at once fascinated by new technology and determined to retain their anachronistic ways of life. This tension shapes the novels; themselves nostalgic texts, they also satirize the interwar nostalgia for the pastoral.

"WHO IS SHE? WHAT IS THIS BOOK?"

Regional fiction was accorded a special prestige during the interwar years. Anthea Trodd writes: "The classic status enjoyed by rural writing in this period derived from the insistently diffused belief that the real England was rural England [. . .] in which continuity with the past was still clearly visible" (103). A common love of the countryside, as articulated in rural writing, was constructed in political discourse as one basis for national unity. This goes some way toward explaining the popularity of authors as diverse as Flora Thompson, Daphne du Maurier, or Alison Uttley, as well as the honors achieved by writers such as Vita Sackville-West, whose long poem *The Land* (1926) won the Hawthornden Prize, or Constance Holme, whose Westmoreland novels were published in the World's Classics Series. During the 1920s, both Holme and Webb won the prestigious Femina Vie Heureuse Prize,[10] and *Cold Comfort Farm* was awarded this same prize in 1933 despite the fact that it ridicules the previous prizewinners. The Femina prize demonstrates that Gibbons's novel benefited from the status achieved by rural writing in general and partly explains why the novel was more highly regarded during the 1930s than it is today. The erosion of the relationship between the countryside and English national identity later caused a decline in the literary standing of *Cold Comfort Farm* along with other once-popular regional novels.

The deliberations of the Femina prize committee further reveal the ambiguous status of *Cold Comfort Farm*. During the interwar years, the English-language Femina prize was awarded annually by a committee of French women of letters, "for the best work of imagination in English published during the year by an author, whose work has hitherto, in the opinion of the committee, not received sufficient recognition."[11] The winning book was chosen from a list of three submitted by a second committee of English women. (The French-language prize was awarded by an equivalent process.) The minutes of the meetings of the English committee record that *Cold Comfort Farm* was proposed for consideration by none other than Sheila Kaye-Smith, who remarked, "I don't quite know what the French committee would make of it, but it is so witty and a first novel."[12] Almost the whole committee admired the book. G. B. Stern described it as "gorgeous" and Netta Syrett argued: "It is such a very unusual book that I think it ought to get a prize."[13] At a subsequent meeting, Rebecca West proclaimed: "It is the greatest comic novel of the age," and Syrett referred to it as "magnificent."[14] For the final short list, Rosamond Lehmann's *Invitation to the Waltz* was selected as the first choice, Elizabeth Bowen's *To the North* as the second, and *Cold Comfort Farm* as the third. Several members of the committee expressed surprise when Stella Gibbons won, some of them because they had not thought that her style of humor would make sense in France, and others (including Margaret Kennedy) because they thought Lehmann's book a finer piece of work.[15]

In general, the minutes indicate that the English committee placed significant emphasis on pleasure and accessibility in their selection of books. Although a number of the winning and short-listed books have since been confirmed in the modernist canon (including fiction by Woolf, Katherine Mansfield, E. M. Forster, and Dorothy Richardson), few of them were radically experimental. Most of the books which won the prize might broadly be described as realist and/or comic narratives, and many would now be classified as middlebrow. Representative winning authors during the interwar years are Bradda Field, Elizabeth

Jenkins, Evelyn Waugh, and Stella Benson. Virginia Woolf, who had been awarded the prize for *To the Lighthouse,* disliked this tendency toward rather middlebrow texts. Forgetting that she had once admired Gibbons's poetry, she wrote to Elizabeth Bowen: "I was enraged to see that they gave the £40 to Gibbons. Who is she? What is this book? And so you can't buy your carpet." [16] In her next letter to Bowen, she admitted: "Now I come to think of it, I remember Stella Gibbons writing a poem we liked, and so asked her to send us some to print; I can't help thinking you and Rosamond had a better claim." [17]

Stella Gibbons's response to the award reveals how little she had sought or experienced public notice. In her correspondence with the honorary secretary of the committee, Winifred Whale, she warmly expresses her surprise and pleasure: "I am, of course, very honoured and extremely delighted by the award," but misapprehends the nature of the presentation ceremony, asking if it is a private meeting and whether she might bring her husband. It was in fact a large invitation-only event, which was always reported in the *Times* and other newspapers. Gibbons's subsequent letters to Whale reveal her alarm at the prospect of the acceptance speech: "I am rather miserable about the speech, and I should be most grateful if you would suggest something about which I could talk." [18] Following her award, Gibbons was invited to become a member of the prize committee, but declined on grounds that she was too busy; [19] the real reason may have been her tendency to resist the institutions of canon-making, which of course include literary prizes. Of all the writers considered in this book, she was the least publicly visible and the least active in the contemporary literary culture. She did establish friendships with some other writers, including Margaret Kennedy, whose work she admired. [20] But in other respects, she remained apart from the literary scene.

The most valuable insights into her attitudes in this respect are provided by Reggie Oliver:

> One of the most curious aspects of Stella's character was that in many ways she wanted to be simpler and more ordinary than she actually was. It could be seen in her hatred of publicity: she much preferred being Mrs. Webb to Stella Gibbons. I remember her telling me in the late 1970s how she had found [. . .] a nice greengrocer's and was very cross that someone had told the people in the shop that she was an authoress. She was afraid of going there again in case she was treated as an oddity or, worse still, a celebrity. (160)

Montgomery, Delafield, and Kennedy likewise changed their names on marriage and, from that point on, effectively maintained two separate identities, each using her maiden name as an authorial persona and her married name for private life.[21] But they, like the American authors considered in this study, cooperated (to varying degrees) with their own construction as celebrities: participating in high-profile activities such as broadcasting, public lecturing, or cinema, mixing with other authors and well-known personalities, and regularly consenting to interviews and media profiles. Stella Gibbons, by contrast, strongly resisted the operations of celebrity culture. Her intense preoccupation with publicity, social performance, and eccentricity in her fiction was balanced by her determined rejection of such things in her own life. Oliver writes:

> Quite suddenly in 1932 Stella found that she was famous. Celebrity bewildered her, and throughout her life she was indifferent, occasionally even hostile, to it. Though, later on, she enjoyed the mild distinction that a Fellowship of the Royal Society of Literature conferred, she never courted honours or publicity, and on at least one occasion she turned down the opportunity to appear on television. She did not even greatly care for the chances fame offered for her to meet other famous people. Interviewing for the *Evening Standard* had perhaps inured her to their glamour. (126)

It was in 1950 that Gibbons was made a Fellow of the Royal Society of Literature, but this was not otherwise the most prosperous period of her career: some of the books she published in the early 1950s were disparaged or ignored by critics.

Her fortunes began to improve, however, in 1954, when Malcolm Muggeridge invited her to write for *Punch,* and she was a regular contributor until the late 1960s. Her 1956 novel *Here Be Dragons,* which was about fifties bohemian culture, was very successful. She continued to publish novels for the next fourteen years, although her last two books remained unpublished since she no longer felt able to cope with the anxiety of exposing her work to editors and critics. *Cold Comfort Farm* remained popular throughout the century and has never gone out of print. Its most famous line, "I saw something nasty in the woodshed," has become a catchphrase. Gibbons continued to receive fan letters to the end of her life, particularly during the period following the adoption of her novel as a set text for the British A-level syllabus in

1978. Gibbons also received many invitations to speak about the novel at universities and other institutions, and despite her dislike of publicity, she sometimes accepted these.

Cold Comfort Farm has been adapted as a stage play, a musical, a radio drama, and two films, thereby reaching a still larger audience.[22] The 1995 BBC television version, directed by John Schlesinger, met with unexpected success when it was released in American art cinemas the following year. Grossing $5 million, it forced a subsequent big-screen release in Britain in 1997. The popularity of the Schlesinger film in America was likely due to its evocation of the comic English eccentricity which apparently fascinates U.S. audiences. The film seems to have contributed to the gradual recuperation of *Cold Comfort Farm* as a classic. Penguin produced three new editions in eight years,[23] and the novel was reinstated on the British A-level syllabus in 2001.[24] While virtually no published criticism on Gibbons appeared before the end of the twentieth century, the first years of the twenty-first have seen a modest but noticeable increase in critical interest.[25]

Gibbons's choice to remain on the fringes of metropolitan literary culture, as an observer rather than an active participant, might be connected with her choice to live all her life in the North London suburbs. She grew up in Kentish Town, later moving to nearby Hampstead. This environment is explored in several of her books, notably *Enbury Heath* (1935), *Miss Linsey and Pa* (1936), *Here Be Dragons* (1956), *A Pink Front Door* (1959), *The Charmers* (1965), *Starlight* (1967), and *The Woods in Winter* (1970). Like Stevie Smith, an exact contemporary of hers at the North London Collegiate School who also remained in the area for her whole life, Gibbons appreciates the suburb, but resists complete identification with it. In the work of both authors, affectionate celebration of the pleasures of the suburb coexists with a certain distaste for its repeating structures and its geographical and social conformity.[26] There are no suburbs in *Cold Comfort Farm*, only the two extremes of central London and deepest Sussex. Yet, as Raymond Williams suggests in his phrase "suburban uneasiness," Gibbons's ambiguous identification with the suburb is emblematic of *Cold Comfort Farm*'s complex attitude toward rural England.

In itself, however, the suburb is not a place of uneasiness for Gibbons; rather, it is a place of comfort and familiarity, both as somewhere to live and as somewhere to set her fiction. It is a chosen vantage point, ideal for achieving a balanced perspective on both country and city.

Some of her elitist contemporaries contemptuously associated the suburb with the middlebrow and the feminine: T. S. Eliot announced that his new *Criterion* was directed against "suburban democracy" (John Carey, 52), while Louis Macneice wrote of "Suburb-dwellers, spinsters, schoolteachers, women secretaries, proprietresses of teashops," noting that such women turned to theater for "an uncritical escape from their daily lives" (87).[27] I would argue, by contrast, that the suburb can be productively associated with the middlebrow, and both can be viewed as sites of subtle yet far-reaching subversion and challenge.[28] For Gibbons, as for some of her contemporaries, the middlebrow, like the suburb, offered a special point of view from which to observe both high and popular culture, and also to reflect on and redefine the middlebrow itself. This point of view disrupts accepted critical paradigms; Gibbons effectively locates herself in a literary no-man's-land, between urban high modernism and pure pastoral, between the experimental and the realist. Raymond Williams's comment on *Cold Comfort Farm*—"what has to be said about that odd work is not easy" (253)—is perhaps representative of the uncertainty of literary historians and critics when faced with *Cold Comfort Farm*.

7 | "Wildest hopes exceeded"
E. M. Delafield's Diary
of a Provincial Lady

In February 1931, E. M. Delafield published the first installment of a series called "Women in Fiction" in *Time and Tide*. It identified the types of women likely to feature in "the dialect novel":

> The malignant grandmother [. . .] dominates the book, and all the people in it, and the destinies of every one of them, and is almost always the victim of a disease, or at least a disability, that keeps her in bed, or anyway in a chair. Briefly, the general rule is that her sons should be weaklings and degenerates and her daughters neurotic victims of sex-repression, but her grandchildren, curiously enough, are fearfully strong characters, and end by defying her. [. . .] The younger women in dialect novels have the most terrifically strong passions. Either it's the old homestead, [. . .] or the Squire's oldest son, or perhaps their own oldest son. ("Women in Fiction")

This is precisely the plot of *Cold Comfort Farm,* and all the characters Delafield mentions are included in Gibbons's novel exactly as described. The piece appeared just before Gibbons began work on her book, and as an occasional contributor to *Time and Tide* herself, she may well have read it. It might have crystallized the ideas she had gained through her own extensive reading of agricultural fiction. More importantly, the piece draws attention to the affinities between the two authors. Like Gibbons, Delafield had an eye for pattern, in terms of both literary convention and ordinary social language; and like her she was a skilled parodist and imitator. In her journalism, Delafield parodied the style of numerous writers, while in her Provincial Lady books, she convincingly evoked the conversation of a whole range of social types. Lady Rhondda (later Viscountess Rhondda, and editor of *Time and Tide*) comments in her obituary of Delafield that her literary parodies "were amongst her best work, but the Provincial Lady, and indeed most of her lighter work, was also in fact parody—parody of life," adding: "One was, I think, more conscious of her amazing ear and memory for words than one is of that of most writers" (Rhondda, Obituary). Delafield—like Gibbons and also Dorothy Parker—creates humor through the very predictability of what her characters say. Yet the styles of these authors would never be mistaken for one another; paradoxically, in the rendering of the phrases of ordinary social intercourse, each found her own distinctive voice.

Delafield's best-known work, *The Diary of a Provincial Lady*, began as a serial in *Time and Tide* from December 1929 onwards, and before the end of 1930, its popularity led to publication in book form. It became a best seller, making its author internationally famous and giving rise to three sequels, *The Provincial Lady Goes Further* (1932), *The Provincial Lady in America* (1934), and *The Provincial Lady in Wartime* (1939).[1] The protagonist's first journal entry immediately reveals her characteristic combination of wit and exasperation, literary and domestic reference.

> *November 7th.*—Plant the indoor bulbs. Just as I am in the middle of them, Lady Boxe calls. I say, untruthfully, how nice to see her, and beg her to sit down while I just finish the bulbs. Lady B. makes determined attempt to sit down in armchair where I have already placed two bulb-bowls and the bag of charcoal, is headed off just in time, and takes the sofa.
>
> Do I know, she asks, how very late it is for indoor bulbs? September, really, or even October, is the time. [. . .] We talk some more about bulbs, the Dutch School of Painting, Our Vicar's Wife, sciatica, and *All Quiet on the Western Front*. (DPL, 3)

The diaries are invariably described as chronicles of ordinariness and domesticity, and their heroine as a representative "type." When the first book appeared, an anonymous notice in *Time and Tide* commented that Delafield had "created a complete and therefore composite portrait of, not only one woman, but a type of women, a state of society, a phase of life."[2] In the *Irish Times,* a reviewer of the 1944 omnibus edition of the *Provincial Lady* books remarked: "Miss Delafield's life in a country village [. . .] *was* the life of every such Englishwoman at the time" (Lane). Nicola Beauman, introducing the 1984 Virago reprint, begins: "*The Diary of a Provincial Lady* is about ordinariness." She adds, "E. M. Delafield's heroines behave in exactly the same way as thousands of other Englishwomen living in the country in the period between the two World Wars" (vii). These various statements might be partially true if the conception of Englishwomen is limited to the upper middle classes. But even within this group, Delafield's heroine is decidedly out of the ordinary. Compare her, for example, with the protagonist of Jan Struther's *Mrs. Miniver* (1939), another best-selling novel concerned with the everyday experiences and musings of a British wife and mother. While Mrs. Miniver is contentedly engrossed in domesticity and maternity, the Provincial Lady protests against the demands and restrictions of these roles, and, crucially, escapes them to a certain extent. She may be a part-time housewife, but she is also a woman of letters, and the very fact that she writes a diary differentiates her from Mrs. Miniver, whose story is told in the third person.

The Provincial Lady's personality and perspective are fundamentally defined by her relationship with literature; books and reading are referred to continually. *The Provincial Lady Goes Further* opens with the information that the narrator has published a highly successful book, at which point her tentative self-construction as a writer receives affirmation through public recognition. As the series of novels unfolds, she is increasingly identified with her professional role, which moves her away from her domestic setting, introduces her to London literary society, and eventually takes her to the States on a book tour. The diaries provide a detailed account of the pleasures and perils of literary celebrity, but despite her success, the Provincial Lady retains a modesty about her abilities and a reluctance to be identified as "literary" or "intellectual," which marks her perspective as middlebrow. This is reaffirmed by her taste in books and her skepticism toward both high and popular culture.

The fact that the Provincial Lady becomes an author is one of the primary explanations for the critical tendency to collapse the distinction between Delafield herself and her fictional heroine, as, for example, in the title of Violet Powell's biography, *The Life of a Provincial Lady;* in Beauman's reference to the Provincial Lady as Delafield's "*alter ego*" (Introduction, xii); and in Maurice McCullen's dubious argument that "her best work comes directly out of her own experience and requires the aid of biography for satisfactory explanation" (x).[3] Certainly, the many correspondences between the experiences of author and character cannot sensibly be ignored, yet the conflation of the two must be resisted. The Diaries are not real autobiographical writing, but comic, satiric texts, published for money and deliberately constructed to appeal to particular audiences (especially to the largely female, middle-class readership of *Time and Tide*). Neither are these books the sum of Delafield's work—in fact, her output of fiction and journalism was immense and heterogeneous, ranging far beyond the outlook of the Provincial Lady. Her contributions to *Time and Tide* range from parodies to ghost stories, and from comic sketches to perceptive book reviews. She became a director of the paper in 1927, and from then on almost every issue contains a piece by her.

Most of her twenty-nine novels were well received, and some are extremely accomplished. They are difficult to characterize collectively, but many center on family life and explore the relationships between the generations. Also, the question of women, war, and employment arises in novels such as *The War Workers* (1918) and *Late and Soon* (1943), while others consider women's lack of career opportunities during peacetime. Among Delafield's best books are *Consequences* (1919) and *Thank Heaven Fasting* (1932), which center on young upper-middle-class women who are brought up to view marriage as their only purpose, yet go through several London seasons without obtaining a husband. These novels' narrow concentration on one subject reproduces the narrowness of the heroines' lives, but the two books ultimately take very different directions. Alex, the protagonist of *Consequences*, enters a convent and then commits suicide, while Monica in *Thank Heaven Fasting* joyfully accepts the dull suitor who proposes as she nears thirty, a conclusion which, though labeled "The Happy Ending" in the chapter heading, is perhaps almost as bleak as that of the earlier novel. The terrible emptiness of the lives of Alex and Monica provides an important counterbalance to the Provincial Lady's experience. Her life—though rather repetitive—is nevertheless fulfilling, and a richer cultural experience is available to her than to most of Delafield's other heroines. Monica, for example, is only taken to art galleries in order that she may have something to discuss with gentlemen, and dutifully expresses nothing but received opinions: "'I liked the Sargeants,' said Monica, knowing that this was the right thing to say" (*Thank Heaven*, 19). Even when in her twenties, she is not permitted newspapers and must ask permission before reading library books. Delafield often presents reading as a luxury, a joy, and a comfort, although it occasionally becomes a difficult duty, especially where experimental writing is concerned. In all her fiction, taste in books is an important indicator of character, and in the *Provincial Lady* books especially, reading is of central importance, and intertextual relationships are established with a variety of authors.

"COULD I WRITE A PLAY MYSELF?"

In the first volume of her diary, the Provincial Lady identifies herself primarily as a reader rather than a writer. Literature mediates the way she sees the world: she often quotes from her favorite authors, imagines herself as a literary character, or compares her own experiences with those depicted in books:

> am struck—as often—by enormous dissimilarity between journeys undertaken in real life, and as reported in fiction. Can remember very few novels in which train journey of any kind does not involve either (a) hectic encounter with member of opposite sex, leading to tense emotional issue; (b) discovery of murdered body in hideously battered condition, under circumstances which utterly defy detection; (c) elopement between two people each of whom is married to somebody else, culminating in severe disillusionment, or lofty renunciation.
>
> Nothing of all this enlivens my own peregrinations. (DPL, 89)

Despite the absence of melodramatic plot possibilities, the diarist embarks upon a lengthy and detailed account of her journey, in which she skillfully turns her fellow travelers into fictional characters and the events en route into comic episodes:

> American young gentleman sits opposite, and elderly French couple, with talkative friend wearing blue beret, who trims his nails with a pocket-knife and tells us about the state of the wine-trade. [. . .]
>
> Towards eleven o'clock we all subside into silence, except the blue beret, who is now launched on tennis-champions, and has much to say about all of them. American young gentleman looks uneasy at mention of any of his compatriots [. . .] Just as we all—except indefatigable beret, now eating small sausage rolls—drop one by one into slumber, train stops at station and fragments of altercation break out in corridor concerning admission, or otherwise, of someone

evidently accompanied by large dog. This is opposed by masculine voice repeating steadily, at short intervals, *Un chien n'est pas une personne.* (DPL, 89–90)

Even as she remarks on the differences between her own journeys and those described in fiction, the Provincial Lady is herself creating a fictional journey through her narrative, and thus is in the process of becoming a writer. There is, perhaps, a suggestion here of Virginia Woolf's influential 1924 essay "Mr. Bennett and Mrs. Brown," which tells of an encounter in a railway carriage with an unknown woman, who immediately starts to impose herself as a character, "making someone begin almost automatically to write a novel about her" (*Collected*, 324). In general terms, of course, Delafield's work by no means corresponds to the new conception of fictional form which Woolf recommends. Yet *The Diary of a Provincial Lady* accords with Woolf's essay in that it implicitly affirms the value of the everyday, of ordinary people, as literary subject matter. Woolf says to her reader: "In the course of your daily life this past week you have had far stranger and more interesting experiences than the one I have tried to describe. You have overheard scraps of talk that filled you with amazement. You have gone to bed at night bewildered by the complexity of your feelings" (*Collected*, 336). Complex feelings are not Delafield's specialism, but astonishing "scraps of talk" form the substance of many of the Provincial Lady's diary entries, including her description of the train journey.

At another point in Delafield's text, the subtle commentary on literary method takes on a specifically gendered dimension:

Notice, and am gratified by, appearance of large clump of crocuses near the front gate. Should like to make whimsical and charming reference to these, and try to fancy myself as "Elizabeth of the German Garden," but am interrupted by Cook, saying that the Fish is here, but he's only brought cod and haddock, and the haddock doesn't smell any too fresh, so what about cod?

Have often noticed that Life is like that. (DPL, 37)

The Provincial Lady's attempt to imagine herself into the role of a literary woman is destroyed by the intrusion of domestic issues, and these markedly female concerns themselves become the subject of the writing. The passage dramatizes the disparity between the pressurized, frustrating nature of her daily existence and the leisured, outdoor idyll of "Elizabeth," heroine of Elizabeth von Arnim's novel *Elizabeth and Her German Garden* (1898). Elizabeth's role as author nevertheless provides a model for the Provincial Lady's own. The novel takes the form of her diary, which, like the Provincial Lady's, combines domestic detail with feminist commentary and features a comically sexist husband. The reference to von Arnim can be read as one of the early stages in the Provincial Lady's self-construction as a writer, and already her diary is being inscribed in a specific literary tradition.

Delafield's narrator directly suggests that success in literature is partly a result of circumstances: "Could I write a play myself? Could we *all* write plays, if only we had the time?" (DPL, 19). This concern with the practical circumstances of literary production forges a link with Woolf's *A Room of One's Own* (1929). Two substantial extracts from Woolf's book appeared in *Time and Tide* in November 1929 [4] (the month before the Provincial Lady's first diary entry), and the paper also printed an admiring review by Theodora Bosanquet. Several articles in later issues take *A Room of One's Own* as a reference point for commentaries on women's writing,[5] and it is, I would argue, an important intertext for *The Diary of a Provincial Lady*. Woolf asks, "What conditions are necessary for the creation of works of art?" (*Room*, 38), and time, money, respect, space, and privacy are among the elements she identifies, all of which are likewise considered in the Provincial Lady's diary. Delafield's heroine, though, never commands the £500 a year recommended by Woolf, and while she affirms the value of a room of her own when renting a small flat in London, she also manages to work at the family home, writing in shared rooms and in the spaces between domestic tasks. A further contrast might be drawn in that Woolf preserves the idea of "genius" as the foundation for artistic creation— the word recurs twenty-one times in her essay; whereas Delafield's narrator articulates a more democratic concept of authorship as something of which "all" are potentially capable. This comment enacts a resistance to the modernist view that true authors belong to a natural elite. Woolf herself, it is true, praises an (imaginary) woman writer who is "no 'genius'" (138), but who succeeds in breaking with convention because "she wrote as a woman" (140). Yet while she denies her imagined writer genius, she endows her with rather remarkable qualities of mind, "natural advantages of a high order [. . .] a sensibility that was very wide, eager and free [and . . .] ranged, too, very subtly and curiously, among almost unknown or unrecorded things" (139). Delafield, on the other hand, describes the transformation into an author of a woman who is simply intelligent, witty, and determined.

Despite her self-consciousness about her authorial agency, the Provincial Lady does not, in the first volume of the *Diary*, make any overt reference to her own role as narrator. Not, that is, until the very last page, when she records an exchange between herself and her husband: "Robert says, Why don't I get into Bed? I say, Because I am writing my Diary. Robert replies [. . .] that In his opinion, That is Waste of Time" (121). The diary has long been considered an appropriate literary form for women because of its private nature and episodic narrative form (it can be written in moments of leisure between domestic tasks). But the opening of the first sequel volume, *The Provincial Lady Goes Further*, reveals that the heroine has published a book, and the reader may wonder whether this is *The Diary of a Provincial Lady* itself. As a document intended for public consumption, rather than a private record, the diary might now be thought a dangerously "unfeminine" undertaking. The Provincial Lady attempts to counter this by insisting on the modesty of her ambitions, opening *The Provincial Lady Goes Further* with the statement "Life takes on entirely new aspect, owing to astonishing and unprecedented success of minute and unpretentious literary effort, published last December, and—incredibly—written by myself" (PLF, 125). The word "unpretentious" is a key term in the definition of the English middlebrow, which is characterized by a resistance to pretension in all its forms. The narrator's astonishment at the success of her work is a disarming gesture, a disavowal of any aspiration to literariness, yet it also indicates her difficulty in imagining herself into the role of writer. Over the course of the sequels, however, she becomes more secure in her identity as author. In the first book, the narrator primarily figures as a wife and mother, only emerging as a (potential) author through occasional subtle features in her self-construction. In the later volumes, by contrast, she is treated as a professional writer by those she meets, and thus issues of authorship, celebrity, and their relation to gender come much more clearly into focus.

"Aunt Mary hopes my writing does not interfere with home life"

As a successful author, the Provincial Lady is rewarded by new social opportunities, increased self-esteem, and a larger income. But she has to contend with feelings of doubt concerning her talent, embarrassment about her inadequate literary knowledge, and guilt over her possible neglect of family responsibilities, as well as with the disapproval of those around her. She records one particularly hostile response: "Singular letter from entire stranger enquires whether I am aware that the doors of every decent home will henceforward be shut to me? Publications such as mine, he says, are harmful to art and morality alike" (PLF, 127). The letter-writer is, presumably, accusing the Provincial Lady of transgressing the bounds of acceptable feminine behavior by allowing her writing to enter the public domain, and also of compromising aesthetic standards in the interests of high sales. Closer to home, her integration in the village community is threatened by her new professional status, and reactions range from distrust to a jealousy which leads her neighbors to undervalue the work of authorship. She writes: "Note curious and rather disturbing tendency of everybody in the neighbourhood to suspect me of Putting Them into a Book"; recounting in the same entry that "Our Vicar's Wife [. . . says] that she has never had time to write a book herself, but has often thought that she would like to do so. Little things, she says—one here, another there—quaint sayings such as she hears every day of her life as she pops round the parish— *Cranford*, she adds in conclusion" (PLF, 126).[6] In constructing writing as a hobby rather than as legitimate employment, the Provincial Lady's neighbors imply that she is indulging herself at the expense of her conjugal and maternal responsibilities. Some of them make this explicit: "Aunt Mary hopes that my writing does not interfere with home life and its many duties" (PLF, 227). The Provincial Lady takes pains to demonstrate that the reverse is in fact true: "literary projects entirely swamped by hourly activities concerned with children, housekeeping, sewing, letter-writing [and] Women's Institute meetings" (PLF, 218).

Until she begins to amass serious profits from her best-selling books, Delafield's narrator is continually harassed by domestic crises and worries over money. She repeatedly pawns her jewelry and even has to defer paying for the milk from month to month. She is always active and frequently exhausted. This contrasts markedly with the comfortable life of Jan Struther's Mrs. Miniver: on one day, she receives in the post "a card for a dress-show; a shooting invitation for Clem; two dinner-parties; three sherry-parties; a highly aperitive notice of some chamber-music concerts; and a letter from Vin at school" (n.p.). After reading these: "She rearranged the fire a little, mostly for the pleasure of handling the fluted steel poker, and then sat down by it. Tea was already laid: there were honey sandwiches, brandy-snaps, and small ratafia biscuits; and there would, she knew, be crumpets." The excess apparent in these listed items of mail and food suggests a fantasized idyll: Mrs. Miniver is provided with cultural stimulation, glamorous social opportunities, abundant food, and efficient servants whose labor is obscured by passive constructions ("Tea was already laid"; "there would [. . .] be crumpets"). She takes up a domestic implement only for aesthetic reasons, and the absence of her children obviates the need for the work of mothering. Mrs. Miniver's easeful lifestyle removes any stimulus to be creative, whereas the Provincial Lady's creativity is at least partly born of financial necessity and concern for her children. At first, she seriously underestimates the exchange value of her writing: "Cheque arrives from publishers [. . .] Wildest hopes exceeded" (PLF, 127). But once the extent of her potential earnings becomes clear, her work need no longer be considered a frivolous distraction from her duty to husband and family.[7] It becomes instead part of those duties, enabling her to provide for her family even as it also allows her to escape them through prolonged visits to her London flat. At the same time, the work of writing becomes an addition to her existing burden of caring for her family.

Although the demands of writing and family life sometimes conflict for Delafield's protagonist, domesticity is also presented as something which can nourish creativity. Even during periods alone in London, details of household equipment, expenditure, and visitors still find their way into her journal entries, and when she is resident in the country, her harassed, continually interrupted existence provides her primary subject matter. Her episodic diary form with its abbreviated style actually fits Woolf's recommendation in *A Room of One's Own* that "women's books should be [. . .] framed so that they do not need long hours of steady and uninterrupted work. For interruptions there will always be" (117). Interruptions, indeed, are a recurrent theme of Delafield's narrative:

> Astounding and enchanting change in the weather, which becomes warm. I carry chair, writing-materials, rug, and cushion into the garden, but am called in to have a look at the Pantry Sink, please, as it seems to have blocked itself up. Attempted return to garden frustrated by arrival of note from the village concerning Garden Fête arrangements, which requires immediate answer, necessity for speaking to the butcher on the telephone, and sudden realisation that

Laundry List hasn't yet been made out, and the Van will be here at eleven. (DPL, 73–74)

Jane Dowson characterizes the tone of the diaries as "suspiciously stoical in their accounts of the trivial routines of women," adding that they "tread a fine line between light entertainment and satirical parody" ("Humming"). Similarly, Alison Light notes that "Delafield's browbeaten heroine is both an embodiment of, and a rebellion against prewar expectations for women of her class, groomed solely for marriage and motherhood" (117).[8] Certainly, the resigned, humorous tone of the diary entry just quoted does not quite conceal a degree of resentment, and the entry itself is apparently a means of relieving the writer's feelings. The protest against conventional gender roles emerges in a more direct form in serious novels such as *Consequences* and *Thank Heaven Fasting*, but the muted rebellion contained in the popular, comic Provincial Lady books reached a much larger audience. Contemporary reviewers did not, though, tend to note this aspect of the diaries. Most described them as witty, absurd, or diverting and referred to the warmth, humanity, and lovableness of the heroine. Among the many reviews and obituaries collected among the E. M. Delafield papers at the University of British Columbia, only one refers to her "deep interest in the social conditions of [women's] lives," and even this reviewer thought such feminist concerns were only visible in "her more serious novels," not in her best-known works.[9]

"CAN I POSSIBLY BE WORTH ALL THIS?"

The Provincial Lady in America, like its predecessor, opens with an expression of amazement at the narrator's own success:

> Incredulous astonishment on receiving [. . .] courteous and charming letter from publishers in America. They are glad to say that they feel able to meet me on every point concerning my forthcoming visit to the United States, and enclose contract for my approval and signature. [. . .] Read contract about fourteen times running [. . .] Can I possibly be worth all this? (263)

During her tour of the States, her attitude continually wavers between alarm at the "responsibility of proving [herself] worthy of all this attention" (299) and resentment over the lack of attention paid her in the UK—"realise estimation in which professional writers are held in America" (287); "have hazy idea of writing letter home to explain that I am evidently of much greater importance than any of us have ever realised" (300). The praise she receives from her overseas audience will clearly never be replicated in her home country, still less in the village where she is personally known. The very familiarity of the characters and the fictional world she created made her, in England, rather less exciting than a writer such as Anita Loos, whose reception in London attested to the exotic glamor with which the British public had invested her.[10] The reverse applied to Delafield; on the appearance of her fourth novel, *Consequences,* in 1919, the *New York Times Book Review* remarked, "Miss Delafield's three previous novels [. . .] have made her well known among lovers of English fiction and seekers of the unusual in this country."[11] This may partly explain Delafield's appeal to American audiences: she doubtless possessed for them a quirky charm which appeared distinctively English, and offered insight into a social class and way of life which did not exist in America.

The Provincial Lady's increased celebrity in the States actually reduces her autonomy. She is treated as the property of her publishers, and their representative, Pete, controls her movements: "Pete [. . .] unfolds terrific programme of activities he has planned for me in Boston. Assent to everything but add that the thing I want to do most of all is to visit the Alcott House at Concord, Mass. At this Pete looks astounded, and replies that this is, he supposes, merely a personal fancy, and so far as he knows no time for anything of that kind has been allowed in the schedule" (PLA, 329). Pete's astonishment derives partly from the Provincial Lady's unexpected self-assertion: her "personal" self is not supposed to intrude; her task is simply to promote book sales by performing the role of successful author and embodying the genteel, provincial Englishness of her novels. Also, Pete is surprised that she should be interested in an author such as Louisa May Alcott.

The next development overturns his judgment:

> Most extraordinary revolution in everybody's outlook—excepting my own—by communication from Mr. Alexander Woollcott. He has, it appears, read in a paper [. . .] that my whole object in coming to America was to visit the Alcott House, and of this he approves to such an extent that he is prepared to Mention It in a Radio Talk, if I will immediately inform him of my reactions to the expedition.

> Entire *volte-face* now takes place in attitude of Pete, Fanny and everybody else. If Alexander Woollcott thinks I ought to visit Alcott House, it apparently becomes essential that I should do so [. . .] Result of it all is that the members of the Alcott-Pratt family are approached, they respond with the greatest kindness, and offer to open the house especially for my benefit. (332)

The undeserved influence of the Algonquin Round Table critics (as satirized in *Gentlemen Prefer Blondes*) is here given a specifically gendered dimension—the eccentric decision of a male critic to favor two authors of popular domestic fiction (Alcott and the Provincial Lady) instantly confers on them a level of status and power they could not achieve on their own merits. The processes by which critical and media agents contribute to the production of literary value, and the arbitrary nature of such processes, are here deliberately exposed. The demand for what would now be called "sound bites" from celebrities is emphasized in Woollcott's request for immediate reactions, but his invitation of the Provincial Lady's opinions invests her with a degree of authority. As Joe Moran points out, "celebrity in the United States has been conferred on authors who have the potential to be commercially successful and penetrate into mainstream media, but are also perceived as in some sense culturally 'authoritative'" (6). This deference for the views of famous authors, even on subjects beyond their expertise, is also evident in an earlier scene in *The Provincial Lady in America*. Before the narrator has even disembarked at New York, she is approached by journalists "and asked if I will at once give my views on The United States, the American Woman and Modern American Novels. Young man says that he wishes to take my photograph, which makes me feel like a film star—appearance, unfortunately, does nothing to support this illusion" (286).

The Provincial Lady's preoccupation with her appearance and image is an important element of Delafield's analysis of the experience of celebrity. Conscious of the more unappealing stereotypes of authors, she takes endless trouble with her clothes, hair, and makeup, especially when attending a literary gathering. Like Gibbons's Flora Poste, she deliberately dresses conventionally; this is part of their assertion of a middlebrow identity, in contrast to the deliberate eccentricity of highbrows. In several of Delafield's other texts, this issue becomes more explicitly gendered, as she deplores the tendency to estimate attractiveness in women as inversely related to intelligence. The heroine of

Consequences is warned by her mother: "don't go and get a reputation for being *clever,* whatever you do. People do dislike that sort of thing so much in a girl" (129). *Consequences* is set at the end of the nineteenth century, a period when writing and intellectual pursuits were often perceived as the refuge of women who were not desirable to men, and it was feared that too much education compromised a woman's femininity and unfitted her for the roles of wife and mother. The unfavorable stereotyping of bluestockings, initiated in the eighteenth century, persisted through the Victorian period and, as one of Delafield's 1934 sketches for *Punch* suggests, well beyond it: "'Remember that woman in Singapore who'd written a book?' 'By Jove, yes! Plainest woman I ever saw in my life'" ("As Others Hear Us," 506). Publishing a book, even in the 1930s, implied a degree of self-assertion which many considered unfeminine, and Woolf remarks in *A Room of One's Own* that women writers "sought ineffectively to veil themselves by using the name of a man. Thus they did homage to the convention [. . .] that publicity in women is detestable" (76). Delafield may have protested about the continuing power of this convention in her writing, but her own practice "did homage" to it, since her pen name disguised her gender and marital status. Her identity was thereby symbolically fragmented into her three names: Edmée Elizabeth Monica de la Pasture, E. M. Delafield, and later Mrs. Paul Dashwood.

Was the use of a pen name due to a desire to veil herself? Quite possibly, given the preoccupation with personal reputation and the effects of fame discernible in the Provincial Lady's diaries. But an American reviewer of one of Delafield's early novels suggests a different reason:

> As the daughter of Lady Clifford, whose novels, published [. . .] while she was writing as Mrs. Henry de la Pasture, have been widely read in both England and the United States, an immediate interest in her books would have awaited her. But with characteristic English independence she chose to forgo all this possible prestige and to win whatever interest and acclaim might be her fortune solely upon her own merits.[12]

The pen name could, equally, indicate a rejection of the legacy of the mother, either in literary or personal terms. Elizabeth de la Pasture is said to have been unduly dominant and aggressive in the family home. Also, her books are very different from her daughter's, and for

Delafield to publish under her own name might have suggested a continuity of the sort to be found between George du Maurier's and his granddaughter Daphne du Maurier's novels.[13]

Delafield does not give her writer-heroine any name at all.[14] This might be read as a strategy, to construct her as a representative, ordinary "everywoman," and perhaps to indicate her tendency to self-effacement (as in the case of the nameless heroine of Daphne du Maurier's *Rebecca,* or the protagonist of *Mrs. Miniver,* whose Christian name is withheld until the very last word of the text). The Provincial Lady is, to a certain extent, a representative upper-middle-class wife, a social "type." But she is not so limited as the "types" Delafield delineated in her contributions to *Time and Tide* ("persons with Symptoms, mothers of children, owners of Pekinese dogs, promoters of Movements," et cetera[15]) or the ones Dorothy Parker sketched for American audiences in *Vanity Fair* (Debutantes, Dowagers, and so on). Her namelessness connects to Delafield's resistance to the idea of the writer as a solitary genius with a special vocation. Her view of writing as a profession, whose prerequisites are simply intelligence, commitment, and fresh ideas, and whose primary goals include economic profit, permits a conception of the author as everywoman. For the purely commercial writer, the author's signature is a brand name. For the highbrow, it supposedly designates a unique locus of genius, entirely separate from all other literary producers, though as Aaron Jaffe points out, this ideal conceals the operation of another kind of logic, since "certain modernists worked to create and expand a market for elite authorial signatures" (1).[16] The middlebrow author, once again, locates herself between these two poles.

There is a curious tension between the fact that the Provincial Lady has made a name for herself as an author and the fact that she doesn't have a name at all. At a literary party, she is given a "small label, bearing name by which I am—presumably—known to readers of *Time and Tide*" (PLF, 228). This line actually draws attention to the heroine's namelessness, as well as humorously playing on the affinity between the Provincial Lady and Delafield herself, a well-known contributor to *Time and Tide.* But Delafield's name was less widely recognized than that of the Provincial Lady. An anonymous reviewer remarked in 1930 that the Provincial Lady "has, through her diary, become the intimate friend of hundreds of people."[17] The value invested in Delafield herself as a public figure was different: her reputation was not founded solely on this popular series. Her status as a contributor to *Punch,* a director of *Time and Tide,* a regular broadcaster on BBC radio, and a respected feminist spokesperson[18] made her an eminent presence on the literary and social scene, whose name—though invented—carried a certain cultural authority for the middlebrow audience.

"MOST ALARMINGLY LITERARY"

Delafield's texts both exemplify and examine the middlebrow perspective. The Provincial Lady affirms her middlebrow outlook in numerous ways, notably through her skepticism toward both highbrow and lowbrow culture, her self-conscious modesty about her own intelligence and literary abilities, and her enthusiasm for the cultural institutions and books which formed the canons of middlebrow taste.

Most obviously, Delafield's narrator defines herself as middlebrow through her reading preferences—she finds modernist writing difficult and is not well acquainted with the classics of English poetry; she approves of accessible Victorian and twentieth-century fiction; and she dislikes sensationalism. Conversations with highbrows prove a trial: "Am asked what I think of *Harriet Hume* but am unable to say, as I have not read it. Have a depressed feeling that this is going to be another case of *Orlando,* about which was perfectly able to talk most intelligently until I read it, and found myself unfortunately unable to understand any of it" (DPL, 5). The disarming gesture of lamenting her own inadequacy as a reader only partly conceals an underlying attack on the obscurity of modernist texts. Delafield may engage with *A Room of One's Own,* but she rejects, through the Provincial Lady, Woolf's more formally experimental texts. Both *Orlando* (1928) and Rebecca West's *Harriet Hume* (1929) are fantasy narratives, but the Provincial Lady exhibits a strong preference for realist fiction. The writers she identifies as congenial include Vicki Baum, Dorothy Whipple, Hugh Walpole, Mrs. Belloc Lowndes, and L. A. G. Strong—a heterogeneous yet distinctly middlebrow selection. She records that a vigorously literary spinster demands of her: "What, for instance, have I read within the last two years. I reply weakly that I have read *Gentlemen Prefer Blondes,* which is the only thing I seem able to remember" (DPL, 100). In another doubled gesture, the narrator, in the very act of self-deprecation, actually affirms the value of her own aesthetic preferences and of the books she admires—*Gentlemen Prefer Blondes* is judged as memorable, as opposed to *Orlando,* which is impenetrable. Pierre Bourdieu illuminates this point: "Every critical affirmation contains, on the one hand, a recognition of the value of the work which occasions it, which is thus designated as a worthy object of legitimate discourse [. . .] and on the other hand an affirmation of its own legitimacy. All critics declare not only their judgement of the work but also their claim to the right to talk about it and judge it. In short, they take part in [. . .] the production of the value of the work of art" (*Field*, 36).

Further, in having her narrator repeatedly celebrate the very genre of middlebrow fiction to which her own work belongs, Delafield proclaims the legitimacy of her text. The Provincial Lady's reading choices clearly identify the literary heritage of Delafield's work in terms of nineteenth-century fiction (Dickens, Alcott, Charlotte Yonge, Susan Warner), English comic writing (Lewis Carroll, E. F. Benson), and published or fictional diaries (*Gentlemen Prefer Blondes, The Diary of a Nobody,* and the journals of Miss Weeton). Delafield thus invokes the authority of tradition to reinforce the status of her own book, but simultaneously challenges existing hierarchies of literature. She refuses to privilege modernist writing above domestic realist fiction, and the only book of Virginia Woolf's which the Provincial Lady claims to enjoy is *Flush,* the very one which was least admired by Woolf's more intellectual contemporaries.

Through her fictional diaries, Delafield negotiates between admiration for Woolf and dislike of the perceived obscurity of some of her texts. Delafield's attitude replicates the ambiguity of *Time and Tide*'s response to Woolf and Bloomsbury. The journal printed admiring reviews of Woolf's work and occasional contributions from her (see, for example, "The Sun and the Fish"), but also allowed space—particularly in the correspondence columns—to those who found high modernist writing impenetrable. In 1927, a series of cartoons satirized members of the Bloomsbury Group; in one, a picture entitled "Mrs. Woolf is Visited by some Uncommon Readers" represents the author encountering several burly, cheerful American men. The parodic caption by Sylvia Townsend Warner concludes:

> But it is impossible to fix the mind upon bananas, for in the harbour were streamers waving, steamers bathing, banded funnels with their sea-going tilt. Meanwhile the waxen fruit bought in the Caledonian Market remained perfectly immobile. And now, having passed the gloom and the felted silence of the archway at Euston, these young men were assuring her that they had read all her books and found them most congenial. (Warner)

If these are uncommon readers, the cartoon suggests, then the majority of people will find Woolf's work rather uncongenial, as the Provincial Lady does.

Time and Tide, like *Vanity Fair,* was broadly aligned with the literary middlebrow, but was also responsive to modernist art. A literary and political weekly founded in 1920, it not only featured contributions from writers such as Delafield, Winifred Holtby, Vera Brittain, and Naomi Mitchison, but also from modernist writers, including Wyndham Lewis, D. H. Lawrence, Edith Sitwell, David Garnett, and T. S. Eliot. The Provincial Lady finds the paper refreshing in its breadth of reference, but also reassuring in its accessibility. She dislikes journals produced by literary coteries: "Unknown benefactor sends me copy of new Literary Review, which seems to be full of personal remarks from well-known writers about other well-known writers. This perhaps more amusing to themselves than to the average reader. Moreover, competitions most alarmingly literary, and I return with immense relief to old friend *Time and Tide*" (DPL, 117).[19] *Time and Tide* and the Provincial Lady may both be middlebrow in their tastes, but the middlebrow was a capacious formation, and embraced a strikingly broad range of art and literature, and an equally various set of opinions on politics and culture.

As Nicola Humble argues, questions about women's reading became a major preoccupation in the period from the 1920s to the 1950s and can be discerned in the fiction of the period: "Middlebrow novels repeatedly portray scenes in which women discuss books, list their favourite authors, or imagine themselves into the plots of their favourite novels" (9). The Provincial Lady generally refers to books without giving the names of their authors, suggesting a direct address to a reader who shares her own reading experience and preference. She pronounces on literature confidently within the controlled space of the diary, where she addresses an implied reader who is perfectly congenial, but in public often appears ashamed of her tastes. On visiting Boston Common, she reflects: "Chief association with the Common is [Alcott's] *An Old-Fashioned Girl,* in which heroine goes tobogganing, but do not refer to this" (PLA, 330). A conversation with a very intellectual man leaves her once again embarrassed over a preference for children's books: "He personally finds that the Greeks provide him with escapist literature. Plato. Should not at all wish him to know that *The Fairchild Family* performs the same service for me—but remember with shame that E. M. Forster, in admirable wireless talk, has told us *not* to be ashamed of our taste in reading" (PLW, 412). Mary Martha Sherwood's *The History of the Fairchild Family; or, The Child's Manual* (1818) is a volume whose excessive and rigid didacticism, together with the horrid punishments meted out to the disobedient children, renders it unintentionally comic.[20] It is also, however, a lively, readable text, and Sherwood was a popular and prolific author. The Provincial Lady doubts that even Forster would approve her taste in this instance, and experiences a doubled sense of shame—both at her preference for an accessible commercial author and at her own embarrassment over it.

The embarrassment of the middlebrow reader within the novel parallels the potential embarrassment of the implied middlebrow reader *of* the novel, and the quoting of Forster's injunction is perhaps an attempt to counter this. Mary Grover argues that one of the characteristic features of the middlebrow novel is "the explicit dramatisation of the text's cultural status" and of the author's "cultural subordination." Delafield does this with a curious mixture of pride and humility: she records her protagonist's sense of inadequacy as a reader and a writer, but this is also a defensive maneuver. It indicates her awareness that she, like other middlebrow writers, risked being attacked by intellectuals for her supposed cultural aspirations. Such an attack is briefly suggested in the text when the narrator has trouble persuading a female academic to chair a debate: "Am informed by a side-wind that Distinguished Professor has said she Hates me" (PLF, 228). The Provincial Lady's consciousness of the antagonism between the intellectual elite and the producers of middlebrow culture is further indicated during her wartime diaries: her reaction to the news that the Ministry of Information has a scheme for making use of intellectuals is: "Should like to yell back in reply that I am not an Intellectual and don't wish to be thought one" (PLW, 477–478).

This disavowal, expressed by turns in apologetic and defiant tones, is given a more critical edge in the episodes satirizing the perceived pretentiousness of highbrow culture. Told she is to meet at a dinner the author of a novel named *Symphony in Three Sexes* (an amusing variation on the vaguely modernist-sounding *Symphony in Three Keys* written by Lewis in *The Constant Nymph*), the Provincial Lady requests his book at the library, "although doubtfully. Doubt more than justified by tone in which Mr. Jones replies that it is not in stock, and never has been" (DPL, 9). The book is clearly a form of highbrow sensationalism; at the dinner, the Provincial Lady is advised by her hostess to get the author "on to the subject of *perversion,* as he is always so amusing about it" (DPL, 11). Deliberate obscurity is likewise ridiculed when the Provincial Lady learns from an acquaintance that the novel just completed by a serious young author called J. L. is to be entitled *Poached Eggs to the Marble Arch*. She makes a misplaced effort to appear serious herself—"I bend my head appreciatively as if to say that's exactly the sort of name I should have *expected* from a really good modern novel"—but is disconcerted when her acquaintance "observes thoughtfully that he thinks it's an utterly vague and off-putting title. But, he adds candidly, he isn't absolutely sure he's got it right. It might be *Poached Eggs ON the Marble Arch* or even *Poached Eggs AT the Marble Arch*" (PLW, 499–500). The Provincial Lady's occasional, unsuccessful attempts to simulate an intellectual perspective are always productive of satiric humor. Although apparently at her own expense, it is ultimately directed at intellectuals themselves, as in this instance, in which her own behavior is far less ludicrous than J. L.'s title.

One of the sketches in Delafield's widely read *Punch* series, "As Others Hear Us," satirizes avant-garde pretension through a conversation about modern writing:

> "Pattern is what I'm getting at."
>> "I think that's so absolutely progressive and right."
>> "Oh, so do I. Nothing matters except pattern."
>> "Oh, and rhythm."
>> "Oh, yes, and rhythm. And of course utter starkness."
>> "Oh, one absolutely must be stark." ("When Bloomsbury Meets")

This conversation, like J. L.'s title, is virtually meaningless: the speakers simply parrot the stock phrases of aspiring Bloomsbury-ites. This piece recalls Stella Gibbons's satire of the conventionality of intellectual and bohemian conversation, as represented by Mr. Mybug. Both authors mock the social behavior of imitative would-be authors. *The Diary of a Provincial Lady* pokes fun at Bloomsbury in the person of a nasty young man "who Writes," named "Jahsper" (DPL, 104), and the description of him is, as Humble points out, one of the earliest middlebrow references to Bloomsbury (30). But although the Provincial Lady takes against Jahsper, she herself rents a flat in Doughty Street, which is in Bloomsbury, and attends numerous parties in that area. It is her firsthand knowledge of the London literary scene which authorizes her mockery of it. To quote Humble again: "Middlebrow fiction laid claim to the highbrow by assuming an easy familiarity with its key texts and attitudes, while simultaneously caricaturing intellectuals as self-indulgent and naïve" (29).

Delafield's sketch "When Bloomsbury Meets" also draws attention to would-be modernists' nervous contempt for popular culture and their attempts to distance themselves from it through overambitious experimentation:

> "My dear, that woman with the *emerald* nose got a fortune for just doing a rotten story for the films. I know it for an absolute fact."
>
> "How utterly bogus! I know for a *fact* she can't write. Who is she?"
>
> "Darling, I've not the faintest. Only I want to know exactly what you think of this new technique of mine because I believe it's going to revolutionize the whole art of fiction."

This language, though, is more reminiscent of the idiom of Evelyn Waugh's Bright Young Things than it is of Bloomsbury discourse. Delafield (like Stella Gibbons) targets, not so much the actual Bloomsbury Group, but its imitators, who include high-society would-be bohemians, and pseudointellectuals. But the fact that Bloomsbury style is susceptible to imitation is partly explained by its own complicity with commerce. Jane Garrity points to Bloomsbury's promotion of itself as "modernist spectacle" through British *Vogue* ("Selling," 29) and argues that "The Group authorized the magazine to circulate its fashionable lifestyle in the commercial marketplace" (30). Once Bloomsbury is considered as a reproducible, marketable style, its highbrow dedication to art for its own sake is compromised, and it thus comes into the purview of middlebrow parodists and satirists like Gibbons and Delafield.

The attitude of superiority is a primary target of middlebrow mockery of the highbrow. *Punch's* obituary of Delafield remarks on this aspect of her work, referring to "her power to detect and expose humbug self-importance, careerism and conceit."[21] The Provincial Lady, for example, subscribes to two book clubs and dislikes her neighbor Lady Boxe for being "always so tiresomely superior about Book of the Month, [. . .] taking up attitude that she does not require to be told what to read" (DPL, 6). To some extent, this comment identifies Delafield's own work with the middlebrow field of literature from which the book clubs generally selected, and indeed, *The Diary of a Provincial Lady* was the Book Society's Book of the Month for December 1930. Yet, while Delafield certainly does not ridicule book clubs in the way that Anita Loos does, nevertheless the Provincial Lady is gently mocked for her dependence on book clubs and her anxious efforts to read the books everyone else has read. The Provincial Lady's choice of *Time and Tide* as her preferred periodical functions in a similar way and also produces an interesting self-reflexivity, since the columns in which she refers to *Time and Tide* initially appeared in its pages.

"YOU WOULDN'T UNDERSTAND"

Just as Anita Loos was told by William Faulkner: "you have builded better than you knew" (32), so Delafield was believed not to have fully understood the achievement of her own text. She wrote in a 1937 essay: "Nothing was as thoroughly baffling as the remark made long afterwards, by a woman to whom I was trying to explain why the Diary was not really my best piece of work: 'Ah,' she said, with a pity-ing smile, 'I don't suppose you have the least idea of why it's good. You wouldn't understand'" ("The Diary," 126–127). Like many readers, the woman apparently considers Delafield to be simply voicing, rather than analyzing, the perspective of her heroine. She may also identify author and heroine so closely that she fails to recognize the Provincial Lady as a comic character, with exaggerated foibles. Like Faulkner in his letter to Loos, Delafield's interlocutor constructs a route of com-munication between a sophisticated text and a sophisticated reader which excludes the author.

Delafield's frustration at being known for just one book, and one she did not herself consider her best, was shared with Loos, Montgom-ery, Gibbons, and Kennedy, all of whom were known primarily for one surprise best seller. Several of them also feared that the writing of se-quels devalued their original achievement: Montgomery, for example, whilst proud of her early *Anne* novels, began to consider her own ar-tistic integrity to be compromised by the pressure on her to produce sequels and felt herself "dragged at Anne's chariot wheels" (*Green Ga-bles Letters,* 74). Sequels are almost universally viewed as a sign of capitulation to market pressures, as the critical contempt for the later volumes in many popular series amply demonstrates. Such books, it is assumed, are in some sense based on a "recipe," which associates them with commercial products. As Delafield noted: "The Provincial Lady brought me a lot of work, and would have brought me more still if I had been willing to use the same formula over and over again" ("The Diary," 131–132).

Much of the humor of the *Diary of a Provincial Lady* can be traced directly to Delafield's earlier comic writing in *Time and Tide*. "Conversation in the Country," for example, published in *Time and Tide* in 1928, features many of the staples of the Provincial Lady's diaries (committee meetings, rock-buns, Our Vicar's Wife, bulbs, servants, and weather), but remains an ephemeral sketch. The Provincial Lady columns, though composed of exactly the same material, are unified by the perspective of a recognizable character with an identifiable prose style. This made them more memorable and created a desire for further installments. Sequels are usually generated by audience demand to know more of the adventures of a particular character or family (Anne, Just William, the Whiteoaks of Jalna, Alcott's March sisters, or indeed the Provincial Lady), a requirement which apparently betokens a naïve reading strategy and aligns the literary series with soap opera. Yet the recurrence of a familiar character is not enough in itself to lower the literary status of a text. Serious modernist artists often resurrected characters in several novels (the most obvious example would be Joyce's Stephen Dedalus), and some modernist fictions even have sequels of a kind, in the form of the "roman-fleuve"—Dorothy Richardson's *Pilgrimage* (1913–1938) or Anaïs Nin's sets of linked novels, *Winter of Artifice* (1939) and *Cities of the Interior* (1959), for instance. But the continuation of these series is justified on the basis of the *author's* long-term exploration of individual consciousness, rather than the *reader's* demand for the "further adventures" of a character, and thus modernist authors seek to preserve themselves from the taint of the marketplace.

Delafield's and Loos's use of episodic fictional forms complicates the matter further. *Gentlemen Prefer Blondes* started out as a short story, and further episodes were generated and published in a magazine. Eventually it reached book length, and then it was continued by a sequel, *But Gentlemen Marry Brunettes*. Similarly, *The Diary of a Provincial Lady* began as a short-term magazine series, but proliferated to the length of four volumes. Delafield remarked: "there is no particular reason why a Diary should not go on just as long as its writer has strength to hold the pen" ("The Diary," 129). Both Delafield's and Loos's books were also self-replicating in that they inspired imitations. For example, a year after *Gentlemen Prefer Blondes* appeared, an author signing herself "Melita Noose" published *Blondes Prefer Gentlemen: A Satire*. The heroine of this rather accomplished parody, Lavender, is an English Lorelei from a country village, who plays up her old-fashioned innocence to good effect. In Delafield's case, the earliest imitations were those of the enthusiastic readers of *Time and Tide*. For the paper's weekly competition on 5 July 1930, Delafield set the task of writing a page from the diary of the Provincial Lady's husband, and the winning entries do recognizably evoke the character of Robert.[22] In the correspondence columns, one of the letters in praise of the Provincial Lady features a poem composed of references to the recurrent features of her diary: Lady B; the cat, Helen Wills; tea; weather; bulbs; et cetera (van Raalte). More intriguingly, Delafield's series of parodies, "The Sincerest Form . . . ," which worked from originals including G. B. Stern, Hugh Walpole, Beverley Nichols, E. Arnot Robertson, Clemence Dane, and Rosamond Lehmann, also included a parody of her own Provincial Lady series. This peculiar form of self-reflexivity exaggerates the foibles and stylistic mannerisms of the character so that she becomes ridiculous rather than lovable. Instead of trying to grow bulbs, the fake Provincial Lady attempts to cultivate mustard and cress on a flannel:

> *December 20:* Still no signs of mustard and cress. Pink flannel not improved by coal-dust, so remove it to middle of the tennis-court. Just as I have spread it out carefully, various distinguished visitors arrive and look astonished. Consult them about mustard and cress and write down their advice in little red notebook.
> *December 21:* Cook gives notice, and mustard and cress still invisible.
> *December 22:* House parlourmaid gives notice, but mustard and cress is sprouting. ("The Sincerest Form")

In 1961, Delafield's daughter, R. M. Dashwood, published a book called *Provincial Daughter,* whose title deliberately signals its literary descent, and whose style is closely imitative of the Provincial Lady's idiom. Only the altered details of domestic life (the absence of servants, the new household technologies, the styles of food and clothing) mark Dashwood's book as a product of a later era than her mother's. As with many highly successful books, the perceived freshness and novelty of the original text were in fact the reason for the sequels, parodies, and imitations which consolidated the status of *The Diary of a Provincial Lady* as a commodity. Yet, ironically, the distinctiveness of Delafield's style was derived from her own consummate skills as an imitator.

Maurice McCullen describes *The Diary of a Provincial Lady* as "the evolutionary culmination of formal experimentation" (68). Although he does not explain this further, it may indeed be possible to read Delafield's fictional diaries as formally experimental, though to a lesser extent than, say, Anita Loos's. Delafield's particular innovations relate to the comic, colloquial idiom developed through her grammatical abbreviations and eccentric use of capital letters, lists, and dashes; as well as her techniques for representing general conversation without attributing particular comments:

> We all say *(a)* that we have read *The Good Companions, (b)* that it is a very *long* book, *(c)* that it was chosen by the Book of the Month Club in America and must be having immense sales, and *(d)* that American sales are What Really Count. We then turn to *High Wind in Jamaica* and say *(a)* that it is quite a short book *(b)* that we hated—or, alternatively, adored—it *(c)* that it Really Is exactly *Like* Children. A small minority here surges into being, and maintains No, they Cannot Believe that any children in the World wouldn't ever have *noticed* that John wasn't there any more. [. . .] I talk to pale young man with horn-rimmed glasses [. . .] about Jamaica, where neither of us has ever been. (DPL, 10–11)

This rendering of conventional social language is made humorous not only by its predictability, but also by the inauthenticity and contradictory nature of the opinions expressed. When the Provincial Lady attributes speech to specific people, it still frequently evokes a stereotype: "But, says Emma, [. . .] Will I come with her to really delightful evening party in Bloomsbury, where every single Worth While Person in London is to be assembled?" (PLF, 221). In this way, the cliques and social types of the novel are defined discursively, through the multiple voices embedded into the narrative.

There is, though, little obvious affinity between Delafield's form of experimentation and that of high modernist writing. Struther's *Mrs. Miniver,* by contrast, while not stylistically experimental, occasionally participates in the modernist project of deconstructing the boundaries between self and world. On the first day of spring, Mrs. Miniver

> felt as though she and the outside world could mingle and interpenetrate; as though she was not entirely contained in her own body but was part also of every other person in the street; and, for that matter, of the thrush singing on a tree in Eaton Square, the roan dray-horse straining to take up the load at Grosvenor Place, the cat stepping delicately across Buckingham Palace Road. (n.p.)

This clearly recalls Clarissa Dalloway's sense "that somehow in the streets of London, on the ebb and flow of things, here, there, she survived, Peter survived, lived in each other, she being part, she was positive, of the trees at home; of the house there, ugly, rambling all to bits and pieces as it was; part of people she had never met" (Woolf, *Mrs. Dalloway*, 10). Yet in the text as a whole, the boundaries of Mrs. Miniver's self remain fairly well-defined, and the narrative stays centered in her consciousness; whereas Woolf moves between the minds of her several characters, enacting Clarissa's theory of the interconnectedness of people. Struther's experimentation with the representation of consciousness is limited in comparison with that of canonized modernists, yet her indebtedness to Woolf is evident. Initially signaled by her choice of title, it is reinforced in the very first line of the novel: "It was lovely, thought Mrs. Miniver, nodding good-bye to the flower-woman and carrying her big sheaf of chrysanthemums down the street with a kind of ceremonious joy, as though it were a cornucopia" (n.p.). *Mrs. Dalloway*, of course, also opens in the middle of a scene, and with a reference to the purchase of flowers. Mrs. Miniver, like her predecessor, repeatedly overlays her present experience with sudden flashes of memory, and yet Struther's evocation of the period of her heroine's childhood is entirely nostalgic and has none of the complexity of Woolf's exploration of prewar England, and of the nature of memory. Mrs. Miniver's cozy complacency and her entire acceptance of conventional feminine roles distance her greatly both from the unsettled Clarissa and the modestly ambitious, occasionally resentful Provincial Lady.

Delafield's talent was amply recognized during her lifetime. Her early novel *Tension* (1920) was considered for the Femina Vie Heureuse Prize, but when her 1937 book *Nothing Is Safe* was suggested for consideration, members of the committee dismissed it on the basis that, as Kate O'Brien commented: "she has had far too much recognition to be eligible." The prize was intended to reward writers whose work had received insufficient attention.[23] Yet in the same year, Delafield noted in an account of the genesis of the Provincial Lady that the number of letters she received from readers, together with the many offers of work from editors, "served to give one some idea of what the post-bag of a real celebrity must be like" ("The Diary," 132). This odd construction, using "one" as if to distance and generalize her experience, suggests that even in 1937 she was not quite able to identify herself as a "real celebrity."

Four years after Delafield's death, an omnibus edition of the Provincial Lady books was issued. Many of the reviews valued the diaries for their insight into "a forgotten way of life, [. . .] effectively killed by the war."[24] The more admiring among the reviews began a process of attempted canonization. Viscountess Rhondda wrote in *Time and Tide* that all Delafield's work was topical, adding: "But first class topical work is seldom ephemeral." She considered the Provincial Lady's diaries "vividly alive," and predicted: "E. M. Delafield has written [. . .] greater books than this. She has written none more likely to endure" ("E. M. Delafield"). The reviewer for *The Spectator* wrote: "The late Miss E. M. Delafield's *Provincial Lady* has entertained many thousands of readers; but she has sometimes been belittled and dismissed as a stock figure of fun. It cannot be too strongly emphasised that enormous skill, subtlety and power of selection have gone to create this seemingly mild and commonplace character." But, like Viscountess Rhondda, the reviewer also argues for the recuperation of Delafield's other work, judged as superior:

> it is not, I think, as the creator of the Provincial Lady that E. M. Delafield should be remembered. Some of her best books, now out of print [. . .] are: *The Chip and the Block, Consequences, Jill,* and *A Reversion to Type.* These novels are remarkable for their ingrained but reasonable pessimism, pin-point observation and startling bursts of sardonic humour; it is high time they were reprinted.[25]

Another review referred to Kate O'Brien's preface to the omnibus volume as "a first attempt to assess E. M. Delafield's place in literature, and assuredly it is a high place."[26]

The optimism of these reviewers, however, proved rather unfounded; in the postwar decades Delafield's reputation rapidly waned, and critics forgot her, at least until J. B. Priestley's 1976 book *English Humour*[27] devoted five pages (largely consisting of lengthy quotations) to Delafield. His chapter on feminine humor covers only four authors in total, the others being Austen, Gaskell, and Nancy Mitford, so that the inclusion of Delafield is an effective form of consecration. Although Delafield has, in recent decades, attracted only minimal critical attention, the *Diary* continues to be read, republished, and serialized on the radio.[28] A new edition of the first volume appeared in the Prion humor series in 2000, with an introduction by Jilly Cooper. Cooper's lack of cultural authority must reduce the impact of her designation of

Delafield as a "genius," but the precise nature of her commendation—"here is a very subtle and deliberate talent at work, naturally satirical, with a marvellous ear for dialogue and an unerringly accurate social sense" (viii)—does capture the reasons for Delafield's continuing appeal. In the same year that Prion's *Diary of a Provincial Lady* appeared, Persephone Books, a publisher committed to publishing neglected novels from the earlier part of the twentieth century, brought out an edition of *Consequences.* The rest of her work, however, is out of print.

Maurice McCullen, author of the only book-length critical study of Delafield's work, describes her as "one of England's finest, most famous journalists" (41), and the *Diary* as "more than a best-seller [. . .] a forgotten classic" (x–xi). McCullen, whose book is designed to rehabilitate his subject and give full appreciation to her gifts for irony, humor, and characterization, rather undermines his project with his final sentence: "E. M. Delafield, distinguished woman of letters, deserves a place, however small, in the Great Tradition" (129). The attempt to insert the writers considered in the present study into a conventional, Leavisite literary tradition is doomed to failure, as is evident in the attitude of critics such as McCullen, who cannot help applying the adjective "small" even as he extols the merits of his chosen author. The best-selling, celebrity women writers of the early twentieth century refuse to be confined by the parameters of traditional criticism and canon-construction, and if their work is measured against dominant literary models, it will always appear to fall short. Their varied literary projects expand beyond conventional definitions of the novel, and they draw on, and respond to, a whole range of high-culture and popular literary models. It is, therefore, productive to read these authors in relation to their more consecrated peers and forebears, but it is also essential to read them on their own terms, and in the context of the particular conditions under which they wrote. As Woolf put it, "delightful as the pastime of measuring may be, it is the most futile of all occupations, and to submit to the decrees of the measurers the most servile of attitudes" (*Room*, 160).

CONCLUSION

In 2002 and 2004, the BBC series *Before the Booker* asked which novels would have won the Booker prize if it had existed before 1969. Each program focused on one particular year, ranging from 1818 to 1966, identifying four contenders for each supposed prize. American authors were permitted, although they would not have been eligible for the real Booker prize. The books selected for 1925 were Kafka's *The Trial*, Woolf's *Mrs. Dalloway*, Fitzgerald's *The Great Gatsby*, and Loos's *Gentlemen Prefer Blondes*. For 1932, they were Huxley's *Brave New World*, Waugh's *Black Mischief*, Faulkner's *Light in August*, and Gibbons's *Cold Comfort Farm*. In each case, three "classics" are pitted against one female-authored best seller occupying a marginal position in the canon. The classics, and the male authors, were victorious: the winners were *The Great Gatsby* and *Light in August*. Nevertheless, the selection of *Gentlemen Prefer Blondes* and *Cold Comfort Farm* for the contest suggests that their significance to early-twentieth-century literature and their continuing interest for contemporary readers are finally beginning to be acknowledged.

Raymond Williams describes *Cold Comfort Farm* as an "odd work" (253), and Susan J. Leonardi applies the same word to Kennedy's *The Constant Nymph*, noting: "Genius in women this odd text will not allow" (153). The books analyzed in this study are frequently considered as odd, because they disrupt the usual categories of interwar literary history. Reasons for this include the generic instability of the novels, their achievement of both critical acclaim and commercial success, and their unusual cross-audience appeal (variously, to intellectuals and mass readerships; men and women; children and adults). These factors are compounded by their uneasy relationship with the (male) literary establishment and their complex attitudes to modernist and experimental art. Also, the largely humorous, nonpolitical content and broadly realist style of these authors' work are discontinuous with the literary trends of an era remembered primarily in terms of the later phases of high modernism together with the politically engaged literature of the Thirties. It seems that literary-historical accounts of the interwar years have largely left these authors out because they do not fit with the broad paradigms used by critics.

Assumptions about gender, popularity, and literary value are also part of the explanation for the marginalization of all the writers considered in this book. The separation between high and popular culture that became entrenched during the heyday of literary modernism continues to inform our judgments about the literature of the 1920s and 1930s, as does the association of the popular and middlebrow with the feminine. This study has sought to detach the middlebrow from its pejorative associations, redefining it as a productive and deliberately chosen standpoint, an intermediate area of cultural production with significant relationships to both high and popular culture. What is needed is a concept of the middlebrow which allows for the slipperiness, complexity, and multiple satiric targets of texts such as *The Diary of a Provincial Lady* or *The Constant Nymph*, or journals such as *Time and Tide* or *Vanity Fair*, which dramatize their own cultural status by reflecting on and satirizing not only highbrow pretension and lowbrow entertainment but also the more limiting formations of middlebrow culture itself. Broadly speaking, the authors I chose, and the journals they published in, found the middlebrow an effective position from which to negotiate their relationship to contemporary culture, both elite and popular. At the same time, middlebrow texts seek in various ways to avoid classification in terms of cultural hierarchy, and in so doing, challenge the separation between high-, middle-, and low-brow which remains entrenched in critical discourse.

While the books considered here are accessible, comic, and often lighthearted, they nevertheless make significant demands on readers. Narrators are untrustworthy; perspectives shift; multiple parodic styles combine and clash; literary and cultural allusions abound and are sometimes rather specialized; the targets of satire are difficult to identify; and the meanings of terms such as "civilized," "vulgar," "refined," and "educational" are systematically destabilized. On the one hand, the texts tend to offer readers positions of superiority, flatteringly constructing them as intelligent, metropolitan, culturally literate, able to discriminate, as Gibbons puts it, between "literature" and "sheer flapdoodle" (*Cold Comfort,* 7), or in Parker's terms, between "a Matisse painting and a Spanish omelette" (Fish, 41). On the other, the reader often finds herself denied a secure location from which to evaluate ideas and characters, uncertain whether her judgments and tastes are being endorsed or mocked by the text.

Much of the complexity of these texts is a result of their preoccupation with style, including styles of writing, speech, clothing, and social performance. This attention to style is connected in various ways with the phenomenon of literary celebrity. One of the primary sources of humor in *Anne of Green Gables,* for example, is the incongruousness, in prosaic Avonlea, of Anne's flowery and allusive way of expressing herself, yet Anne's construction of Avonlea as pastoral idyll determined the nostalgic, Romantic meanings which were invested in Montgomery's own celebrity image. Delafield's Provincial Lady and Loos's blonde adventurer Lorelei Lee each exist entirely through the distinctive idioms of their diaries, and both styles were frequently imitated. Much of the comedy of both novels is at the expense of the protagonists; nevertheless, the authors became so closely identified with their heroines that they were reinvented in their images through the media. Delafield and Loos were expected to perform the fictional roles they had created, and to some extent, they complied.

In her autobiographies, Loos at times plays on the widely circulated image of herself as a youthful, frivolous good-time girl in order to disarm her readers and claim their indulgence. But in the same texts, she constructed herself as widely read, highly intelligent, and contemptuous of popular culture and particularly of Hollywood, where she had launched her career. Tensions such as these can frequently be discerned in women writers' negotiations with celebrity. Richard Dyer identifies the inherent contradictions within the "star image," which, he argues, is constituted by "the finite multiplicity of meanings and affects they embody and the attempt so to structure them that some meanings and affects are foregrounded and others are masked" (3). The conflicts between these different meanings threaten the image with fragmentation (72). At the same time, it is possible to make capital from the contradictions, as Loos herself did by exploiting the disjunction between her childlike appearance on the one hand and her intellectual abilities and success in the literary marketplace on the other. Similarly,

Dorothy Parker played off her reputed bitchiness against her rhetorical embracing of sentimentalism.

Mae West, the most effective self-publicist among the women compared in this study, was also the one most concerned to mystify her private life. Curiosity about her was intensified by her refusal to satisfy enquiries and by her unreliable and contradictory statements in interviews and autobiographical texts. Toward the end of her life, in the late 1970s, West was asked by the writer Charlotte Chandler: "Do you find Hollywood greatly changed now?" West replied: "The star system's gone. I was a real star. The star is someone who has a love affair with her audience. They want to know everything about you, but they can't because you have mystery and romance" (65–66). It is the appearance of romance and mystery which allows multiple meanings to be invested in the celebrity image. As Richard Schickel puts it, celebrity is "the principal source of motive power in putting across ideas of every kind—social, political, aesthetic, moral," and celebrities themselves are not just used "for something as simple as advertising a product. They are turned into representations for much more inchoate longings" (x–xi). West's image was, in fact, literally used to advertise products (such as shoes and perfume), but she has also been identified as a focus for presumably conflicting fantasies relating to gay camp, heterosexual promiscuity, interracial sex, urban lowlife sensation, female power, and excessive wealth. L. M. Montgomery, whose public image contrasts with West's in every possible way, nevertheless illustrates the same point. Her fame led to her appropriation into a remarkably diverse range of cultural narratives concerned with wholesomeness, a nostalgia for the pastoral, cultural nationalism, the Protestant work ethic, literary idealism, and Maritime tourism.

In previous studies of celebrity, female authors have been largely ignored, but gender is a crucial factor in celebrity culture, and authors such as those considered here are highly significant in the history of fame. Their careers break with traditional models of female authorship and initiate new ways of understanding women in relation to literary culture and the public sphere. Important differences are revealed by the comparisons between North American and British writers. Broadly speaking, Mae West, Anita Loos, and Dorothy Parker created themselves as celebrities fairly deliberately and strategically, even though they negotiated various anxieties related to gender and publicity along the way. Stella Gibbons, E. M. Delafield, and Margaret Kennedy, by contrast, constructed themselves largely against, or in defiance of, their fame; privacy, modesty, and commitment to the alternative female roles of wife and mother are fundamental to their personal narratives. L. M. Montgomery comes somewhere in between—she adopted some of the strategies of fame which her American peers used to advance their careers, but she was also highly committed to private life and domestic duty. Her journals inscribe this tension, and were themselves crucial to her self-construction as celebrity and her attempt to exert control over her literary legacy.

In journals and autobiographies, writers such as Montgomery, Loos, and West censored their own lives, suppressing some aspects and foregrounding others in order to deflect criticism and disapproval, and inscribe their celebrity images for posterity in particular ways. This kind of self-censorship can be connected to the more public forms of moral policing prevalent in the interwar decades. Michael North points out that "sharing the threat of censorship brought literary experiment and popular culture together" (150). Certainly, censorship threatened writers such as Joyce, Lawrence, and e. e. cummings as much as it did Hollywood producers. High-profile censorship cases were less frequently focused on works which we might classify as middlebrow, and yet the writers studied in this book were all menaced by moral disapproval and attempts at suppression. Mae West, due to her association with the stage and with Hollywood, is a special case, and her performances and writing were continually subject to state censorship and moral condemnation. But the other writers, too, were sometimes seen as dangerous. *Cold Comfort Farm* was banned by the Irish Free State for endorsing the use of contraception, while *The Constant Nymph* shocked readers (including some of Kennedy's relatives) because of its representation of teenage sexuality. *Gentlemen Prefer Blondes* criticizes censorship, yet ironically, Anita Loos's husband and male mentors considered that the suggestiveness of the story could damage her reputation, and felt that she should not publish it. More than one editor saw Dorothy Parker's outspokenness and uninhibited style as a threat to the reputations of their magazines. Her risqué lingerie captions were suppressed, while her outspoken theater reviews cost her her job at *Vanity Fair*. Even E. M. Delafield, whose work seems fairly harmless by today's standards, received hostile correspondence from readers who considered her work immoral because of its feminist perspective, an experience she projected onto her fictional author, the Provincial Lady.

The work of these authors, of course, is no longer censored. Yet it is suppressed in a different way, by paradigms of literary history and criticism which allow it no place. The authors considered in this study demand attention in the context of contemporary reassessments of modernism and modernity. Among them are some of the iconic figures of the twentieth century; between them they produced some of the most discussed books of the interwar years. Their careers and their texts offer many and various insights into the cultural history of the period, and considering these authors alongside the canonized writers of literary modernism significantly modifies our understanding of literary culture, especially in terms of the construction of hierarchies of value and the making of literary stars.

Notes

Introduction

1. Glass offers a similar argument in relation to high modernist writing, noting that "Personality continued to function as a factor in the literary field, even if one of the interpretative tenets of that field was to bracket it from the successful work of art. [. . .] Much as modernist artists were interested in appearing disinterested, their personality tended to inhere in their ability to escape personality through rendering it as style" (6).

2. Huyssen, treating everything which is not high culture as mass culture, points to "the notion which gained ground during the nineteenth century that mass culture is somehow associated with woman, while real, authentic culture remains the prerogative of men" (47) and argues that "the universalizing ascription of femininity to mass culture always depended on the very real exclusion of women from high culture and its institutions" (62). His analysis has been influential, though aspects have been challenged by feminist critics. For example, Garrity argues that he "neglects to take into account the ambivalent position of the woman writer for whom the lure of mass culture was arguably a more complex, if not strictly enabling, historical development," because of the increasing female audience for mass cultural products, and the opportunities for women to enter the literary marketplace as writers ("Selling," 31).

3. Humble and Light, among others, read early-twentieth-century women's fiction primarily in terms of the domestic and the personal. Light explores an "intimate and everyday species of conservatism which caught the public imagination between the wars" and which led, in fiction, to the development of "an idiom more about self-effacement and retreat than bombast and expansion" (11). She does rightly argue that her project of "making a space for subjectivity [. . .] must call in question what is seen as history," and therefore "attacks that opposition of the private and the public which structures and determines [. . .] categories of knowledge" (4). Her focus, nevertheless, remains on the literature of

private emotion, whereas other recent books on interwar and wartime writing counter this, concentrating on authors who are opposed to the privileging of private consciousness over the social and public. See, for example, Lassner, *British Women Writers;* Maslen.

4. See Deen; Humble; Light; and the essays in Botshon and Goldsmith; Earnshaw; Grover and Hopkins. Bluemel makes an important contribution to the study of the nonmodernist literature of the period, although she does not mention the term "middlebrow" or examine its relationship to her proposed new category of "intermodern."

5. Harold Ross, prospectus for *The New Yorker,* issued in 1924. Cited in Burstein, 239.

6. Mencken's essay "The Sahara of the Bozart" was first published in 1920. Loos refers to it in "The Biography of a Book" (xl).

7. To cite just three examples, Ardis situates canonical literary modernism in relation to other cultural forces (including middlebrow art and British feminism and socialism); and Ayers also considers high modernist alongside nonmodernist and popular texts, focusing on their engagement with a shared context of social, political, and cultural issues. Bluemel has coined the term "intermodernism" to describe writers who "do not fit into the Oxbridge networks or values that shaped the dominant English literary culture of their time because they have the 'wrong' sex, class, or colonial status" and "remain on the margins of celebrated literary groups." She adds: "When intermodernists experiment with style or form, [. . .] their narratives are still within a recognizably realist tradition" (5). She identifies George Orwell, Inez Holden, Stevie Smith, and others as examples. Important feminist scholarship has also expanded conventional understandings of modernism (see especially Scott, *Refiguring* and *The Gender of Modernism*).

8. Huyssen and other scholars refer back to Fredric Jameson's work, especially his 1979 essay "Reification and Utopia in Mass Culture," which points to the dialectical interdependence of modernism and mass culture, and of course to the earlier research of Adorno and the Frankfurt school.

9. See especially: Rainey; Wicke; and also two collections, one edited by Willison, Gould, and Chernaik; the other by Dettmar and Watt. A different kind of challenge is offered by Jaffe, who argues that modernism should be considered a form of cultural production, and that it therefore participates in the mass phenomenon of celebrity (88–90).

10. See, for example, Jaffe 89. Huyssen himself notes such borrowings, only to dismiss them: "From Courbet's appropriation of popular iconography to the collages of cubism, [. . .] from Madison Avenue's conscious exploitation of modernist pictorial strategies to postmodernism's uninhibited learning from Las Vegas, there has been a plethora of strategic moves tending to destabilize the high/low opposition from within. Ultimately, however, these attempts have never had lasting effects" (16).

11. John Carey also constructs modernism in this way, but North is explicitly responding to Huyssen. Carey does write about clerks and suburbs, but identifies them with the modernist's concept of "the mass." He makes no distinction between middlebrow and mass culture, and rarely uses the word "middlebrow."

12. There are, of course, books on West which analyze her stardom, but these pay scant attention to her role as author. Also, critics have begun to discuss Montgomery and Parker in terms of their celebrity status (see Helal; Miller; York), indicating that interest in female literary stars is awakening. As for the other authors, I am, as far as I am aware, the first to read them in relation to celebrity and publicity.

13. As an example, in the special issue of *M/C Journal: A Journal of Media and Culture* on fame (November 2004), just one of the sixteen articles focuses on a literary topic (Harry Potter).

14. See in particular: Austin and Barker; Boorstin; Dyer; Gamson; Marshall; Schickel; Turner; Rojek. Also very important, as a foundation for many later analyses of personality as performative, is Susman. I have found all these books most useful, but have not drawn directly on all of them in my discussion, only those which are particularly relevant. Celebrity is only one of the aspects of women and literary culture discussed in the book, and so I have not had space to engage in detail with more sociologically oriented work on fame, or with material which relates only to contemporary culture.

15. Peaches Browning was an American actress. In 1925, at age fifteen, she met a fifty-one-year-old property tycoon who had advertised that he wanted to adopt teenage girls. He then divorced his wife to marry Peaches. She failed to obtain a divorce the following year, and when he died in 1934, she inherited his estate. Wallis Simpson, of course, was the twice-married American woman for whom Edward VIII abdicated the British throne.

16. Fine counts 138 American writers who, having already established at least the beginnings of a literary career in New York, traveled to Hollywood between 1927 and 1938 (12).

17. Robert Sherwood wrote: "While the movies have developed several great directors, many fine actors, and two or three first-rate financiers [. . .] they have, in their thirty-year existence, developed only one writer who is worthy of mention; that lone exception is the gifted Miss Anita Loos" (432).

18. However, when Woolf became a best-selling author, she did appear on one cover of *Time,* but this was not until 1937. On the way Bloomsbury was promoted, see Garrity, "Selling."

19. See Gerson, "Canadian Women Writers"; Hammill, *Literary Culture,* 48–51, 107–111.

20. All these institutions and initiatives are discussed in detail in Rubin; the book club is analyzed by Radway.

21. Selling ex-library books at reduced prices controversially violated the Net Book Agreement and led to the Times Book Club war of 1906.

22. An encyclopedia of British women's writing in the first half of the twentieth century, which I recently coedited, included individual entries for 187 writers. See Hammill, Miskimmin, and Sponenberg.

23. Examples include Marjorie Hillis's *Live Alone and Like It,* a best seller from 1936, and Rose Henniker Heaton's *The Perfect Hostess* (1931), both reprinted in 2005, by Virago and Conran Octopus, respectively.

24. West, *Mae West on Sex, Health and ESP* (18). Parker's reply was made to *The New Yorker,* and is recorded by Silverstein (67) in his compendium of her witticisms.

1

1. Among the best examples are her poems "The Far-Sighted Muse" (1922) and "Figures in Popular Literature" (1922). Sam Goldwyn was remembered to have said to Parker: "You're a great writer [. . .] but you haven't got a great audience and you know why? Because you don't want to give people what they want. [. . .] there's no money in wisecracks. People want a happy ending" (Kanin, 284).

2. The title was likely inspired by a 1915 Broadway play, *Our Mrs. McChesney,* based on stories by Edna Ferber.

3. Entries in the *OED* for which Parker's usage is given as the earliest include "bobbed hair," "sex appeal," and "what the hell" (Silverstein, 57).

4. This game was, famously, played at the Algonquin (see Silverstein, 63).

5. In comparison with writers more firmly associated with modernism, Parker has received very limited critical attention. But among the authors considered in this study, Parker and Montgomery have attracted the largest amount of scholarly discussion. The articles on Parker mentioned in this paragraph are the most relevant to my project; several more have recently appeared, and others date back to the 1970s and 1980s. Three books on her work have been published (Kinney; Melzer; Pettit, *A Gendered Collision*), and she is also discussed in a number of books with a wider remit.

6. "Crossing many genres, and widely diffused throughout public speech about sex and gender, Modern Love [. . .] focus[ed] on the social identities of its lovers to the virtual exclusion of any notion of private self [. . .]. Foundational to the ideology of Modern Love was the assumption that gender relations were permanently and intrinsically flawed. [. . .] Modern Love rendered a vision of heterosexuality toward which one could only assume a stance of cynical detachment" (Miller, 764).

7. A small number of pieces signed Dorothy Rothschild or Dorothy Rothschild (Parker) appeared in *Vogue,* among them a humorous piece on knitting (Parker, "Each Thought") and a poem (Parker, "The Lady"). They do not fit with the general tone of the magazine.

8. *Vogue* 48.7 (1 October 1916): 101. All references are to American *Vogue.*

9. *Vogue* 47.10 (15 May 1916): 85.

10. *Vogue* 50.2 (15 July 1917): 66.

11. *Vogue* 47.11 (1 June 1916): 44.

12. *Vogue* 47.10 (15 May 1916): 49.

13. *Vogue* 47.11 (1 June 1916): 82.

14. *Vogue* 47.10 (15 May 1916): 79.

15. Two earlier humorous weeklies had borne the title *Vanity Fair,* one in New York (1860–1863) and one in London, from 1868. This last eventually merged with *Dress* magazine to form Nast's *Vanity Fair,* which—though influential—was never commercially successful and became a casualty of the Depression. In 1983, the magazine was relaunched.

16. *Vanity Fair* 5.5 (January 1916): 11.

17. An advert stated: "In London alone there are seventeen papers like the 'Sketch' and the 'Tatler.' In America there is not one. [. . .] It is along the lines of

these English publications that we have planned 'Dress and Vanity Fair.'" Advert in *Vogue* 42.7 (1 October 1913): 16.

18. *Vogue* 47.10 (15 May 1916): 33. It was not until February 1938 that it devoted an issue to American fashion. It should be noted, though, that American *Vogue* was the original magazine, and the European editions came later.

19. *Vogue* 42.7 (1 October 1913): 16.

20. Silverstein notes that almost all of those who comprised "the nucleus of the Round Table [. . .] were from somewhere else," but were "desperately anxious to be taken for Manhattan sophisticates" (22).

21. "We Nominate for the Hall of Fame," *Vanity Fair* 12.1 (March 1919): 44. Nominees from the 1920s included Douglas Fairbanks, Virginia Woolf, Havelock Ellis, Marcel Proust, Pablo Picasso, Marie Laurencin, and Serge Diaghileff.

22. For example, Parker's 1926 story for *The New Yorker*, "Oh! He's Charming," satirizes a conceited, rude author, but the adoring, yet self-centered, fan who pesters him at a party is yet more tiresome than he is.

23. The book predates Emily Post's *Etiquette* by two years, but by 1920 there was already an extensive literature of etiquette and conduct.

24. The captions are not individually attributed to Parker, Crowninshield, or Chappell. These, though, are probably Parker's, as they are similar to some of her credited captions to Fish drawings in *Vanity Fair*.

25. Silverstein speculates that this is a play on "Hell on Wheels" (60).

26. Advert in *Vogue* (15 May 1913): 133. *Vogue* did not display volume and issue numbers until June 1916.

27. Loos compared *Smart Set* and *Vanity Fair*: "Crownie's magazine, together with *Smart Set,* had an enormously civilizing effect on the United States; but while Mencken's policy was to boot our native land into an awareness of culture, Crownie's was to lead us there with a gentle, properly gloved hand" (*Girl*, 145).

28. For example, in 1930 she told reporters that she was not a wit but "only a hardworking woman, who writes for a living and hates writing." Reported in the *New York Telegram* (1 February 1930), quoted in Meade, 209. In a 1956 interview, she said she had never managed to be a wit: "There's a hell of a distance between wisecracking and wit. Wit has truth in it; wisecracking is simply calisthenics with words" (Capron, 10).

29. By the late 1930s, however, Parker had become better known in Hollywood, through working on scripts for several high-profile films. Like Anita Loos, she commanded an unusually large salary for a writer in Hollywood. For details see Kinney, 53–56.

30. These include her "Songs of Hate," some first published in *Vanity Fair* and others in *Life* and reprinted in *The Uncollected Dorothy Parker* (194–246); and her set of parodies, "Oh Look! I Can Do It Too," first published in *Vanity Fair* and reprinted in *The Uncollected Dorothy Parker* (86–87).

31. See Kinney, 104–111, for a full discussion of her influences.

32. Maugham remarks: "A carping critic of these stories might suggest that their author on occasion shows an inclination to imitate Dorothy Parker, but I as an admiring friend would answer stoutly that she could not have a better

model" (602). Kinney considers Benchley a better drama critic than Parker because he is "less self-conscious" (155), and describes certain of Parker's poems as "straining self-consciously" (112).

33. The novel is Charles Brackett's *Entirely Surrounded* (1934). The plays are: Donald Ogden Stewart's *The Crazy Fool* (1925); George Oppenheimer's *Here Today* (1932); Philip Barry's *Hotel Universe* (1932); George S. Kaufman and Moss Hart's *Merrily We Roll Along* (1934); Ruth Gordon's *Over Twenty-One* (1944); and Laurel Ollstein's *Laughter, Hope, and a Sock in the Eye* (1990).

34. The title was likely inspired by a book of reminiscences, *The Vicious Circle* (1951), by Margaret Case Harriman, daughter of Frank Case, who was the Algonquin Hotel's manager during the 1920s.

2

1. The title of the magazine was spelled this way from 1867 until 1929.

2. A Missouri farmer's daughter whose popularity at the height of her career had rivaled Mary Pickford's, White was given to falsifying the facts of her life to create legends around herself, and her autobiography is highly dubious.

3. There are affinities between this text and some of Parker's signed stories ("From the Diary of a New York Lady," for example, or "Lady with a Lamp"). Also, more than one critic has tentatively attributed "Extracts from a Secretary's Diary" to Parker. See Rahne Alexander's online bibliography of Parker's magazine articles at http://www.xantippe.com/dorothy/bibliography/articles.html (consulted 18 July 2005).

4. Like Lorelei (who starts out as a secretary), this diarist—while none too bright herself—manages to show up the obtuseness and self-absorption of those around her. The diary has touches of the Lorelei style, with its frequent redundancy and repetition. The secretary says of her boss: "when I take his funny letters, I try to look amused. I can tell that they are funny because he laughs at them himself" (Jones, 100). Compare Lorelei, trying to butter up a rich old bore: "I laughed, very, very loud and I told Piggie he was wonderful the way he could tell jokes. I mean you can always tell when to laugh because Piggie always laughs first" (*Blondes*, 41).

5. While Pettit's connection between Parker and Loos is interesting, her reading of *Gentlemen Prefer Blondes* misses most of the subtleties of the novel. She considers Loos to have unwittingly made Lorelei cleverer than she intended, thereby failing in her aim to satirize provincial stupidity.

6. Another comparison might be drawn with Parker's 1933 story for *The New Yorker*, "From the Diary of a New York Lady." While not stylistically comparable to *Gentlemen Prefer Blondes*, this story does replicate Lorelei's round of identical social engagements, as well as her complete lack of interest in anything beyond her immediate surroundings.

7. Feminist attitudes to the film differ sharply: Arbuthnot and Seneca argue that it "can be read as a feminist text" (112), which "celebrates women's pleasure in each other" (113), while Turim attacks Hawks's transformation of the female body into "sex object" and "commodity" (106).

8. As Elaine Showalter points out, "A country taking new pride in its cultural heritage after the war saw only weakness and sentimentality in the contribution women had made to our national literature. In the years following the [First World] war, women writers were gradually eliminated from the canon of American literature as it was anthologized, criticized, and taught" (824).

9. There are signs that it has begun. The Folio Society reissue of *Blondes* in 1985 initiated its recuperation as a classic of American literature, and the 1990s saw new editions of Loos's work and seven scholarly articles wholly or partially about *Blondes* (see Barreca, Churchwell, Hegeman, Matthews, Pettit, von Ankum, Wittmann). Reference books and survey studies published in the middle decades of the century omitted Loos, but in more recent literary companions and surveys she tends to be mentioned briefly.

10. Wharton to Gaillard Lapsley, 11 April 1926, Wharton, 491.

11. Wharton to John Hugh Smith, letters dated 14 and 26 January 1926, Edith Wharton Collection, Yale University Rare Book and Manuscript Library, YCAL MSS 42, Series II, Box 26, Folder 807.

12. Quoted in Gary Carey, 108. Blom notes that when Loos wrote to Wharton suggesting she had overpraised the novel, Wharton replied: "I meant every word I wrote about 'Blondes'" (39). The editors of her letters quote, in a footnote, a further letter to Hugh Smith, pronouncing *Blondes* "the greatest novel since *Manon Lescaut*" (Wharton, 491).

13. Cover blurb from the first British edition, quoted in Clive Bloom, 91.

14. Likewise, in his letters, Mencken "does not overpraise the more cerebral aspects of Loos's brilliant satire" (Schrader, 7). See Bruccoli, 129, for a further account of Mencken's reactions.

15. Aspects of Huyssen's argument have been challenged in recent years (see my introduction for details). However, his analysis of the gendering of mass culture as feminine remains important to our understanding of cultural production in the early twentieth century.

16. Loos recalls that the newsstand sales of *Harper's Bazar* tripled during the serialization, and that the magazine gained a new male audience ("Biography," xli). Wittmann states that in the United States *Blondes* attracted primarily a male audience (36).

17. The letter is dated "Something Febry 1926" (Faulkner, 32).

18. Astonishingly, Faulkner's patronizing approach is replicated in a 1997 essay by a female critic, who twice refers to subtle effects which Loos has "unwittingly" achieved, and remarks that the novel "contains more wisdom than perhaps Loos intended" (Pettit, 49, 50, 51).

19. Definitions of best sellers in terms of sales achievements vary, and some books were best sellers in the UK but not the United States, or vice versa. Frank Luther Mott lists books believed to have a total sale of 1 percent of the population of continental America for the decade in which they were published. For the 1920s, his table includes (with the exception of P. G. Wodehouse) only writers of formulaic popular fiction, who are no longer read today. He also lists books which nearly made the 1 percent mark, including *Blondes* as well as *The House of Mirth, The Age of Innocence, Main Street,* and *Babbitt* (102–120). Rosen lists the ten best-selling novels of 1925 in America, including *The Profes-*

sor's House and *A Mother's Recompense* (82). In *Fiction and the Reading Public,* Q. D. Leavis chooses *A Passage to India* as a representative 1920s "highbrow best-seller" (247).

20. Loos dramatized *Blondes* for the New York stage in 1926, and it toured successfully. She scripted both the 1928 and the 1953 films, as well as the 1955 film *Gentlemen Marry Brunettes.* With Joseph Fields she wrote the book for a musical version of *Blondes* in 1949. Commercial spin-offs included a comic strip, dress material, and a wallpaper design (Loos, "A Musical Is Born," 59).

21. She even became literally commodified when she was photographed alongside a new Ford (Stendhal, 141).

22. All language errors in quotations from Loos's fiction are Lorelei's.

23. On the Book-of-the-Month Club and American middlebrow culture, see Radway; Rubin.

24. Clive Bell, Edmund Wilson, John McClure, and Burton Rascoe all compared Eliot's poems to jazz in the early 1920s. For details, see North, 146.

25. On the extent of Loos's fame, see Kobal, 80. On the reception of *A Girl Like I,* see Loos, *Anita Loos Rediscovered,* 206.

26. As well as mentioning the gift in her tribute to Huxley, she also refers to it in *Kiss Hollywood Goodbye* (161), this time naming the perfume.

3

1. Both claimed to have been born in 1893. Recent research suggests that Loos was in fact born in 1888. One of West's biographers, Fergus Cashin, develops a hypothesis that she, too, was born in 1888; however, more reliable sources agree on 1893.

2. I have checked as many such encyclopedias as possible. Even the supplement to John Foster Kirk's *Allibone's Critical Dictionary of English Literature and British and American Authors,* which lists thirty-seven thousand authors, among them twenty-eight surnamed "West," omits Mae West, though it includes such entirely obscure figures as George West, author of *Methodism in Marshland* (1866), and Maria A. West, author of *The Romance of Missions* (1875).

3. For details, see Curry, 24. Curry reprints publicity photographs for West's film *Belle of the Nineties* showing her dictating dialogue and consulting with the cameraman, director, and censorship expert.

4. According to Helfer, it was never on the *Publishers Weekly* best seller lists ("Mae West," 299). However, it certainly achieved high sales and convinced the Shubert organization that a play based on it would be profitable (Leider, 226). West claims that *She Done Him Wrong* sold ninety-five thousand copies (*Goodness,* 188).

5. There is only Lette's introduction to the Virago reprints (the same introduction, identical except in one paragraph, prefaces both *She Done Him Wrong* and *The Constant Sinner*), together with some paragraphs of more useful discussion in two books: Hamilton devotes several pages to *The Constant Sinner* (137-146) and a paragraph to *Pleasure Man* (230); Leider comments on *The Constant Sinner* (223-226) and *She Done Him Wrong* (190-191).

6. The racial politics of her fiction are sometimes problematic. She includes characters who voice strongly racist views (though they would not have been considered extreme at the time), but the narrators do not endorse these opinions and sometimes point out their cruelty. At the same time, her most attractive characters are always white, and her imagery repeatedly associates black people with animals.

7. Compare Cole Porter's lyrics for "You're the Top," from the 1934 musical *Anything Goes,* in which he lists icons from both high and popular culture in an attempt to capture the value of the inexpressible "she," comparing her to a Botticelli, a Shakespeare sonnet, an Arrow collar, the feet of Fred Astaire, and the moon over Mae West's shoulder.

8. Leider, 116, quoting from her own interview with Ron Fields, 28 March 1994.

9. On imitations of West, see footnote 19 below. Following the success of the film of *She Done Him Wrong,* West inspired a Betty Boop cartoon, "She Wronged Him Right," and in 1935 she was the model for Disney's Jenny Wren in "Who Killed Cock Robin?" West insisted that she was only imitated because "I was an original" (Chandler, 65).

10. This association is discussed at length by Pitman. See in particular pp. 59–61.

11. A comparison with *Gentlemen Prefer Blondes* is also pertinent here. The anxieties about imitation and reproduction evident in the text of the novel, epitomized in Lorelei's preoccupation with distinguishing diamonds from paste jewelry, echo the conditions of its production and reproduction in the form of sequels, musical and film versions, and spin-off consumer goods. Although Loos did not literally perform the role of Lorelei on stage or celluloid, she did perform it in her later writing, adopting the Lorelei persona in articles and letters. See Chapter 1 for fuller discussion, and see Churchwell on the anxieties of imitation in *Gentlemen Prefer Blondes.*

12. Cinema, of course, proved the most powerful medium for circulating West's image. Not only could it be reproduced, like a photograph; it also incorporated movement, like a stage play.

13. West, *Diamond Lil.* Quoted in Hamilton (247) from the script.

14. The three pieces were entitled "Making Love to Mae West" and appeared in *Picturegoer* (10 and 30 December 1933; 6 January 1934). Leider remarks that Grant may have written the articles under pressure from Paramount, or to advance his own career, or else out of genuine regard for West, and that it is possible that he did not write them but merely signed them (273).

15. "In Brooklyn, police reserves had to be called out to keep the fans in order, and continuous performances, beginning at 9 A.M. and ending at 5 in the morning, had to be scheduled to accommodate the crowds" (Leider, 283).

16. This exchange is quoted from the film by Curry (88).

17. The reformers' emphasis on containing transgressive sexuality was essential to the maintenance of middle-class dominance, which depended on the assertion of family values and traditional morality. At the same time, reform placed limits on the free enterprise system, which was so much cherished in America during this era, and this forced the industry to adopt tactics which

would turn censorship to its advantage. As Curry explains, the enforcement of the Production Code strengthened the central trade organization, the Motion Picture Producers and Distributors Association, and fostered oligopolistic trade practices (56).

18. Brooks to Ricky Leacock, *Lulu in Berlin* transcript, pp. 27–28. Quoted in Paris, 530.

19. In 1928, Dorothy Sands in the *Grand Street Follies* impersonated West (Bordman, 439); shortly afterwards Grace Hayes used an impression of Diamond Lil as a vaudeville act, but West threatened her with a lawsuit unless she dropped it (Leider, 197). In 1960, West went to court to establish her exclusive rights to the Lil name. She initially lost, and a supper-club performer, Marie Lind, was allowed to continue her Diamond Lil act. Four years later, this ruling was reversed, and no other performer could thereafter masquerade as Lil (Leider, 202). The only imitator West countenanced was her sister, whose Diamond Lil act Mae West describes as "the best imitation of me ever done to that time" (*Goodness,* 165).

20. For recent articles on this topic, see Finney; Helfer, "The Drag"; Ivanov; Schlissel.

21. The photograph, taken at the Steichen exhibit at Eastman House, Rochester (5 August 1979), appears in the picture section in Paris (pages unnumbered).

22. Letter to a cousin, Patricia Calvert, September 1967. Quoted in Paris, 456.

23. See Cashin, 7, 17; Fleming and Fleming, 280. The painting was by Florence Kinzel, done in 1934.

24. McCorkle lists: Marilyn Monroe, Brigitte Bardot, Anita Ekberg, Jayne Mansfield, Dolly Parton, Bette Midler, Patti LaBelle, Madonna, RuPaul, and Fran Drescher (49). She might have added Barbra Streisand in *Hello, Dolly!* (1969).

25. In an interview, Carter said of her heroine: "Fevvers is basically Mae West with wings. I'm a great admirer of Mae West. The way Mae West controls the audience-response towards herself in her movies is quite extraordinary" (Haffenden, 88).

26. By the Hourglass Group, at the Gershwin Hotel (December 1999–January 2000). Dir. Elyse Singer; starring Carolyn Baeumler.

4

1. In this chapter, I draw on Montgomery's scrapbook of reviews, covering the period 1911–1936, and derived from a clipping service. L. M. Montgomery Collection, University of Guelph, XZ5 MS A001-3, referred to hereafter as "Scrapbook." Pages in the scrapbook are numbered; my parenthetical references are page numbers.

2. For details of seventeen later films and television adaptations, see Lefebvre, "L. M. Montgomery: An Annotated Filmography."

3. On the 1934 film, see Sheckels. On Sullivan, see Frever; Gates and Gillis; Hersey; Howey; Kotsopoulos; Lefebvre, *"Road to Avonlea";* Poe; Tye. On the CBC's *Emily of New Moon,* see Gittings.

4. The articles on celebrity are Pike, "Mass Marketing," and York. Montgomery's life and autobiographical writing are touched on by numerous other critics.

5. Montgomery, *Selected Journals* I, 259–260. Future references to the published journals will be abbreviated to SJ, followed by the volume and page numbers.

6. "Put On Her Red Mittens to Write in the Cold," Scrapbook (211). The item, unlabeled, is pasted between others dated September and November 1923. The contributing reader's address is in Toronto, suggesting an Ontario paper.

7. The Scottish system of church government by presbyters was originally developed by Puritans in the late sixteenth century, and the Puritan influence continued in later centuries. Because of the influx of Scottish immigrants to Maritime Canada, the Presbyterian Church was particularly strong there. It was central to Montgomery's life, but despite her commitment to her church, it is clear from her writing that she was unable to accept certain aspects of its ideology. See Reid; Rubio, "L. M. Montgomery: Scottish-Presbyterian Agency in Canadian Culture."

8. See Radway; Rubin.

9. For discussion, see Gittings, 188; Lawson, 158, 164.

10. This piece, unlabeled, is pasted in the scrapbook (86–87), adjacent to items from October 1915. It is reprinted in Devereux (ed.), *Anne of Green Gables,* 365–370, but Devereux has not been able to discover its source either. My quotations appear on 366 and 370 in her edition.

11. See Tiessen and Tiessen on Montgomery's negotiation with cultural hierarchy in these letters.

12. Rubio and Waterston give the fullest account of the textual evolution of the journal (Introduction to SJ III). See York on Montgomery's awareness of "the likely future value of objects associated with her" (113).

13. On Ostenso and de la Roche's celebrity, see Hammill, "Sensations."

14. Numerous critics have explored this topic in relation to the journal and the Anne and Emily novels. Among the more detailed and recent discussions are Roberta Buchanan; Campbell; Pike, "(Re)Producing"; Rubio, "Subverting."

15. "Canadian Author Delights Her Audience," Scrapbook (189). Unlabeled but dated by the content and pasted next to other items from 1921.

16. See Karr, passim, for discussion of this issue in relation to Montgomery and her peers.

17. Morley Callaghan Papers, National Archives of Canada. Quoted in Neijmann, 148.

18. Corse claims that "Unlike high-culture literature, popular-culture literature lacks a *national* symbolic value" (130), since popular literature, in seeking to appeal to the widest possible audience, eliminates the kinds of markers of national specificity which permit a work to be selected into a national canon. In Montgomery's case, it is not that her texts contain no markers of national specificity, but that her markers do not correspond to those identified by critics. During the 1960s and 1970s, thematic criticism established paradigms of Canadian national identity relating to survival in a hostile environment, which excluded Montgomery's more sunny vision of her country (see Åhmansson, 51–52; Hammill, *Literary Culture,* 84–85).

19. "New Literary Star," Scrapbook (23). Unlabeled but pasted between items dated 1911. Further quotations in this section are from the same source.

20. The name of Isle St. Jean was changed to Prince Edward Island in 1798, some years after the British deported the Acadian inhabitants. The reference to

the Isle of Man sets Montgomery up against Hall Caine (1853–1951), author of best-selling novels with Manx settings.

21. As Gates and Gillis note: "Prince Edward Island has reinvented its rural economy as a *performance* of a rural economy, the purpose of which is to provide a vision of 'Anne's' Prince Edward Island" (189).

22. Mme. Albani was included in the book of profiles of great Canadian women written by Montgomery, Marian Keith, and Mabel Burns McKinley.

23. "The Greatest Living Canadians," Scrapbook (221). Not labeled, but between items dated March and June 1924.

24. "Who Are the Twelve Greatest Canadian Women?" *Border Cities Star,* Scrapbook (202–204). Not dated but adjacent to items dated 1923.

25. "Twelve Greatest Women of Canada," *The Digest,* Scrapbook (204). Not dated but pasted underneath the *Border Cities Star* item.

26. Grace Kingsley, "Flashes: Enter Mary Minter," Scrapbook (148). Not labeled but from a Los Angeles paper. The film was released on 15 November 1919, and the premiere was at Miller's California Theater.

27. *Photoplay* (February 1920), reprinted in *Taylorology* 24 (December 1994), http://www.silent-movies.com/Taylorology/Taylor24.txt (consulted 2 January 2005).

28. *Harrison's Reports* (22 November 1919), available at http://www .geocities.com/cyberanne/marymilesminter.html (consulted 2 January 2005).

29. *Moving Picture World* (22 November 1919), available at http://www .geocities.com/cyberanne/marymilesminter.html (consulted 2 January 2005).

30. A good example is de la Roche's immensely popular Jalna books. Their Loyalist ideology aligns the Canadian idyll of Jalna with solid English tradition and opposes this to the pretentious, oversophisticated social world of New York, which is visited by several of the characters. See Hammill, "Sensations."

31. *Moving Picture World* (22 November 1919), available at http://www .geocities.com/cyberanne/marymilesminter.html (consulted 2 January 2005).

32. Huggan proposes several ways of understanding "authentic," of which I have quoted just one.

33. http://www.geocities.com/cyberanne/marymilesminter.html (consulted 2 January 2005).

34. As Montgomery wrote in 1929 on a return visit to the Island, following the conversion of the house into a tourist site: "It seems of no use to protest that it is not 'Green Gables'—that Green Gables was a purely imaginary place. Tourists by the hundred come here" (SJ IV, 9).

5

1. This information appears in the caption to a photo of Kennedy by Lenare, *The Sketch* (6 October 1926), Margaret Kennedy Papers, Somerville College, Oxford, Main Collection, Press Cuttings Scrapbooks, British Reviews.

2. "Personalities and Powers," 1101. To give just two of the many other examples: "*The Constant Nymph* was acclaimed as a masterpiece by many 'highbrow' critics, and it has proved to be a best-seller as well" (Nichols); "Here is a

book that is a literary achievement, as well as a best seller in two continents. The two sorts of success, then, are not so wholly incompatible as some of the high-brows would have us believe" (Over).

3. There is very little published criticism on Kennedy's work. Aside from brief introductions to reprints of her novels, there are: some pages in Humble; some paragraphs in Lassner, "Objects"; a chapter in Melman; a chapter in Leonardi; and a description of *The Constant Nymph* in Cockburn. The only biographical study is Powell's *The Constant Novelist*. While not a scholarly biography, it contains valuable material.

4. In *The Winter's Tale*, the abandoned baby Perdita is found by a shepherd who has just been muttering: "I would there were no age between sixteen and three-and-twenty, or that youth would sleep out the rest" (3.3.59–3.3.60). Perdita is sixteen when she and Florizel fall in love and her true identity is revealed. Sixteen is also the much-emphasized age of Antonia Sanger, who at the start of Kennedy's book has just been seduced.

5. Unpublished letter, 22 June 1925. Quoted in Melman, 77n.

6. Connolly to Noel Blakiston, 20 October 1926; September 1926 (Connolly 178, 173). The published volume of Connolly's letters to Blakiston contains sixteen (indexed) references to the book and its characters.

7. The word "tragic" appears in numerous reviews. *Punch*, for example, referred to "the innocent and tragic figure of Tessa" ("Our Booking Office"). A journalist profiling Kennedy wrote: "one well-known critic to whom I sent [the novel] told me that he had lain awake all night after reading of the death of Tessa" (Evans).

8. Trigorin's name seems to be taken from Chekhov's *The Seagull* (1896). Chekhov's Trigorin is a writer, compulsively dedicated to his work. Although his books are mediocre, he is idolized by the public and has become careless and selfish. His affair with a young actress causes her devoted admirer, Konstantin, to commit suicide. Kennedy's Trigorin is not similar to Chekhov's, but the themes of the two texts are related.

9. Kennedy mentioned that the circus owners might sue in a letter (Margaret Kennedy Papers, Letters to Flora Forster, Folder MK 1-55, Letter 21, 12 January 1925), but in the end they did not. See also Melman, 79; Powell, *Constant Novelist*, 68, on this episode.

10. For example, an American journalist wrote in 1925 that she "may yet, if she will, become a novelist of distinctive rank" (Dodd). Two years later, a critic reviewing *Red Sky* remarked on its author's "distinguished ability, of which much may be expected" (Loveman); while a 1931 review refers to "the great book one assumes the author of *The Constant Nymph* will write one day" (Kendon).

11. Sylvia Lynd's review of *Red Sky at Morning* (1927) is representative: "Few novels have so exquisite a forerunner as *The Constant Nymph* with which to compete. Compared with that, *Red Sky at Morning*, it must be admitted, is far less moving, less inevitable in the progress of its events, and less well stocked with fascinating characters. Compared with any ordinary novel, however, it is very good indeed—finely wrought, just, sensible, perceptive, and witty" (103).

12. Changing critical fashions were also partly responsible for this. While Kennedy's early work was admired by an older generation of critics, the increas-

ing sway of modernist and experimental writers, and their advocates, meant that her style was quickly perceived as somewhat old-fashioned.

13. "Genius," "brilliant," and "masterpiece" occur, for example, in Cumberland (91), Evans, Nichols, and "Our Booking Office." An American review describes her novel as "wholly exceptional" (Broun).

14. Quoted in Melman, 77. The review appeared on 6 December 1924.

15. This list has been compiled from the following sources: Bennett; Brookner, xi; Hartley; Powell, *Constant Novelist,* 67; Gramsci, *Lettere,* 118; Melman, 77. Also Margaret Kennedy Papers, Letters to Flora Forster, Folder MK 1-55, Letter 16, 30 October 1924; Letter 21, 12 January 1925; Letter 22, 13 April 1925. Giraudoux admired the novel so much that he adapted Kennedy and Dean's play *The Constant Nymph* into a French-language musical in 1934.

16. Birrell compared her to Meredith in his review (quoted in Melman, 77). Rebecca West identified Kennedy's literary progenitors as Shakespeare and Galsworthy (209). The comparison to Masefield and Forster comes in an anonymous review in the *New York Evening Post Book Review* (16 February 1925), Margaret Kennedy Papers, Main Collection, Clipping Scrapbooks, American Reviews.

17. "è certamente notevole, sia perché scritto da una donna, sia per l'atmosfera psicologica in cui è concepito e sia ancora per il mondo che descrive" (Gramsci, *Lettere,* 118). The letter does not appear in the English edition of the letters, but is cited in a footnote (Gramsci, *Letters,* 104n).

18. Quoted in Melman, 77, without a reference. Galsworthy and Housman, writers of a traditional stamp, resisted modernist experimentation and so did not acknowledge the earlier achievements of women such as Virginia Woolf or Katherine Mansfield.

19. Margaret Kennedy Papers, Letters to Flora Forster, Folder MK 1-55, Letter 24, 25 April 1925.

20. Ibid., Letter 51, 30 December 1929.

21. Ibid., Letter 39, 20 June 1928.

22. Ibid., Letter 43, 10 December 1929.

23. Ibid., Letter 58, 29 December 1932.

24. Ibid., Letter 53, 13 April 1931.

25. Ibid., Letter 16, 30 October 1924.

26. For discussion of the novel's influence on later women writers, see Humble, 152, 159–160. She reads it as "the initiating text in [a] middlebrow cult of familial eccentricity" (152).

27. *The Ladies of Lyndon* in 1981; *Together and Apart* in 1982; *The Constant Nymph* in 1983 (reissued 2000); and *Troy Chimneys* in 1985.

28. Aside from Jane Austen, the authors Kennedy is regularly compared with are men. Fisher, writing in 1969, compares her to Galsworthy (9); while Mannin (86), Melman (passim), and others class her with the male best sellers of the Twenties, notably Michael Arlen and A. S. M. Hutchinson, both authors of emotionally charged novels which have not stood the test of time.

29. For example, *The Heroes of Clone* portrays a woman writer and Kennedy's last novel, *Not in the Calendar: The Story of a Friendship* (1964), is about a deaf girl who is developing into an artist.

30. The 1928 silent film, directed by Adrian Brunel and Basil Dean, starred Mabel Poulton and Ivor Novello. In 1933, Dean directed the first sound version, starring Victoria Hopper and Brian Aherne. The 1943 picture, directed by Edmund Goulding, starred Joan Fontaine and Charles Boyer. There was also a UK television version in 1938, featuring some of the 1933 film cast.

31. Reported by Powell (*Constant Novelist,* 122), without a reference. Probably taken from the journal Kennedy wrote from 1937 to 1939.

32. Letter to Edward Garnett, 2 February 1925 (Galsworthy, 241).

33. Letter to Noel Blakiston, 5 November 1926 (Connolly, 181).

34. Margaret Kennedy Papers, Letters to Flora Forster, Folder MK 1-55, Letter 27, 27 June 1926.

35. The letters from the late 1920s record that Bennett, Moore, Kipling, Hardy, Connolly, Hartley, de la Mare, and Raymond Mortimer all sought introductions to Kennedy after reading her book. Powell records that she also met writers, including Somerset Maugham and E. M. Forster, at literary dinners and events (*Constant Novelist,* 126–127), and she worked with several eminent women writers on the Femina Vie Heureuse prize committee. Through her work as a playwright and scriptwriter, she met many high-ranking actors.

36. An unsigned paragraph in the *Newcastle Daily Journal* (8 October 1931), for example, notes that the novel's hero is based on Coward. Margaret Kennedy Papers, Main Collection, Clipping Scrapbooks, British Reviews.

37. Several such books, by Roth, Updike, DeLillo, and Acker, are analyzed by Moran. He quotes, for example, from Updike's book *Self-Consciousness* (1989): "Celebrity is a mask that eats into the face. As soon as one is aware of being 'somebody' to be watched and listened to with extra interest, input ceases, and the performer goes blind and deaf in his overanimation" (Moran, 92, quoting Updike, 252–253).

38. Margaret Kennedy Papers, Letters to Flora Forster, Folder MK 1-55, Letter 24, 25 April 1925.

6

1. Letter from Woolf to Gibbons, 20 May 1934, Woolf, *Sickle,* 304. Woolf noted in her diary on 22 October 1927 that Dorothy Wellesley, editor of the *Hogarth Living Poets* series, "is investing £200 a year in Stella Gibbons &c." (162). In fact, Gibbons's work did not appear in this series. Her first volume, *The Mountain Beast, and Other Poems* (1930), was published by Longmans. While Hogarth, along with Cape, Chatto and Faber, was among the elite publishers of the period, Longmans was a more commercial operation. *Cold Comfort Farm* was also published by Longmans, and reprinted in 1938 by Penguin, which was "by then the most successful of the new distinctively middlebrow publishing ventures" (English Studies Group, 14).

2. Bluemel says of Gibbons's contemporary Stevie Smith that "the experimental, humorous forms of [her] novels further distance her work from the traditional vision of thirties prose literature," a comment which might also be applied to Gibbons. Bluemel notes that for Smith, "style, humor and racial poli-

tics" are "interconnected, formative, and primary" (29). In Gibbons's case, gender politics are more relevant than racial politics, but they are similarly explored through the politics of literary style.

3. Her work is omitted from many relevant survey studies and reference books. I looked Gibbons up in twenty-one such books, and she was mentioned in only half. For details, see Hammill, "*Cold Comfort.*"

4. Trodd, however, suggests this was a deliberate strategy, saying of Kaye-Smith's *Joanna Godden:* "For the mostly urban reader for whom she is writing, Sussex is picturesque, historical, literary, but she is constantly pointing out that this view is entirely alien to Joanna" (105), who has a more authentic identification with the land.

5. Gibbons wrote a novel called *The Matchmaker,* still more clearly indebted to *Emma.* She also wrote the preface to a 1964 edition of *Emma* by the Heritage Press.

6. A tension might be noted between Flora's rejection of Bloomsbury and British *Vogue*'s effort to promote and reproduce Bloomsbury style. See Garrity, "Selling," on *Vogue* and Bloomsbury.

7. Cunningham, in *British Writers of the Thirties,* notes: "The air and its texts had indeed become largely male preserves. Agatha Christie's air-based stories are as rare in their airmindedness as Stella Gibbons's *Cold Comfort Farm* or Elizabeth Bowen's *To the North*" (173).

8. Bluemel cites some representative titles of the latter variety: *The Fringe of London: Being Some Ventures and Adventures in Topography* (1925) and *Where London Sleeps: Historical Journeying into the Suburbs* (1926), noting that these books "boast an avuncular first-person narrator who is bent on discovering the old or historical (the authentic) within the new suburban terrain" (57).

9. Bluemel focuses on George Orwell, Stevie Smith, Mulk Raj Anand, and Inez Holden, arguing that these writers are "importantly eccentric and radical [. . .] because they consistently resist inhibiting, often oppressive assumptions about art and ideology—about standard relations between literary form and sex, gender, race, class, and empire" (7–8).

10. Holme won it for *The Splendid Fairing* in 1921, Webb for *Precious Bane* in 1926.

11. Femina Vie Heureuse Papers, Cambridge University Library, MS Add. 8900, Item 2/1/1, Terms of reference.

12. FVH Papers, Item 1/2/21, Minutes of Femina Vie Heureuse and Northcliffe Prize Committee, 5 May 1933.

13. FVH Papers, Item 1/2/22, Minutes, 24 October 1933.

14. FVH Papers, Item 1/2/23, Minutes, 14 November 1933.

15. FVH Papers, Item 1/2/26, Minutes, 2 May 1934.

16. Letter from Woolf to Bowen, 16 May 1934, Woolf, *Sickle,* 303.

17. Letter from Woolf to Bowen, 20 May 1934, Woolf, *Sickle,* 304.

18. FVH Papers, Folder 5/5, Letters from Prizewinners, Items 5/5/18 and 5/5/20.

19. Noted in FVH Papers, Item 1/2/38, Minutes, 21 October 1936.

20. I am grateful to Margaret Kennedy's daughter, Mrs. Julia Birley, for this information, sent in a letter on 17 July 2005.

21. Loos generally continued to go by her maiden name, though she sometimes sought to overcome the public/private split by signing herself Anita Loos Emerson. Parker, by contrast, used her first married name to efface her earlier identity as Dorothy Rothschild, retaining "Mrs. Parker" as her public identity even after she married Alan Campbell.

22. In 1965 a musical, *Something Nasty in the Woodshed,* was produced, and three years later the novel was filmed for the first time. It has been adapted for the stage by Paul Doust (first performed in 1991) and read on BBC radio by Kenneth Williams. A BBC radio dramatization was broadcast in May 1981 and issued as the first of several audiobook versions in 1989.

23. The film tie-in edition appeared in 1996, the Modern Classics edition in 2000, and the Essential Penguins edition in 2003.

24. The Assessment and Qualifications Alliance syllabus for Advanced Subsidiary and Advanced English Literature (Specification A), written in 2001 and valid until 2006, includes a module called Literary Connections. It requires the study of two set texts, chosen from a range of options which include *Cold Comfort Farm,* paired with Mary Webb's *Precious Bane* (1925). Gibbons's novel was also set at A-level from 1978 until the early 1980s.

25. One full article on *Cold Comfort Farm* was published in 1978 (Ariail), and from then until the end of the century, only a piece in *Notes and Queries* (Vickers) and some paragraphs in studies of regional writing (Keith; Snell; Williams) discussed the novel. In 2001 and 2002, one essay devoted to *Cold Comfort Farm* (Hammill, "*Cold Comfort*") and two essays comparing it with other texts (Parkins; Horner and Zlosnik) appeared. Humble discusses Gibbons in *The Feminine Middlebrow.*

26. On Stevie Smith's relationship to the suburb, see Bluemel's chapter "Stevie Smith and Suburban Satire" in *George Orwell.* The passage in *Vile Bodies* describing Nina's nausea on looking down from an aeroplane at a view of "straggling red suburb; arterial road dotted with little cars; [. . .] some distant hills sown with bungalows; wireless masts and overhead power cables" (171) is a frequently cited expression of disgust at the expansion of the suburbs in interwar England.

27. More examples can be found in John Carey's chapter "The Suburbs and the Clerks" in *The Intellectuals and the Masses.* On British suburbs in the 1930s, see Dentith; Giles.

28. Bluemel says of Stevie Smith's *Novel on Yellow Paper* (1936) that the "narrative instructs us to look for signs of acute cultural transformation in the thoughts and emotions of a London secretary whose life is built out of the routines of suburban life" (29). Gibbons's Hampstead novels engage in similar projects, although Smith is perhaps more ambivalent about suburbs than Gibbons.

7

1. *The Provincial Lady Goes Further* was published in America as *The Provincial Lady in London.* Quotations from the four books all refer to the Virago edition, and are given with the abbreviations DPL, PLF, PLA, and PLW, unless it is clear from the context which volume is being referred to.

2. Untitled, anonymous review, *Time and Tide* 11.51 (20 December 1930): 1609.

3. McCullen more helpfully remarks that "as she often drew obviously from her own life for subject matter, the 'I' persona became identified with the Provincial Lady—and both with the author herself" (51).

4. *Time and Tide* 10.47 (22 November 1929): 1403–1404; 10.48 (29 November 1929): 1434–1436.

5. Examples include Lady Rhondda's piece, "Mr. Shaw Writes to Me about Conduit Pipes," and Delafield's own series, "Women in Fiction," appearing in February and March 1931.

6. One obituary of Delafield noted that *The Diary of a Provincial Lady* had "been classed with *Cranford.*" Untitled, anonymous obituary, *Glasgow Evening News* (2 December 1943), E. M. Delafield Papers, University of British Columbia, Box 3, File 9.

7. Woolf makes this point explicit, noting that the sudden development of literary activity among women in the later eighteenth century "was founded on the solid fact that women could make money by writing. Money dignifies what is frivolous if unpaid for" (*Room,* 97).

8. Dowson's comment refers both to *The Diary of a Provincial Lady* and *Mrs. Miniver;* but Light contrasts them, finding the undertone of protest to be absent from Struther's text. See Beauman, *A Very Great Profession,* 114, for a further comparison of Delafield and Struther.

9. Untitled, anonymous obituary, the *Times* (3 December 1943), E. M. Delafield Papers, Box 3, File 9.

10. See my introduction for details. Compare Scott and Zelda Fitzgerald's reception in London in 1921, when they were treated like film stars and invited to lunch with Lady Randolph Spencer Churchill. On the Fitzgeralds' celebrity, see Prigozy.

11. Untitled, anonymous review, *New York Times Book Review* (9 November 1919), reprinted in *Consequences* by E. M. Delafield, 419–421 (quotation from p. 419).

12. Ibid.

13. Auerbach comments: "The most potent, if hidden, ghost in the haunted *Rebecca* is not that of the lost wife but that of loving, yearning George du Maurier, with his romanticism twisted into hate" (63).

14. She has, however, been "named" by later readers. Jane Rogers, adapting the diaries for serialization on BBC Radio 4 in 1999, calls the Provincial Lady "Elizabeth," probably because Delafield herself was known by this name. Beauman remarks that Delafield's heroine "would surely be called Laura if she wasn't [. . .] nameless" (Introduction, ix), apparently connecting her with the heroine of the film *Brief Encounter* (1945). Delafield herself says of her protagonist's name: "Undoubtedly it was Mary Smith" ("The Diary," 138), evidently choosing the most commonplace name she can.

15. This list appears in one of Delafield's "Studies in Every-day Life" series ("Conversation in the Country").

16. Jaffe discusses in detail "the circulation of modernist names as rarefied, fungible commodities in economies of great names" (4) and suggests that the

"bundles of associations, qualities and properties" which names such as Eliot, Joyce, or Stein "organize" can actually be described as "products" (12).

17. Untitled, anonymous review, *Time and Tide* 11.51 (20 December 1930): 1609.

18. During the Second World War, the Ministry of Information commissioned Delafield to write a thirty-page booklet about women and the war. As Mc-Cullen points out: "The support of British women, at whom this piece was aimed, was critical for the war effort [. . .]. Delafield's choice as the propagandist who could help unite them testifies to her reputation as a feminist spokeswoman" (90).

19. This comment on the cliquey nature of highbrow literary groupings is reminiscent of Loos's satire of the self-absorbed conversations of the Algonquin Round Table critics.

20. Delafield draws out the comedy of this text in a journalistic piece: "Take Mr. Fairchild. At any moment, his four-year-old son Henry might say to him, 'Pray, papa, what has the Bible to say for and against the practice of dancing?' or Emily enquire, 'What is the process, papa, by which iron is extracted from its ore?' Mr. Fairchild had not only to be prepared to answer these intelligent enquiries, but he had to answer them at immense length, with illustrations, and edifying examples" ("Being a Parent").

21. Anonymous obituary of E. M. Delafield, *Punch* 5366 (8 December 1943): 477.

22. The winning entries were printed in issue 11.29 (19 July 1930): 940.

23. Femina Vie Heureuse Papers, Cambridge University Library, MS AD8900, Box One, Item number 1/2/43, Minutes of Femina and Heinemann Prizes Committee, 24 March 1937. A similar discussion occurred in the meeting of 15 October 1937, item number 1/2/44, when Amabel Williams-Ellis described Delafield as "much too well known."

24. Untitled, anonymous review, *The Sunday Express* (Johannesburg) (30 October 1947), E. M. Delafield Papers, Box 3, File 8. To give another example, the reviewer for the *Irish Times* remarked that "her work [. . .] may remain a social comment as valuable as the novels of Angela Thirkell" (Lane).

25. Untitled, anonymous review, *The Spectator* (24 October 1947), E. M. Delafield Papers, Box 3, File 8.

26. Untitled, anonymous review, *Sphere* (11 October 1947), E. M. Delafield Papers, Box 3, File 8.

27. Priestley published two books with this title, the first in 1929. He notes in his 1976 book: "I am using the title again because it best describes this new book on the very same subject. Though I cannot help sharing some material, what I am not doing is merely bringing up to date the book I wrote so long ago" (8).

28. The most recent serialization, on BBC Radio 4, was of *The Provincial Lady in Wartime,* but it was interrupted after two episodes due to the events of 11 September 2001.

BIBLIOGRAPHY

BOOKS AND ARTICLES

Adams, Franklin P. *The Diary of Our Own Samuel Pepys.* Volume I. New York: Simon and Schuster, 1935.

Agate, James. "A Fine Play." *The Sunday Times* (19 September 1926). Margaret Kennedy Papers. Forster Collection. Clipping File.

Åhmansson, Gabriella. *A Life and Its Mirrors: A Feminist Reading of L. M. Montgomery's Fiction.* Uppsala, Sweden: Acta Universatis Upsaliensis, 1991.

Allen, Brooke. *"Vile Bodies:* A Futurist Fantasy." *Twentieth Century Literature* 40.3 (Fall 1994): 318–328.

Amory, Cleveland, and Frederic Bradlee, eds. *Vanity Fair: A Cavalcade of the 1920s and 1930s.* New York: Viking, 1960.

Arbuthnot, Lucie, and Gail Seneca. "Pre-Text and Text in *Gentlemen Prefer Blondes.*" Erens 112–125.

Ardis, Ann. *Modernism and Cultural Conflict, 1880–1922.* Cambridge: Cambridge University Press, 2002.

———, and Leslie W. Lewis, eds. *Women's Experience of Modernity, 1875–1945.* Baltimore: Johns Hopkins University Press, 2003.

Ariail, Jacqueline Ann. "Cold Comfort from Stella Gibbons." *Ariel: A Review of International English Literature* 9.3 (1978): 63–73.

Auerbach, Nina. *Daphne du Maurier: Haunted Heiress.* Philadelphia: University of Pennsylvania Press, 2000.

Austin, Thomas, and Martin Barker, eds. *Contemporary Hollywood Stardom.* London: Edward Arnold, 2003.

"Author of *The Constant Nymph* Dies." *The Daily Telegraph* (2 August 1967). Margaret Kennedy Papers. Forster Collection. Clipping File.

Ayers, David. *English Literature of the 1920s.* Edinburgh: Edinburgh University Press, 1999.

Barreca, Regina. Introduction to *Complete Stories,* by Dorothy Parker, vii–xix.

————. Introduction to *Gentlemen Prefer Blondes,* by Anita Loos, vii–xxiv.

Beauman, Nicola. Introduction to *The Diary of a Provincial Lady,* by E. M. Delafield, vii–xvii.

————. *A Very Great Profession: The Woman's Novel, 1914–1939.* London: Virago, 1983.

Bennett, Arnold. "Books and Persons: Another Criticism of the New School." *The Evening Standard* (2 December 1926). Margaret Kennedy Papers. Main Collection. Clipping Scrapbooks. British Reviews.

Benton, Megan. "'Too Many Books': Book Ownership and Cultural Identity in the 1920s." *American Quarterly* 49.2 (June 1997): 268–297.

Berton, Pierre. *Hollywood's Canada: The Americanization of Our National Image.* Toronto: McClelland and Stewart, 1975.

"A Best Seller on the Stage." *The Queen* (22 September 1926): 6.

Blodgett, E. D. *Five-Part Invention: A History of Literary History in Canada.* Toronto: University of Toronto Press, 2003.

Blom, T. E. "Anita Loos and Sexual Economics: *Gentlemen Prefer Blondes.*" *Canadian Review of American Studies* 7.1 (1976): 39–47.

Bloom, Clive. *Bestsellers: Popular Fiction since 1900.* Basingstoke, England: Palgrave Macmillan, 2002.

Bloom, Harold, ed. *British Women Fiction Writers: 1900–1960: Volume One.* New York: Chelsea House, 1997.

Bluemel, Kristin. *George Orwell and the Radical Eccentrics: Intermodernism in Literary London.* Basingstoke, England: Palgrave Macmillan, 2004.

Bobak, E. L. "Seeking 'Direct, Honest Realism': The Canadian Novel of the 1920s." *Canadian Literature* 89 (Summer 1981): 85–101.

Boorstin, Daniel. *The Image: A Guide to Pseudo-Events in America.* New York: Atheneum, 1962.

Bordman, Gerald. *American Musical Theatre: A Chronicle.* New York: Oxford University Press, 1986.

Bosanquet, Theodora. Review of *A Room of One's Own* by Virginia Woolf. *Time and Tide* 10.46 (15 November 1929): 1371–1372.

Botshon, Lisa, and Meredith Goldsmith, eds. *Middlebrow Moderns: Popular American Women Writers of the 1920s.* Boston: Northeastern University Press, 2003.

Bourdieu, Pierre. *Distinction: A Social Critique of the Judgement of Taste.* Translated by Richard Nice. Cambridge, Mass.: Harvard University Press, 1984.

————. *The Field of Cultural Production: Essays on Art and Literature.* Edited by Randal Johnson. Cambridge: Polity, 1993.

Bradbury, Malcolm. "Style of Life, Style of Art and the American Novelist in the Nineteen Twenties." In *The American Novel and the Nineteen Twenties,* ed. Malcolm Bradbury and David Palmer, pp. 11–36. London: Edward Arnold, 1971.

Bradlee, Frederic. "Frank Crowninshield: Editor, Man, and Uncle." Amory and Bradlee 11–12.

Braudy, Leo. *The Frenzy of Renown: Fame and Its History.* Second edition. Orig. 1986; New York: Random House, 1997.

Brookner, Anita. Introduction to *The Constant Nymph*, by Margaret Kennedy, ix–xiv.

Broun, Heywood. "It Seems to Me." *New York World* (27 March 1925). Margaret Kennedy Papers. Main Collection. Clippings Scrapbooks. American Reviews.

Brown, John Mason. *Dramatis Personae: A Retrospective Show*. London: Hamish Hamilton, 1963.

Bruccoli, Matthew J. Interview with Anita Loos. In *Conversations with Writers II*, ed. Bruccoli et al., pp. 124–140. Detroit: Gale Research Company, 1978.

Buchanan, Brad. Entry for *Gentlemen Prefer Blondes*. Sage 268.

Buchanan, Roberta. "'I Wrote Two Hours This Morning and Put Up Grape Juice in the Afternoon': The Conflict between Woman and Writer in L. M. Montgomery's Journals." Gammel and Epperly 153–158.

Burstein, Jessica. "A Few Words about Dubuque: Modernism, Sentimentalism, and the Blasé." *American Literary History* 14.2 (Summer 2002): 227–254.

Campbell, Marie. "Wedding Bells and Death Knells: The Writer as Bride in the *Emily* Trilogy." In *Harvesting Thistles: The Textual Garden of L. M. Montgomery*, ed. Mary Rubio, pp. 137–145. Guelph, Ontario: Canadian Children's Press, 1994.

Capron, Marion. "The Art of Fiction No. 13: Dorothy Parker." *The Paris Review* 13 (Summer 1956). Consulted 18 July 2005. <http://www.theparisreview .com/viewinterview.php/prmMID/4933>

Carey, Gary. *Anita Loos: A Biography*. New York: Alfred A. Knopf, 1988.

Carey, John. *The Intellectuals and the Masses: Pride and Prejudice among the Literary Intelligentsia, 1880–1930*. London: Faber and Faber, 1992.

Cashin, Fergus. *Mae West: A Biography*. London: W. H. Allen, 1981.

Cawelti, John. "The Writer as Celebrity: Some Aspects of American Literature as Popular Culture." *Studies in American Fiction* 5.1 (1977): 161–174.

Cella, Laurie J. C. "Narrative 'Confidence Games': Framing the Blonde Spectacle in *Gentlemen Prefer Blondes* (1925) and *Nights at the Circus* (1984)." *Frontiers—A Journal of Women's Studies* 25.3 (2004): 47–62.

Chandler, Charlotte. *The Ultimate Seduction*. Garden City, N.Y.: Doubleday, 1984.

Churchwell, Sarah. "'Lost among the Ads': *Gentlemen Prefer Blondes* and the Politics of Imitation." Botshon and Goldsmith 135–164.

Cockburn, Claud. *Bestseller: The Books That Everyone Read, 1900–1939*. London: Sidgwick and Jackson, 1972.

Coles, Gladys Mary. *The Flower of Light: A Biography of Mary Webb*. London: Duckworth, 1978.

Connolly, Cyril. *A Romantic Friendship: The Letters of Cyril Connolly to Noel Blakiston*. London: Constable, 1975.

Constant Reader [Dorothy Parker]. "Re-enter Margot Asquith—A Masterpiece from the French." *The New Yorker* (22 October 1927). *The Collected Dorothy Parker* 455–458.

Coolidge, Calvin. "Books for Better Homes." *The Delineator* 103 (August 1923): 2.

Cooper, Jilly. Introduction to *The Diary of a Provincial Lady*, by E. M. Delafield, vii–xv. London: Prion Books, 2000.

Corse, Sarah. *Nationalism and Literature: The Politics of Culture in Canada and the United States.* Cambridge: Cambridge University Press, 1997.

Coward, Noël. *Autobiography.* London: Methuen, 1986.

Crowninshield, Frank. Editorial. *Vanity Fair* (March 1914). Amory and Bradlee 13.

Cumberland, Roy. "Margaret Kennedy." *The Schoolmistress* (21 October 1926): 91–92.

cummings, e. e. *Complete Poems, 1904–1962.* New York: Liveright, 1994.

Cunningham, Valentine. *British Writers of the Thirties.* Oxford: Clarendon Press, 1988.

Curry, Ramona. *Too Much of a Good Thing: Mae West as Cultural Icon.* Minneapolis: University of Minnesota Press, 1996.

Dashwood, R. M. *Provincial Daughter.* Orig. 1961; London: Virago, 2002.

Deen, Stella, ed. *Challenging Modernism: New Readings in Literature and Culture, 1914–45.* Aldershot, England: Ashgate, 2002.

Delafield, E. M. "As Others Hear Us." *Punch* (9 May 1934): 506, 508.

———. "Being a Parent." *Time and Tide* 9.20 (18 May 1928): 486.

———. *Consequences.* Orig. 1919; London: Persephone Books, 2000.

———. "Conversation in the Country." *Time and Tide* 9.17 (27 April 1928): 402.

———. *The Diary of a Provincial Lady.* Omnibus edition. Includes *The Diary of a Provincial Lady* (DPL, 1–121); *The Provincial Lady Goes Further* (PLF, 123–260); *The Provincial Lady in America* (PLA, 261–370); and *The Provincial Lady in Wartime* (PLW, 371–529). London: Virago, 1984.

———. "The Diary of a Provincial Lady." Roberts 121–138.

———. "The Sincerest Form . . . Diary of a Provincial (but not necessarily a Lady)." *Time and Tide* 11.51 (20 December 1930): 1605.

———. *Thank Heaven Fasting.* London: Macmillan, 1932.

———. "When Bloomsbury Meets." *Punch* (22 May 1935): 615.

———. "Women in Fiction: The Dialect Novel." *Time and Tide* 12.6 (7 February 1931): 158.

Dentith, Simon. "Thirties Poetry and the Landscape of Suburbia." In *Rewriting the Thirties: After Modernism,* ed. Keith Williams and Steven Matthews, pp. 108–123. Harlow, England: Longman, 1997.

Dettmar, Kevin J. H., and Steven Watt, eds. *Marketing Modernisms: Self-Promotion, Canonization, Rereading.* Ann Arbor: University of Michigan Press, 1996.

Devereux, Cecily. Introduction to *Anne of Green Gables,* by L. M. Montgomery, edited by Devereux, 12–38. Peterborough, Ontario: Broadview, 2004.

———. " 'See my Journal for the full story': Fictions of Truth in *Anne of Green Gables* and L. M. Montgomery's Journals." Gammel, *Intimate Life,* 241–257.

———, ed. *Anne of Green Gables.* By L. M. Montgomery. Peterborough, Ontario: Broadview, 2004.

Dodd, Lee Wilson. "The 'Nymph's' Precursor." *The Saturday Review of Literature* (14 November 1925): 291.

Doherty, Thomas. Review of *Mae West: An Icon in Black and White* by Jill Watts. *American Historical Review* 107.5 (December 2002): 1576–1577.

Dowson, Jane. "'Humming an entirely different tune'? A Case Study of Anthologies: *Women's Poetry of the 1930s*." Earnshaw, no page numbers.

———. *Women, Modernism and British Poetry, 1910–1939*. Aldershot, England: Ashgate, 2002.

D. P. [Dorothy Parker]. "So This Is New York!: The Story of a Warrior's Return." *Vanity Fair* 12.3 (May 1919): 21.

Dyer, Richard. *Stars*. Second edition. Orig. 1979; London: British Film Institute, 1998.

Dyke, Edwin. "Margaret Kennedy on *The Constant Nymph* in an Interview with Edwin Dyke." *The London Magazine* (19 January 1927): 48–51.

Earnshaw, Steven, ed. *Literature and Value. Working Papers on the Web,* Volume II (November 2001). Consulted 12 August 2005. <http://www.shu.ac.uk/wpw/previousissues.html>

Edwardson, Ryan. "A Canadian Modernism: The Pre-Group of Seven Algonquin School." *British Journal of Canadian Studies* 17.1 (2004): 81–92.

Empson, William. *The Complete Poems*. Edited by John Haffenden. Orig. 1955; Harmondsworth, England: Penguin, 2000.

English Studies Group, Centre for Contemporary Cultural Studies, University of Birmingham. "Thinking the Thirties." In *1936: The Sociology of Literature,* ed. Francis Barker et al., pp. 2:1–20. Colchester: University of Essex, 1979.

Epperly, Elizabeth R. "The Visual Imagination of L. M. Montgomery." Gammel, *Making Avonlea,* 84–98.

Erens, Patricia, ed. *Issues in Feminist Film Criticism*. Bloomington: Indiana University Press, 1990.

Evans, C. S. "Romance of a Best Seller: *The Constant Nymph* and Its Creator." *T.P.'s and Cassell's Weekly* New series 6.154 (9 October 1926): 743.

Everett, Barbara. "The New Style of *Sweeney Agonistes*." *Yearbook of English Studies* 14 (1984): 243–263.

Faulkner, William. *Selected Letters*. Edited by Joseph Blotner. London: Scolar, 1977.

Feather, John. *A History of British Publishing*. London: Routledge, 1988.

Fenton, Matthew McCann. "Goodness Had Nothing to Do with It." *Biography* 5.9 (September 2001): 86–91.

Fiamengo, Janice. "Theory of the Popular Landscape in *Anne*." Gammel, *Making Avonlea,* 225–237.

Fine, Richard. *Hollywood and the Profession of Authorship, 1928–1940*. Orig. 1985; Washington, D.C.: Smithsonian Institution, 1993.

Finney, Gail. "Queering the Stage: Critical Displacement in the Theater of Else Lasker-Schüler and Mae West." *Comparative Literature Studies* 40.1 (2003): 54–71.

Fish, [Anne Harriet]. *High Society: The Drawings by Fish. The Prose Precepts by Dorothy Parker, George S. Chappell, and Frank Crowninshield*. New York and London: G. P. Putnam, 1920.

Fisher, Margery. Introduction to *The Constant Nymph,* by Margaret Kennedy, 9–10. Harmondsworth, England: Penguin, 1969.

Fleming, Karl, and Anne Taylor Fleming. *The First Time*. New York: Berkley Medallion Books, 1975.

Frever, Trinna S. "Vaguely Familiar: Cinematic Intertextuality in Kevin Sullivan's *Anne of Avonlea.*" *CCL: Canadian Children's Literature* 91/92 (Fall/Winter 1998): 36–52.

Galsworthy, John. *Letters from John Galsworthy: 1900–1932.* Edited by Edward Garnett. London: Jonathan Cape; New York: Scribner's, 1934.

Gammel, Irene. "Making Avonlea: An Introduction." Gammel, *Making Avonlea,* 3–13.

——, ed. *The Intimate Life of L. M. Montgomery.* Toronto: University of Toronto Press, 2005.

——, ed. *Making Avonlea: L. M. Montgomery and Popular Culture.* Toronto: University of Toronto Press, 2002.

——, and Elizabeth Epperly, eds. *L. M. Montgomery and Canadian Culture.* Toronto: University of Toronto Press, 1999.

Gamson, Joshua. *Claims to Fame: Celebrity in Contemporary America.* Berkeley: University of California Press, 1994.

Garrity, Jane. "Selling Culture to the 'Civilized': Bloomsbury, British *Vogue,* and the Marketing of National Identity." *Modernism/Modernity* 6.2 (April 1999): 29–58.

——. *Step-Daughters of England: British Women Modernists and the National Imaginary.* Manchester: Manchester University Press, 2003.

Gates, Philippa, and Stacy Gillis. "Screening L. M. Montgomery: Heritage, Nostalgia and National Identity." *British Journal of Canadian Studies* 17.2 (2004): 186–196.

Gerson, Carole. "Canadian Women Writers and American Markets, 1880–1940." In *Context North America: Canadian-U.S. Literary Relations,* ed. Camille La Bossière, pp. 107–118. Ottawa: University of Ottawa Press, 1994.

——. "'Dragged at Anne's Chariot Wheels': The Triangle of Author, Publisher and Fictional Character." Gammel and Epperly, 49–63.

Gibbons, Stella. *Bassett.* London: Longmans, 1946.

——. *Cold Comfort Farm.* Orig. 1932; Harmondsworth, England: Penguin, 1982.

——. *Conference at Cold Comfort Farm.* Orig. 1949; London: White Lion, 1973.

Giles, Judy. *The Parlour and the Suburb: Domestic Identities, Class, Femininity and Modernity.* Basingstoke, England: Palgrave Macmillan, 2004.

Gill, Brendan. Introduction to *The Collected Dorothy Parker,* by Dorothy Parker, xiii–xxviii.

Gittings, Christopher. "Melodrama for the Nation: *Emily of New Moon.*" Gammel, *Making Avonlea,* 186–200.

Glass, Loren Daniel. *Authors Inc.: Literary Celebrity in the Modern United States.* New York: New York University Press, 2004.

Gramsci, Antonio. *Lettere dal Carcere.* Edited by Sergio Caprioglio and Elsa Fubini. Torino: Einaudi, 1965.

——. *Letters from Prison.* Selected, translated, and introduced by Lynne Lawner. Orig. 1975; London: Quartet, 1979.

GREC. "Parnassus in Academe: Novelists at Oxford." *Time and Tide* 9.52 (28 December 1928): 1271–1272.

Grover, Mary. "The Reciprocal Antagonisms of Modernism and the Middle-brow." Unpublished conference paper. Modernist Studies Association Conference, Birmingham, England, October 2003.

——, and Chris Hopkins, eds. *The Thirties Now. Working Papers on the Web*, Volume VI (June 2003). Consulted 20 August 2005. <http://www.shu.ac.uk/wpw/previousissues.html>

Haffenden, John. *Novelists in Interview*. London: Methuen, 1985.

Haftmann, Werner. *Painting in the Twentieth Century*. Volume I. Translated by Ralph Manheim. Second edition. Orig. 1961; London: Lund Humphries, 1965.

Hamilton, Marybeth. *The Queen of Camp: Mae West, Sex and Popular Culture*. London: HarperCollins, 1995.

Hammill, Faye. "*Cold Comfort Farm*, D. H. Lawrence, and Literary Culture be-tween the Wars." *Modern Fiction Studies* 47.4 (Fall 2001): 831–854.

——. *Literary Culture and Female Authorship in Canada, 1760–2000*. Amster-dam and New York: Editions Rodopi, 2003.

——. "The Sensations of the 1920s: Martha Ostenso's *Wild Geese* and Mazo de la Roche's *Jalna*." *Studies in Canadian Literature* 28.2 (Spring 2004): 66–89.

——, Esme Miskimmin, and Ashlie Sponenberg, eds. *Encyclopedia of British Women's Writing, 1900–1950*. Basingstoke, England: Palgrave Macmillan, 2006.

Hardy, Thomas. *The Woodlanders*. Edited by Patricia Ingham. Orig. 1887; Harmondsworth, England: Penguin, 1998.

Hartley, L. P. Review of *Red Sky at Morning. Saturday Review* (5 November 1927). Excerpted in Harold Bloom 172–174.

Hegeman, Susan. "Taking *Blondes* Seriously." *American Literary History* 7.3 (1995): 525–554.

Helal, Kathleen. "Celebrity, Femininity, Lingerie: Dorothy Parker's Autobio-graphical Monologues." *Women's Studies* 33 (2004): 77–102.

Helfer, Richard. "The Drag: Mae West and the Gay World." *Journal of Ameri-can Drama and Theatre* 8.1 (Winter 1996): 50–66.

——. "Mae West on Stage: Themes and Persona." Ph.D. diss., City University of New York, 1990.

Hellman, Lillian. Introduction to *A Month of Saturdays: Thirty-One Famous Pieces by "Constant Reader,"* by Dorothy Parker, xi–xxiv. London: Macmil-lan, 1971.

——. *An Unfinished Woman*. Orig. 1969; Harmondsworth, England: Penguin, 1972.

Hersey, Eleanor. "'It's All Mine': The Modern Woman as Writer in Sullivan's *Anne of Green Gables* Films." Gammel, *Making Avonlea*, 131–144.

Horner, Avril, and Sue Zlosnik. "Agriculture, Body Sculpture, Gothic Cul-ture: Gothic Parody in Gibbons, Atwood and Weldon." *Gothic Studies* 4.2 (November 2002): 167–177.

Howey, Ann F. "'She Look'd Down to Camelot': Anne Shirley, Sullivan, and the Lady of Shalott." Gammel, *Making Avonlea*, 160–173.

Huggan, Graham. *The Postcolonial Exotic: Marketing the Margins*. London: Routledge, 2001.

Humble, Nicola. *The Feminine Middlebrow Novel, 1920s to 1950s: Class, Domesticity and Bohemianism*. Oxford: Oxford University Press, 2001.

Huyssen, Andreas. *After the Great Divide: Modernism, Mass Culture, Postmodernism*. Basingstoke, England: Macmillan, 1986.

Ivanov, Andrea J. "Mae West Was Not a Man: Sexual Parody and Genre in the Plays and Films of Mae West." In *Look Who's Laughing: Gender and Comedy*, ed. Gail Finney, pp. 275–297. Langhorne, Pa.: Gordon and Berach, 1994.

Jackson, Crispin. "Stella Gibbons: Author of *Cold Comfort Farm*." *The Book and Magazine Collector* 130 (1995): 18–26.

Jaffe, Aaron. *Modernism and the Culture of Celebrity*. Cambridge: Cambridge University Press, 2005.

Jameson, Fredric. "Reification and Utopia in Mass Culture." *Social Text* 1 (Winter 1979): 130–148.

Jones, L. L. [Dorothy Parker?] "Extracts from a Secretary's Diary. Showing the Narrowness and Bias of a Working Woman's Judgement." *Vanity Fair* 10.8 (October 1918): 60, 100.

Joyce, James. *Letters of James Joyce*. Volume I. Edited by Stuart Gilbert. New York: Viking, 1957.

Kanin, Garson. *Hollywood*. New York: Viking, 1974.

Karr, Clarence. *Authors and Audiences: Popular Canadian Fiction in the Early Twentieth Century*. Montreal and Kingston: McGill-Queen's University Press, 2000.

Keefer, Janice Kulyk. *Under Eastern Eyes: A Critical Reading of Maritime Fiction*. Toronto: University of Toronto Press, 1987.

Keith, W. J. *Regions of the Imagination: The Development of British Rural Fiction*. Toronto: University of Toronto Press, 1988.

Kendon, Frank. "The New Books at a Glance." *John O'London's Weekly* (17 October 1931). Margaret Kennedy Papers. Clipping Scrapbooks. British Reviews.

Kennedy, Margaret. *The Constant Nymph*. 1924. London: Virago, 2000.

——. "The Constant Nymph." Roberts 23–50.

——. *The Heroes of Clone*. London: Macmillan, 1957.

——. *A Long Time Ago*. London: William Heinemann, 1932.

——. "The Novelist and His Public." Paper read 26 October 1961. In *Essays by Divers Hands: Being the Transactions of the Royal Society of Literature*, New Series 32, ed. Joanna Richardson, pp. 72–83. London: Oxford University Press, 1963.

——. *The Outlaws on Parnassus*. London: Cresset, 1958.

——. *Return I Dare Not*. Orig. 1931; New York: Doubleday, 1933.

——. *Together and Apart*. London: Cassell, 1936.

——, and Basil Dean. *The Constant Nymph*. 1926. In *The Years Between: Plays by Women on the London Stage, 1900–1950*, ed. Fidelis Morgan, pp. 172–263. London: Virago, 1994.

Kenner, Hugh. *The Counterfeiters: An Historical Comedy*. Baltimore: Johns Hopkins University Press, 1985.

Kinney, Arthur F. *Dorothy Parker.* Twayne's United States Authors Series. Boston: Twayne, 1978.

Kipling, Rudyard. "The Elephant's Child." In *Just So Stories for Little Children,* 59–76. Orig. 1902; London: Macmillan, 1964.

Kirk, John Foster. *Supplement to Allibone's Critical Dictionary of English Literature and British and American Authors.* Detroit: Gale Research Company, 1965.

Kobal, John. *People Will Talk: Personal Conversations with the Legends of Hollywood.* London: Aurum, 1986.

Kotsopoulos, Aspasia. "Our Avonlea: Imagining Community in an Imaginary Past." In *Pop Can: Popular Culture in Canada,* ed. Lynne Van Luven and Priscilla Walton, pp. 98–105. Scarborough, Ontario: Prentice Hall Allyn and Bacon Canada, 1999.

Lane, Temple. "Dear Madam." Review of the omnibus edition of *The Diary of a Provincial Lady. Irish Times* (25 October 1947). E. M. Delafield Papers. Box 3, File 8.

Lasch, Christopher. *The Culture of Narcissism: American Life in an Age of Diminishing Expectations.* New York: Warner, 1979.

Lassner, Phyllis. *British Women Writers of World War II.* New York: St. Martin's Press, 1998.

———. *Colonial Strangers: British Women Writing the End of Empire.* New Brunswick, N.J.: Rutgers University Press, 2004.

———. "'Objects to Possess and Discard': The Representation of Jews and Women by British Women Novelists of the 1920s." In *Borderlines: Genders and Identities in War and Peace, 1870–1930,* ed. Billie Melman, pp. 245–261. London and New York: Routledge, 1998.

Lathem, Maude. "'Will I Last?' Asks Mae West." *Motion Picture* (June 1934): 28–29, 92–93.

Lawrence, D. H. *Lady Chatterley's Lover.* Orig. 1928; Harmondsworth, England: Penguin, 1997.

———. *The Rainbow.* Edited by Mark Kinkead-Weekes. Orig. 1915; Cambridge: Cambridge University Press, 1989.

Lawson, Kate. "The Alien at Home: Hearing Voices in L. M. Montgomery's *Emily Climbs* and F. W. H. Myers." *Gothic Studies* 4.2 (November 2002): 155–166.

Leavis, Q. D. *Fiction and the Reading Public.* Orig. 1932; London: Chatto and Windus, 1968.

Lefebvre, Benjamin. "L. M. Montgomery: An Annotated Filmography." *CCL: Canadian Children's Literature* 99 (2000): 43–73.

———. "*Road to Avonlea:* A Co-production of the Disney Corporation." Gammel, *Making Avonlea,* 174–185.

Leider, Emily Wortis. *Becoming Mae West.* Orig. 1997; New York and Cambridge, Mass.: Da Capo, 2000.

Leonardi, Susan J. *Dangerous by Degrees: Women at Oxford and the Somerville College Novelists.* New Brunswick, N.J., and London: Rutgers University Press, 1989.

Lette, Kathy. Introduction to *She Done Him Wrong,* by Mae West, v–xii. London: Virago, 1995.

Lewis, R. W. B. *Edith Wharton: A Biography.* London: Constable, 1975.

Lewis, Wyndham. *Time and Western Man.* Edited by Paul Edwards. Orig. 1927; Santa Rosa, Calif.: Black Sparrow Press, 1993.

Light, Alison. *Forever England: Femininity, Literature and Conservatism between the Wars.* London: Routledge, 1991.

Lindsay, Vachel. *The Art of the Moving Picture.* Second edition. Orig. 1915; New York: Liveright, 1970.

Lippmann, Walter. "Blazing Publicity: Why We Know So Much about 'Peaches' Browning, Valentino, Lindbergh and Queen Marie." 1927. Amory and Bradlee 121–122.

Loos, Anita. *Anita Loos Rediscovered: Film Treatments and Fiction.* Edited by Cari Beauchamp and Mary Anita Loos. Berkeley, Los Angeles, and London: University of California Press, 2003.

———. "The Biography of a Book." 1963. Loos, *Gentlemen Prefer Blondes,* xxxvii–xlii.

———. "But Dr. Kinsey, What about Romance?" *The New York Times Magazine* (30 August 1953). Loos, *Fate Keeps On Happening,* 35–38.

———. *But Gentlemen Marry Brunettes.* 1928. Loos, *Gentlemen Prefer Blondes,* 125–243.

———. *Fate Keeps On Happening: Adventures of Lorelei Lee and Other Writings.* Edited by Ray Pierre Corsini. New York: Dodd, Mead, 1984.

———. *Gentlemen Prefer Blondes: The Illuminating Diary of a Professional Lady.* 1925. Reprinted with *But Gentlemen Marry Brunettes.* Illustrated by Ralph Barton. Harmondsworth, England: Penguin, 1998.

———. "A Girl Can't Go On Laughing All the Time." 1980?. Loos, *Fate Keeps On Happening,* 62–65.

———. *A Girl Like I.* Orig. 1966; London: Hamish Hamilton, 1967.

———. *Kiss Hollywood Goodbye.* Orig. 1974; Harmondsworth, England: Penguin, 1979.

———. "Memoir of Aldous Huxley." 1964. In *Aldous Huxley: 1894–1963: A Memorial Volume,* ed. Julian Huxley, pp. 89–97. London: Chatto and Windus, 1966.

———. "Memoirs of a Best-Selling Blonde." Loos, *Fate Keeps On Happening,* 3–6.

———. *A Mouse Is Born.* London: Jonathan Cape, 1951.

———. "A Musical Is Born." *The New York Times* (4 December 1949). Loos, *Fate Keeps On Happening,* 58–61.

———. *No Mother to Guide Her.* Orig. 1930, revised 1960; London: Prion Books, 2000.

Loveman, Amy. Review of *Red Sky at Morning* by Margaret Kennedy. *Saturday Review of Literature* (5 November 1927). Margaret Kennedy Papers. Clipping Scrapbooks. American Reviews.

Luhrs, Marie. "Fashionable Poetry." Review of *Enough Rope* by Dorothy Parker. *Poetry: A Magazine of Verse* 30.1 (April 1927): 52–54.

Lynd, Sylvia. "Four New Novels." *Time and Tide* 8.46 (18 November 1927): 103–104.

McCorkle, Susannah. "The Immortality of Mae West." *American Heritage* 52 (September 2001): 48–57.

McCullen, Maurice L. *E. M. Delafield.* Boston: Twayne, 1985.

McDonald, Peter D. *British Literary Culture and Publishing Practice 1880–1914.* Cambridge: Cambridge University Press, 1997.

Macneice, Louis. *Selected Literary Criticism of Louis Macneice.* Edited by Alan Heuser. Oxford: Oxford University Press, 1987.

Mannin, Ethel. *Young in the Twenties: A Chapter of Autobiography.* London: Hutchison, 1971.

"Margaret Kennedy: Noted Novelist." *The Times* (2 August 1967). Margaret Kennedy Papers. Forster Collection. Clipping File.

Marshall, P. David. *Celebrity and Power: Fame in Contemporary Culture.* Minneapolis: University of Minnesota Press, 1997.

Maslen, Elizabeth. *Political and Social Issues in British Women's Fiction, 1928–1968.* Basingstoke, England: Palgrave Macmillan, 2001.

Matthews, John T. "Gentlemen Defer Blondes: Faulkner, Anita Loos, and Mass Culture." In *Faulkner, His Contemporaries, and His Posterity,* ed. Waldemar Zacharasiewicz, pp. 207–221. Tübingen, Germany: Francke, 1993.

Maugham, W. Somerset. Introduction to *The Portable Dorothy Parker.* 1944. 599–603.

M/C Journal: A Journal of Media and Culture 7.5 (November 2004). Special issue edited by P. David Marshall.

Meade, Marion. *Dorothy Parker: What Fresh Hell Is This?* New York: Villard Books, 1988.

Melman, Billie. *Women and the Popular Imagination in the 1920s: Flappers and Nymphs.* London: Macmillan, 1988.

Melzer, Sondra. *The Rhetoric of Rage: Women in Dorothy Parker.* New York: Peter Lang, 1997.

[Mencken, H. L.] Review of *Gentlemen Prefer Blondes. The American Mercury* (January 1926): 127.

Mencken, H. L. "The Sahara of the Bozart." In *Prejudices: A Selection,* ed. James T. Farrell, pp. 69–82. New York: Vintage, 1958.

Meryman, Richard. "Mae West: Going Strong at 75." *Life* (28 April 1969): 46–56.

Miller, Nina. "Making Love Modern: Dorothy Parker and Her Public." *American Literature* 64.4 (December 1992): 763–784.

Mitchell, Margaret. "Anita Loos: A Chronology." Loos, *Gentlemen Prefer Blondes,* xxix–xxxiii.

Montgomery, L. M. *The Alpine Path: The Story of My Career.* Orig. 1917; Don Mills, Ontario: Fitzhenry and Whiteside, 1975.

———. *Anne of Green Gables.* Edited by Cecily Devereux. Broadview Editions Series. Orig. 1908; Peterborough, Ontario: Broadview, 2004.

———. *Emily Climbs.* Orig. 1925; Harmondsworth, England: Penguin, 1990.

———. *Emily of New Moon.* Orig. 1923; New York: Bantam, 1983.

———. *The Green Gables Letters: From L. M. Montgomery to Ephraim Weber, 1905–1909.* Edited by Wilfrid Eggleston. Toronto: Ryerson, 1960.

————. "Is This My *Anne*." *Chatelaine* (January 1935). In *The Lucy Maud Montgomery Album*, ed. Kevin McCabe, pp. 333–335. Don Mills, Ontario: Fitzhenry and Whiteside, 1999.

————. *L. M. Montgomery's Ephraim Weber: Letters 1916–1941*. Edited by Paul Tiessen and Hildi Froese Tiessen. Waterloo, Ontario: MLR Editions, 2000.

————. *My Dear Mr. M.: Letters to G. B. Macmillan*. Edited by Francis W. P. Bolger and Elizabeth R. Epperly. Toronto: McGraw-Hill Ryerson, 1980.

————. *The Selected Journals of L. M. Montgomery, Volume I: 1889–1910*. Edited by Mary Rubio and Elizabeth Waterston. Toronto: Oxford University Press, 1985.

————. *The Selected Journals of L. M. Montgomery, Volume II: 1910–1921*. Edited by Mary Rubio and Elizabeth Waterston. Toronto: Oxford University Press, 1987.

————. *The Selected Journals of L. M. Montgomery, Volume III: 1921–1929*. Edited by Mary Rubio and Elizabeth Waterston. Toronto: Oxford University Press, 1992.

————. *The Selected Journals of L. M. Montgomery, Volume IV: 1929–1935*. Edited by Mary Rubio and Elizabeth Waterston. Toronto: Oxford University Press, 1998.

————. "The Way to Make a Book." 1915. Devereux, *Anne of Green Gables*, 365–370.

————, Marian Keith, and Mabel Burns McKinley. *Courageous Women*. Toronto: McClelland, 1934.

Moran, Joe. *Star Authors: Literary Celebrity in America*. London: Pluto, 2000.

Mott, Frank Luther. *Golden Multitudes: The Story of Best Sellers in the United States*. New York: Macmillan, 1947.

"Mysterious Marriages: A Scientific Search into Certain Matings and Mismatings. Sketches by Fish. Diagnosis by Our Staff Psychoanalyst." *Vanity Fair* 15.4 (December 1920): 66–67.

Neijmann, Daisy. "Fighting with Blunt Swords: Laura Goodman Salverson and the Canadian Literary Canon." *Essays on Canadian Writing* 67 (Spring 1999): 138–173.

Nichols, Beverley. "Woad! Celebrities in Undress: XXVI—Margaret Kennedy." *The Sketch* (22 September 1926): 568.

Noose, Melita. *Blondes Prefer Gentlemen: A Satire*. London: Stanley Paul, 1926.

North, Michael. *Reading 1922: A Return to the Scene of the Modern*. New York: Oxford University Press, 1999.

O'Day, Marc. "Mae West." Sage 660.

Oliver, Reggie. *Out of the Woodshed: A Portrait of Stella Gibbons*. London: Bloomsbury, 1998.

Opdycke, Mary Ellis. Review of *The Constant Nymph*. *New Republic* (15 April 1925). Excerpted in Harold Bloom 168–169.

"Our Booking Office: By Mr. Punch's Staff of Learned Clerks." *Punch* 167 (17 December 1924): 698.

Over, Mark. Untitled paragraph. *The Outlook* (27 June 1925): 431.

Paris, Barry. *Louise Brooks*. Orig. 1989; London: Mandarin, 1991.

Parker, Dorothy. "But the One on the Right." *The New Yorker* (19 October 1929). Parker, *Complete Stories*, 132–135.

———. *The Collected Dorothy Parker*. Orig. 1973; Harmondsworth, England: Penguin, 2001.

———. *Complete Stories*. Edited by Colleen Breese. Orig. 1995; Harmondsworth, England: Penguin, 2003.

———. "The Cradle of Civilization." *The New Yorker* (21 September 1929). Parker, *Complete Stories*, 129–131.

———. "Each Thought a Purl, Each Purl a Prayer." *Vogue* 50.8 (15 October 1917): 51, 144.

———. "The Far-Sighted Muse." *Life* (9 March 1922). Parker, *Uncollected Dorothy Parker*, 125.

———. "Figures in Popular Literature." *Life* (19 January 1922). Parker, *Uncollected Dorothy Parker*, 115–120.

———. "The First Hundred Plays Are the Hardest." *Vanity Fair* (December 1919). Amory and Bradlee, 34–35.

———. "From the Diary of a New York Lady." *The New Yorker* (25 March 1933). Parker, *Complete Stories*, 191–194.

———. "The Garter." *The New Yorker* (8 September 1928). Parker, *Complete Stories*, 99–101.

———. "Just around Pooh Corner." *The New Yorker* (14 March 1931). Parker, *Collected Dorothy Parker*, 437–441.

———. "Kindly Accept Substitutes." *The New Yorker* (21 February 1931). Parker, *Collected Dorothy Parker*, 434–437.

———. "The Lady in Back." *Vogue* 48.9 (15 November 1916): 128.

———. "Lady with a Lamp." *Harper's Bazaar* (April 1932). Parker, *Collected Dorothy Parker*, 144–150.

———. "The Little Hours." *The New Yorker* (19 August 1933). Parker, *Complete Stories*, 204–208.

———. "The Midwinter Plays." *Vanity Fair* 11.6 (February 1919): 39, 74.

———. *A Month of Saturdays: Thirty-One Famous Pieces by "Constant Reader"* (Dorothy Parker). London: Macmillan, 1971.

———. "News Item." Parker, *Collected Dorothy Parker*, 109.

———. "No More Fun." *The New Yorker* (21 March 1931). Parker, *Collected Dorothy Parker*, 441–443.

———. "Our Office: A Hate Song." *Vanity Fair* 12.3 (May 1919): 6, 8.

———. "Plays of War and Peace." *Vanity Fair* 11.5 (January 1919): 33, 70, 72.

———. *The Uncollected Dorothy Parker*. Edited by Stuart Silverstein. Orig. 1996; London: Duckbacks, 2001.

———. "Valedictory." Parker, *Collected Dorothy Parker*, 446–450.

Parkins, Wendy. "Moving Dangerously: Mobility and the Modern Woman." *Tulsa Studies in Women's Literature* 20.1 (Spring 2001): 77–92.

Parsons, Deborah. *Streetwalking the Metropolis: Women, the City and Modernity*. Oxford: Oxford University Press, 2000.

Perelman, S. J. *The Last Laugh*. New York: Simon and Schuster, 1981.

"Personalities and Powers: Miss Margaret Kennedy." *Time and Tide* 7.49 (3 December 1926): 1100–1101.

Pettit, Rhonda. *A Gendered Collision: Sentimentality and Modernism in Dorothy Parker's Poetry and Fiction*. Madison, N.J.: Farleigh Dickinson University Press, 2000.

———. "Material Girls in the Jazz Age: Dorothy Parker's 'Big Blonde' as an Answer to Anita Loos's *Gentlemen Prefer Blondes*." *Kentucky Philological Review* 12 (1997): 49–54.

Pevere, Geoff, and Greig Dymond. *Mondo Canuck: A Canadian Pop Culture Odyssey*. Scarborough, Ontario: Prentice Hall, 1996.

Pike, E. Holly. "Mass Marketing, Popular Culture, and the Canadian Celebrity Author." Gammel, *Making Avonlea*, 238–251.

———. "(Re)Producing Canadian Literature: L. M. Montgomery's Emily Novels." Gammel and Epperly 64–76.

Pitman, Joanna. *On Blondes*. London: Bloomsbury, 2003.

Poe, K. L. "Who's Got the Power?: Montgomery, Sullivan and the Unsuspecting Viewer." Gammel, *Making Avonlea*, 145–159.

Powell, Violet. *The Constant Novelist: A Study of Margaret Kennedy, 1896–1967*. London: Heinemann, 1983.

———. *The Life of a Provincial Lady*. London: Heinemann, 1988.

Priestley, J. B. *English Humour*. London: Heinemann, 1976.

Prigozy, Ruth. "Introduction: Scott, Zelda and the Culture of Celebrity." In *The Cambridge Companion to F. Scott Fitzgerald*, ed. Prigozy. Cambridge: Cambridge University Press, 2002.

Purves, Libby. Interview with Stella Gibbons. *Woman's Hour*. BBC Radio 4 (May 1981).

———. "The Road to Cold Comfort Farm." *Listener* 105 (14 May 1981): 639.

Radway, Janice. "The Scandal of the Middlebrow: The Book-of-the-Month Club, Class Fracture, and Cultural Authority." *South Atlantic Quarterly* 89 (1990): 703–736.

Rainey, Lawrence. *Institutions of Modernism: Literary Elites and Public Culture*. New Haven, Conn.: Yale University Press, 1998.

Reid, W. Stanford. *The Scottish Tradition in Canada*. Toronto: McClelland and Stewart, 1976.

[Rhondda, Margaret Haig]. "E. M. Delafield, by The Editor." *Time and Tide* (13 December 1947). E. M. Delafield Papers. Box 3, File 8.

Rhondda [Margaret Haig]. "Mr. Shaw Writes to Me about Conduit Pipes." *Time and Tide* 11.27 (5 July 1930): 854–856.

———. Obituary of E. M. Delafield. *Time and Tide* (11 December 1943). E. M. Delafield Papers. Box 3, File 9.

Roberts, Denys Kilham, ed. *Titles to Fame*. London: Thomas Nelson, 1937.

Rojek, Chris. *Celebrity*. London: Reaktion, 2001.

Rose, Frank. *The Agency: William Morris and the Hidden History of Show Business*. New York: Harper Business, 1995.

Rose, Margaret A. *Parody: Ancient, Modern and Postmodern*. Cambridge: Cambridge University Press, 1993.

Rosen, Marjorie. *Popcorn Venus: Women, Movies and the American Dream*. New York: Coward, McGann and Geohegan, 1973.

Ross, Claire J. "Putting Over a Prima Donna: Some Reflections on the Gentle Art of Press Agenting." *Vanity Fair* 12.1 (March 1919): 100, 102.

Rubin, Joan Shelley. *The Making of Middlebrow Culture.* Chapel Hill: University of North Carolina Press, 1992.

Rubio, Mary. "L. M. Montgomery: Scottish-Presbyterian Agency in Canadian Culture." Gammel and Epperly 89–105.

———. "Subverting the Trite: L. M. Montgomery's 'Room of Her Own.'" *CCL: Canadian Children's Literature* 65 (1992): 6–39.

———, and Elizabeth Waterston. Introduction to Montgomery, *Selected Journals, Volume III,* x–xxv.

———, and Elizabeth Waterston. Introduction to Montgomery, *Selected Journals, Volume IV,* xi–xxxi.

Ryan, Marion. "The Mysterious Margaret Kennedy." *The Queen* (3 June 1925): 26–27.

Sage, Lorna, ed. *The Cambridge Guide to Women's Writing in English.* Cambridge: Cambridge University Press, 1999.

Schickel, Richard. *Intimate Strangers: The Culture of Celebrity in America.* Second edition. Orig. 1985; Chicago: Ivan Dee, 2000.

Schlissel, Lillian. "Mae West and the 'Queer Plays.'" *Women's History Review* 11.1 (2002): 71–87.

Schrader, Richard J. "'But Gentlemen Marry Brunettes': Anita Loos and H. L. Mencken." *Menckeniana: A Quarterly Review* 98 (Summer 1986): 1–7.

Schwinn, Walter K. "The Constantly Selling Nymph." *Springfield [Mass.] Union* (3 May 1925). Margaret Kennedy Papers. Press Cuttings Scrapbooks. American Reviews.

Scott, Bonnie Kime. *Refiguring Modernism Volume I: The Women of 1928.* Bloomington: Indiana University Press, 1995.

———, ed. *The Gender of Modernism: A Critical Anthology.* Bloomington: Indiana University Press, 1990.

Shakespeare, William. *The Winter's Tale.* The Arden Edition. Orig. 1611; London: Methuen, 1963.

Shear, Claudia. *Dirty Blonde.* Unpublished playscript in author's personal collection. First performed 1999.

Sheckels, Theodore F. "Anne in Hollywood: The Americanization of a Canadian Icon." Gammel and Epperly 183–191.

Sherwood, Robert. "Renaissance in Hollywood." *American Mercury* 16.64 (April 1929): 432.

Showalter, Elaine. "Women Writers between the Wars." *The Columbia Literary History of the United States,* ed. Emory Elliott, pp. 822–841. New York: Columbia University Press, 1988.

Silverstein, Stuart. Introduction to *The Uncollected Dorothy Parker,* 11–76. Orig. 1996; London: Duckbacks, 2001.

Smith, Clara. "New Fiction." *Time and Tide* 12.40 (3 October 1931): 1134, 1136.

Snell, K. D. M. Introduction. *The Regional Novel in Britain and Ireland, 1800–1990,* ed. Snell, pp. 1–53. Cambridge: Cambridge University Press, 1998.

Spender, Dale. *Time and Tide Wait for No Man.* London: Pandora, 1984.

Stein, Gertrude. *Everybody's Autobiography.* New York: Random House, 1937.

Stendhal, Renate, ed. *Gertrude Stein in Words and Pictures: A Photobiography.* Originally published in German, 1989. London: Thames and Hudson, 1995.

Steyn, Mark. "Mae Days." *New Criterion* 18.7 (March 2000). Consulted 10 August 2004. < http://www.newcriterion.com>

Struther, Jan. *Mrs. Miniver.* 1939. Internet edition. Edited by Robert Maxtone Graham. 2001. Consulted 1 March 2005. <http://digital.library.upenn.edu/ women/struther/miniver/miniver.html>

Susman, Warren. *Culture as History: The Transformation of American Society in the Twentieth Century.* New York: Pantheon, 1984.

Tiessen, Paul, and Hildi Froese Tiessen. "Epistolary Performance: Writing Mr. Weber." Gammel, *The Intimate Life,* 222–238.

Trodd, Anthea. *Women's Writing in English: Britain, 1900–1945.* Harlow, England: Addison, 1998.

Turim, Maureen. "Gentlemen Consume Blondes." Erens 101–111.

Turner, Graeme. *Understanding Celebrity.* London: Sage, 2004.

Tye, D. "'Multiple Meanings Called Cavendish': The Interaction of Tourism with Traditional Culture." *Journal of Canadian Studies* 30.1 (Spring 1994): 122–134.

Updike, John. *Self-Consciousness: Memoirs.* New York: Knopf, 1989.

van Raalte, George. Letter. *Time and Tide* 11.40 (4 October 1930): 1232.

Vickers, Jackie. "Cold Comfort for Ethan Frome." *Notes and Queries* 40.4 (December 1993): 498–500.

Von Ankum, Katharina. "Material Girls: Consumer Culture and the 'New Woman' in Anita Loos' *Gentlemen Prefer Blondes* and Irmgard Keun's *Das Kunstseidene Mädchen.*" *Colloquia Germanica* 27.2 (1994): 159–172.

Vreeland, Diane. Introduction to *The Vogue Poster Book,* [no pagination]. New York: Harmony Books, 1975.

Wagenknecht, Edward. *The Movies in the Age of Innocence.* Norman: University of Oklahoma Press, 1962.

Walker, Alexander. *The Celluloid Sacrifice: Aspects of Sex in the Movies.* London: Michael Joseph, 1966.

Wallace, Diana. *Sisters and Rivals in British Women's Fiction, 1914–1939.* Basingstoke, England: Palgrave Macmillan, 2000.

———. *The Woman's Historical Novel: British Women Writers, 1900–2000.* Basingstoke, England: Palgrave Macmillan, 2005.

Walpole, Hugh. "New Writers and Their Novels." *T.P.'s and Cassell's Weekly* 10.244 (30 June 1928): 297–298.

Warner, Sylvia Townsend. "Mrs. Woolf is Visited by some Uncommon Readers." Illustration by Paul Bloomfield. *Time and Tide* 8.47 (25 November 1927): 1057.

Waugh, Evelyn. *Vile Bodies.* Orig. 1930; Harmondsworth, England: Penguin, 1938.

Wells, Helen [Dorothy Parker]. "The Autobiography of Any Movie Actress, Set Down in the Regulation Manner." *Vanity Fair* 13.6 (September 1919): 33, 110.

West, Mae. *The Constant Sinner.* Orig. 1930; London: Virago, 1995.

———. *Goodness Had Nothing to Do with It.* Orig. 1959; London: Virago, 1996.

———. *Mae West on Sex, Health and ESP.* London and New York: W. H. Allen, 1975.

———. *Pleasure Man.* Orig. 1975; London: Corgi, 1976.

———. Preface to *Pleasure Man,* 7–8. Orig. 1975; London: Corgi, 1976.

———. *She Done Him Wrong.* Originally published as *Diamond Lil* in 1932. London: Virago, 1995.

West, Rebecca. "Notes on Three Novels." *The Saturday Review of Literature* (17 October 1925): 207–209.

Wharton, Edith. *The Letters of Edith Wharton.* Edited by R. W. B. Lewis and Nancy Lewis. New York: Scribner's, 1958.

"What They Read." Book review column. *Vogue* 67.10 (15 May 1926): 150, 152, 160.

Wicke, Jennifer. *Advertising Fictions: Literature, Advertisement and Social Reading.* New York: Columbia University Press, 1998.

Williams, Raymond. *The Country and the City.* Orig. 1973; London: Hogarth, 1985.

Willison, Ian, Warwick Gould, and Warren Chernaik, eds. *Modernist Writers and the Marketplace.* London: Macmillan, 1996.

Wilson, Edmund. "Dorothy Parker's Poems." *New Republic* (19 January 1927): 256.

Wittmann, Livia Z. "Erfolgschancen eines Gaukelspiels: Vergleichende Beobachtungen zu *Das Kunstseidene Mädchen* (Irmgard Keun) und *Gentlemen Prefer Blondes* (Anita Loos)." *Carleton Germanic Papers* 11 (1983): 35–49.

Woolf, Virginia. *Collected Essays. Volume I.* London: Hogarth, 1966.

———. *The Death of the Moth, and Other Essays.* London: Hogarth, 1942.

———. *The Diary of Virginia Woolf. Volume II: 1925–1930.* Edited by Anne Olivier Bell. Assistant editor Andrew McNeillie. Harmondsworth, England: Penguin, 1982.

———. *Mrs. Dalloway.* 1925. London: Grafton, 1976.

———. *A Room of One's Own.* London: Hogarth, 1929.

———. *The Sickle Side of the Moon: The Letters of Virginia Woolf. Volume V: 1932–1935.* Edited by Nigel Nicolson. Assistant editor Joanne Trautmann. London: Hogarth, 1979.

———. "The Sun and the Fish." *Time and Tide* 9.5 (3 February 1928): 99–100.

Woollcott, Alexander. *While Rome Burns.* New York: Viking, 1934.

York, Lorraine. "'I Knew I Would "Arrive" Some Day': L. M. Montgomery and the Strategies of Literary Celebrity." *CCL: Canadian Children's Literature* 113/114 (Spring–Summer 2004): 98–116.

ARCHIVAL SOURCES

E. M. Delafield Papers. Main Library Special Collections. University of British Columbia.

Edith Wharton Collection. Yale University Rare Book and Manuscript Library. YCAL MSS 42.

Femina Vie Heureuse Papers. Cambridge University Library. MS Add. 8900.

Margaret Kennedy Papers. Somerville College, Oxford.

L. M. Montgomery Collection. University of Guelph. XZ5 MS A001-3.

INDEX

Lightning Source UK Ltd.
Milton Keynes UK
UKHW011851030920
369309UK00001B/44